SPACE AND
NATIONAL SECURITY

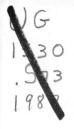

PAUL B. STARES

SPACE AND
NATIONAL SECURITY

THE BROOKINGS INSTITUTION
Washington, D.C.

Copyright © 1987

THE BROOKINGS INSTITUTION

1775 Massachusetts Avenue, N.W., Washington, D.C. 20036

Library of Congress Cataloging-in-Publication data:

Stares, Paul B.
  Space and national security.
  Includes bibliographical references and index.
  1. Anti-satellite weapons—United States.
2. Anti-satellite weapons—Soviet Union.   3. Astro-
nautics, Military—United States.   4. Astronautics,
Military—Soviet Union.   5. United States—Military
policy.   I. Title.
UG1530.S73   1987   358'.17   87-14694
ISBN 0-8157-8110-5
ISBN 0-8157-8109-1 (pbk.)

9 8 7 6 5 4 3 2 1

For Rodney, Susanne, Anthea, and Peter

Foreword

WHETHER the United States should proceed with the development of antisatellite weapons is one of the most pressing and consequential defense issues facing the nation. The Reagan administration believes that the United States must have an antisatellite capability to deter attacks against its spacecraft and to counter the threat from Soviet military uses of space. An advanced U.S. antisatellite system is currently scheduled to become operational by 1990. But the competition in antisatellite weapons that would most likely follow could endanger the many benefits the United States now derives from its space systems. In particular, the presence of sophisticated weapons able to impair or destroy satellites used for nuclear command and control could seriously undermine strategic stability in periods of heightened tension between the superpowers.

In this book, Paul B. Stares examines the officially stated rationales for deploying antisatellite weapons and assesses their long-term consequences for U.S. national security. He surveys how the superpowers use space for military purposes and appraises the value of satellites for each side. He also assesses the threats to U.S. and Soviet space systems and the countermeasures that can be employed to reduce their vulnerability. After evaluating the potential usefulness of antisatellite weapons in a range of wartime contingencies, he analyzes the feasibility of arms control in space. Stares concludes that there is at present no urgent need for a U.S. antisatellite system and recommends instead a variety of unilateral and bilateral measures to preserve the security of U.S. space assets.

Paul Stares, a research associate in the Brookings Foreign Policy Studies program, gratefully acknowledges the valuable comments and suggestions of John D. Steinbruner, Bruce G. Blair, William J. Durch,

Donald L. Hafner, Nicholas L. Johnson, John E. Pike, William B. Quandt, and Jeffrey T. Richelson, all of whom painstakingly reviewed the manuscript in its entirety. Additional comments and assistance were provided by Pete Didisheim, Lisa B. Mages, Michael K. MccGwire, and Lieutenant Colonel Gregory S. Parnell. Special thanks are owed to Joshua M. Epstein for the quantitative analysis in chapter 4, and to Christine C. de Fontenay and Robert W. Davis II of the Brookings Social Science Computation Center for their support throughout the study. The author is also grateful to Jeanette Morrison for editing the manuscript, Stephen K. Wegren and James E. McKee for verifying its factual content, and Thomas T. Somuah for typing its many drafts. Max Franke prepared the index.

The book was begun while the author was a Rockefeller Foundation International Relations Fellow. Brookings is grateful to the Carnegie Corporation of New York and the John D. and Catherine T. MacArthur Foundation for financial support.

The views expressed in this study are those of the author and should not be ascribed to the persons or foundations whose assistance is acknowledged, or to the trustees, officers, or other staff members of the Brookings Institution.

BRUCE K. MACLAURY
President

June 1987
Washington, D.C.

Contents

Figures

Abbreviations
and Acronyms

ABM	antiballistic missile
AFB	Air Force base
AFSATCOM	Air Force Satellite Communications System
AFSCF	Air Force Satellite Control Facility
AFSCN	Air Force Satellite Control Network
ALMV	Air-Launched Miniature Vehicle
ASAT	antisatellite; antisatellite weapon
ASW	antisubmarine warfare
BMD	ballistic missile defense
BMEWS	Ballistic Missile Early Warning System
BSTS	Boost Surveillance and Tracking System
C^2	command and control
C^3I	command, control, communications, and intelligence
CSOC	Consolidated Space Operations Center
DARPA	Defense Advanced Research Projects Agency
DEW	directed-energy weapon
DMSP	Defense Meteorological Satellite Program
DSCS	Defense Satellite Communications System
DSP	Defense Support Program
ECM	electronic countermeasure(s)
EHF	extremely high frequency
ELF	extremely low frequency
EMCON	emission control (''radio silence'')
EMP	electromagnetic pulse
EORSAT	electronic ocean reconnaissance satellite
ERIS	Exo-atmospheric Re-entry Vehicle Interception System
FLTSATCOM	Fleet Satellite Communications System
FOBS	fractional orbital bombardment system
FOSIC	Fleet Ocean Surveillance Center
GEODSS	Ground-based Electro-Optical Deep Space Surveillance system

Glonass	Global Navigation Satellite System
GPS	Global Positioning System (Navstar)
HF	high frequency
HF/DF	high-frequency direction finding
HOE	Homing Overlay Experiment
ICBM	intercontinental ballistic missile
INF	intermediate-range nuclear forces
IONDS	Integrated Operational Nuclear Detection System
IRBM	intermediate-range ballistic missile
ITV	Instrumented Test Vehicle
KEW	kinetic energy weapon
KH	Keyhole
LCC	launch control center
Leasat	Leased Satellite System
LES	Lincoln Experimental Satellite
LF	low frequency
LORAN	long-range aids to navigation
LPAR	large phased-array radar
LWIR	long-wave infrared
MGT	mobile ground terminal
Milstar	Military Strategic and Tactical Relay System
MIRACL	Mid-infrared Advanced Chemical Laser
MV	Miniature Vehicle
NASA	National Aeronautics and Space Administration
NAVSPASUR	Naval Space Surveillance System
Navstar GPS	Navigation System Time and Ranging Global Positioning System
NCA	national command authorities
NDS	Nuclear Detection System
NOAA	National Oceanic and Atmospheric Administration
NORAD	North American Aerospace Defense Command
NOSS	Navy Ocean Surveillance System
N-ROSS	Navy–Remote Ocean Sensing System
NTM	national technical means (of verification)
NUDETS	nuclear explosion detection sensors
OTH	over-the-horizon
PARCS	Perimeter Attack Radar Characterization System
RORSAT	radar ocean reconnaissance satellite
SAC	Strategic Air Command
SAR	synthetic aperture radar
SCF	satellite control facility
SDI	Strategic Defense Initiative
SDS	Satellite Data System
SGEMP	system-generated electromagnetic pulse
SHF	superhigh frequency
SIGINT	signals intelligence
SIOP	Single Integrated Operational Plan

SLBM	submarine-launched ballistic missile
SOSS	Soviet ocean surveillance system
SOSUS	Sound Surveillance System
SPADOC	Space Defense Operations Center
SRAM	short-range attack missile
SSBN	nuclear ballistic missile submarine
SSN	nuclear attack submarine
SSTS	Space Surveillance and Tracking System
SURTASS	Surface Towed-Array Sensor System
TACAMO	Take Charge and Move Out (US Navy airborne command post)
TDRSS	Tracking and Data Relay Satellite System
TENCAP	Tactical Exploitation of National Capabilities
UHF	ultrahigh frequency
VDL	video data link

SPACE AND
NATIONAL SECURITY

CHAPTER ONE

Introduction

OF THE areas critical to U.S. national security, outer space is the least understood. The military satellites that are routinely launched for intelligence gathering, early warning, arms control monitoring, communication, navigation, and weather forecasting—to name the most significant applications—contribute in vital ways to America's defense. The Soviet Union likewise makes extensive use of space systems.

For more than twenty-five years, U.S. and Soviet military satellites have operated in a virtual sanctuary, with the superpowers making only half-hearted and sporadic efforts to develop weapons to disable each other's space assets. This state of affairs is unlikely to last for much longer, however, unless the superpowers reach some agreement on constraining the development of antisatellite (ASAT) weapons. Although the Soviet Union has proposed that ASAT weapons be banned, the Reagan administration believes a ban would not be in the interests of the United States. A U.S. ASAT system is now nearing completion, with deployment expected within the next few years.

Whether the United States should proceed with the deployment of antisatellite weapons is the subject of this book. The implications of going ahead are enormous. At stake is not only the security of each side's space systems in wartime, but the possibility that the *threat* of their loss would inject dangerous uncertainties into each superpower's calculations during a severe crisis. The use of ASAT weapons, furthermore, could escalate a conflict in undesirable and uncontrollable ways.

Unfortunately, this issue has not received the scrutiny it merits, largely because it has been eclipsed by the debate on the Strategic Defense Initiative. Begun in 1983 the SDI, or "Star Wars" program as

1

it is popularly known, is investigating ways to defend America against ballistic missile attack. Although the program has raised the concern that antimissile weapons may be deployed in space, that prospect is not likely to be realized for at least another decade. The antisatellite issue, on the other hand, deserves immediate attention before the United States commits itself to a new avenue of the arms race without fully considering whether there is an alternative, more prudent strategy.

The Evolution of the Antisatellite Issue

Since 1977 the United States has been developing an air-launched heat-seeking missile that is designed to home in on a target satellite and destroy it by force of impact. With further testing this system could be ready for deployment in 1990 at an estimated cost of $4 billion. In March 1987 the U.S. Air Force announced plans to upgrade the capabilities of the system, which may lead to the modification of land-based Pershing II missiles for the ASAT mission.[1]

To a large extent, the U.S. ASAT program was initiated in response to an operational if limited Soviet antisatellite capability. The Soviet ASAT system uses an enormous liquid-fueled booster to launch an interceptor satellite into the immediate vicinity of its quarry, whereupon a fragmentation charge is detonated, sending a cloud of shrapnel to disable the target. Though tests of this system were carried out intermittently between 1968 and 1971, it was their resumption in 1976 that led President Gerald R. Ford in the last days of his administration to authorize a new U.S. antisatellite program.[2]

The incoming Carter administration, however, believed that it was in the interests of both superpowers to avoid an antisatellite arms competition and proposed bilateral negotiations with the Soviet Union to prohibit these weapons. Nevertheless, as part of a two-track strategy to provide bargaining leverage at the talks and to hedge against their failure, the U.S. ASAT program was allowed to continue. Though discussions

1. Office of the Assistant Secretary of Defense for Public Affairs, "Secretary of Defense Announces Details of Restructured Anti-Satellite Program," news release, Washington, D.C., March 10, 1987.

2. The United States had actually tested and deployed two nuclear-armed antisatellite weapon systems in the Pacific during the 1960s. By 1975 the last remaining system was fully decommissioned. For more details see Paul B. Stares, *The Militarization of Space: U.S. Policy, 1945–1984* (Ithaca, N.Y.: Cornell University Press, 1985), pp. 157–79.

were eventually held, they proved fruitless and ceased after the Soviet invasion of Afghanistan in 1979.

Part of the reason for the lack of progress was the Soviet Union's apparent unwillingness to dismantle its existing ASAT system. By the early 1980s, however, the U.S. and Soviet positions on ASAT arms control had essentially reversed themselves. Instead of being the reluctant partner, the Soviet Union became the champion of strict limits on space weapons. This change was widely credited to the Soviet Union's interest in curbing the SDI, but in fact it preceded the Reagan administration's initiative. In 1981 the Soviets presented a draft treaty to the UN General Assembly that called for a ban on weapons in outer space. In 1983 they followed this up by announcing a unilateral moratorium on the testing of antisatellite weapons and in a second, more inclusive draft treaty put before the United Nations they also indicated they would dismantle their own system.

The Reagan administration has steadfastly rejected these initiatives and made no effort to respond with counterproposals of its own. The reasons were laid out in a White House report to Congress delivered in March 1984.[3] In essence the administration argues that ASAT arms control can offer little in the way of protection for U.S. satellites. Not only will it be difficult if not impossible to verify the dismantlement of the Soviet ASAT system, but the unavoidable presence of what are termed "residual" antisatellite weapons make specific limits of dubious worth. (The term "residual ASATs" refers to weapons such as intercontinental ballistic missiles and antiballistic missiles that have not been specifically designed to attack satellites but nevertheless can be used for this purpose.) It is argued, therefore, that a U.S. antisatellite capability is essential to deter attacks on U.S. and Allied space systems.

Besides deterring aggression in space, the other stated U.S. rationale for pursuing ASAT development and rejecting arms control is that these weapons are needed to counter the threat from Soviet space systems.[4] That military planners consider certain satellites a threat may come as a surprise to some. After all, they possess no means of attacking either

3. Ronald Reagan, "Report to the Congress on U.S. Policy on ASAT Arms Control," March 31, 1984.

4. Both rationales were first laid out in the public version of National Security Decision Directive–42, signed by President Reagan in July 1982. See "Fact Sheet Outlining United States Space Policy, July 4, 1982," *Public Papers of the Presidents of the United States: Ronald Reagan, 1982* (Government Printing Office, 1983), bk. 2, p. 897.

other objects in space or targets on earth. The predominant image of satellites is that their functions are peaceful and benign.

Indeed, satellites do make an important contribution to international peace and stability. By providing accurate and timely intelligence on one's adversaries, reconnaissance satellites reduce suspicions of warlike intentions and warn of potential threats. They are also invaluable aids for monitoring compliance with arms control accords. Furthermore, a separate class of surveillance satellites designed to detect the launch of ballistic missiles bolsters deterrence by improving the likelihood that either side can retaliate effectively in the event of a surprise attack. Finally, communication satellites ensure that reliable links between the superpowers will be available for crisis management.

The role of satellites, however, is changing in a fundamental way. They are becoming more and more useful for enhancing the war-fighting effectiveness of armed forces. Virtually every type of military operation, from small conventional conflicts to strategic nuclear war, is now likely to involve satellites. Reconnaissance satellites, for instance, are increasingly being used to locate, track, and target military forces such as naval ships. Communication satellites, by being able to receive and rapidly distribute vital information, can improve in radical ways the command and control of military forces and thus their combat performance. And navigation satellites now make it possible to guide the "dumbest" munitions to their targets with nearly perfect precision. In military terms, satellites have become true "force multipliers."

The growing applications of space systems will "change profoundly the conduct of military operations," according to General Robert T. Herres, former commander in chief, U.S. Space Command:

> Commanders operating military forces today conduct operations without many of the uncertainties that plagued their predecessors. Because of the support space based systems provide, commanders have better data on weather conditions and can use such information to their advantage. They know with far more confidence the strength and disposition of the forces they face, and they are more certain of the disposition of their own forces. This knowledge has been historically decisive in the outcome of military operations. It is clear that the use of space can provide a decisive edge. Modern military forces cannot expect success if they are denied that edge while operating against forces who enjoy the support provided by space based systems.[5]

5. Gen. Robert T. Herres, USAF, "The Military's Use of Space Based Systems," *Signal*, vol. 40 (March 1986), p. 48.

As General Herres's final point intimates, the expanding role of military space systems has increased the incentives to deny these benefits to an adversary in wartime. Equally, it has made it more important to protect them from attack. Herein lies a fundamental dilemma for U.S. policymakers that is at the center of the debate over antisatellite weapons. The United States cannot expect to develop the means to counter the Soviet military use of space in wartime without the Soviet Union responding in a similar fashion and threatening U.S. space assets. Yet to forgo a satellite-attack capability allows the Soviet Union to take full advantage of the support from its space systems, with potentially serious consequences for the success of U.S. military operations.

Two schools of thought have evolved over how U.S. military space policy should proceed. One starts from the belief that space is just another military arena where satellites will have to adapt to new threats with new countermeasures in the same way that their counterparts on earth have adapted. Proponents of this view believe, at least by implication, that the United States can stay ahead in this unfolding contest and essentially get the best of both worlds; that is, deny the Soviets the use of their space assets in wartime while simultaneously preserving the security of U.S. space systems. Moreover, they argue that any attempt to constrain the development of antisatellite systems is illogical and unfeasible; illogical because there are no such limitations on weapons capable of attacking, say, high-flying reconnaissance aircraft or early warning radars, and unfeasible because of the unavoidable presence of the residual antisatellite systems mentioned earlier.

The second school considers the laissez-faire approach to antisatellite development dangerously shortsighted and ultimately counterproductive to U.S. interests. It starts from the belief that the United States is more dependent on the services of military satellites than the Soviet Union is and therefore has more to lose in the event of hostilities in space. The proponents of this view remain highly skeptical of the United States' ability to defend its vital space assets in the face of unconstrained antisatellite development by the Soviet Union. In addition to stimulating an expensive and in the end fruitless competition, they believe an ASAT arms race could seriously erode superpower stability during a severe crisis. Specifically, the knowledge that the other side had a highly effective ASAT weapon system capable of crippling one's own vital early warning and strategic communication satellites could become an overwhelming incentive to strike first in a major superpower crisis. They conclude, therefore, that the United States and the Soviet Union should seek an immediate halt to ASAT development and the testing of other weapons in space.

Both sides of the antisatellite debate marshal persuasive arguments yet both leave unanswered some troubling questions. Advocates of the U.S. ASAT program assume that American satellites can be defended against the best efforts of the Soviets to destroy them. But is this a prudent assumption to guide current decisionmaking when space technology is in a constant state of flux and when U.S. hopes of maintaining a decisive lead in other areas of weapons development have often proved illusive? As for those who advocate space arms control, it is fair to ask them how the United States should deal with the threat from Soviet satellites. Ironically, an arms control regime that maintained space as a virtual sanctuary could encourage the deployment of even more threatening types of satellites. For example, the possible development of satellites capable of detecting, tracking, and therefore targeting missile-carrying submarines and mobile ICBMs, which both sides would rely on to ensure retaliation, could make a truly disabling first strike feasible. In this eventuality, possessing an ASAT system could be viewed as positively desirable if not essential.

The Strategic Defense Initiative has added yet another dimension to the antisatellite debate. Because the techniques for disabling satellites and intercepting missiles are very similar, the Reagan administration has become even more reluctant to consider an agreement that might inhibit U.S. freedom to test and deploy antimissile weapons in space, even though such actions are currently prohibited by the Antiballistic Missile Treaty of 1972.[6] Furthermore, given the inherent ASAT capabilities of high-altitude antimissile systems, a vigorous SDI research and development program promises at the very least to complicate negotiations aimed at limiting ASAT weapons and may undermine them totally. At the same time, continuing with the development of antisatellite weapons could jeopardize negotiations to resolve superpower differences over antimissile research. Since 1985 the United States and the Soviet Union have been meeting regularly in Geneva to discuss limits on strategic offensive missiles, intermediate-range nuclear forces (INF), and strategic defense systems. Differences over the SDI have inhibited progress

6. The ABM treaty prohibits the testing and deployment of space-based antiballistic missile systems (article 5). It does not, however, prohibit tests in space of fixed land-based ABM systems. See chapter 5 for more details.

in all but the area of INF arms control. Thus the antisatellite debate affects much larger issues than just the future security of space systems.

Organization of the Study

A necessary starting point for this study is a full appraisal of the current and potential military space programs of the superpowers. Thus chapter 2 compares the general operational characteristics of the two space programs and describes the individual satellite systems by mission category. Such analysis is important for gauging the potential effects of antisatellite weapons in time of war.

It is equally important to understand the changing role of satellites and their growing military value to the superpowers. This is essential not only to assess the incentives for antisatellite weapons development but also to judge the potential consequences of their deployment and possible use. Chapter 3, therefore, examines the contribution of satellites to the security and war-fighting capabilities of the superpowers.

The arguments against antisatellite arms control rest largely on the presence of the Soviets' operational ASAT system and also on their residual capabilities. Chapter 4 assesses these threats to U.S. satellites and the countermeasures available to reduce their vulnerability. The performance of the planned U.S. ASAT system is also analyzed for comparison. Finally, this chapter examines the ASAT weapons that could be deployed in the absence of constraints.

Because the consequences of ASAT threats and attacks will depend greatly on contextual factors, chapter 5 surveys a range of specific conflict scenarios to judge the military utility of antisatellite weapons.

Finally, the feasibility of space arms control is analyzed in light of the most commonly stated reservations about the presence of residual ASAT systems, the adequacy of verification procedures, and the possible effects on the Strategic Defense Initiative. Chapter 6 examines the spectrum of potential arms control options ranging from the most restrictive to the most permissive. The study concludes with a final assessment of the desirability of further ASAT development and presents a list of recommendations for U.S. policy.

CHAPTER TWO

U.S. and Soviet Military Space Programs

THE *Challenger* disaster of January 1986 and the series of catastrophic U.S. launch failures that followed it created a period of almost unprecedented public soul-searching and self-doubt about the U.S. space program. Not since the Soviets became the first nation to launch an artificial satellite in 1957 has the U.S. space effort been subjected to such critical examination. As in the period following the launch of Sputnik, the Soviet space effort has become a natural yardstick by which to gauge the relative performance of the American space program. Judged by selected indicators, the U.S. position looks dismal if not alarming. The Soviets consistently outlaunch the United States, orbit more satellites, and allow their cosmonauts to spend longer periods in space. The commonly drawn conclusions are that the United States has relinquished its acclaimed position as the leading space nation and that the Soviet Union now exploits space more extensively than the United States.

Although the investigation following the launch failures revealed basic problems in the management of the U.S. space program, the assertion that the Soviet Union has overtaken the United States in this area does not stand up to closer examination. This is particularly true for the military exploitation of space, which accounts for the bulk of Soviet space activities. The purpose of this chapter is to compare the military space programs of the superpowers in greater detail to evaluate both their strengths and weaknesses. These differences are highly pertinent to the assessment in later chapters of the vulnerability of each side's military space systems to antisatellite attack. But first it is important to explain the often misunderstood differences between the two space programs.

General Comparisons

Probably the most startling difference is the large disparity in the number of space launches conducted annually by each country. In the year before the *Challenger* accident, the Soviet Union completed a total of 98 space launches to the United States' 17.[1] This imbalance is not, moreover, a recent phenomenon but part of a long-term trend. As figure 2-1 shows, the U.S. annual launch rate peaked in 1966 and declined thereafter, except for minor upturns in the mid-1970s and early 1980s. In contrast, the Soviet Union has steadily increased its annual launch rate, so that by 1967 it had overtaken the United States.

A comparison of total payload weight launched each year by the two countries reveals similar disparities: during the early 1980s the Soviet total was ten times that of the United States, according to the U.S. Department of Defense.[2] This difference is even more pronounced when launches of military payloads are singled out. Between 1957 and 1984 the United States launched roughly 360 specialized military payloads, or only about a third of the Soviets' total of more than 1,100.[3] Another indicator often cited to illustrate the Soviet Union's greater commitment to space development is its continuing interest in *prolonged* manned space flight, which the United States virtually abandoned in the 1970s.[4]

1. Figures derived from Nicholas L. Johnson, *The Soviet Year in Space, 1985* (Colorado Springs, Colo., Teledyne Brown Engineering), pp. 72–78; U.S. National Aeronautics and Space Administration, Goddard Space Flight Center, *Satellite Situation Report*, vol. 25 (NASA, December 1985); and "U.S. Space Launches in 1985," *Aerospace Daily*, January 16, 1986, pp. 85–88. Roughly two-thirds of both were for military purposes: 67 percent for the USSR, 64 percent for the United States. The percentage of U.S. military launches in 1985 represented a sharp increase over the previous year's figure of 38 percent.

2. U.S. Department of Defense, *Soviet Military Power, 1983* (Government Printing Office), p. 65.

3. Marcia S. Smith, *Space Activities of the United States, Soviet Union, and Other Launching Countries/Organizations: 1957–1984* (Library of Congress, Congressional Research Service, 1985), p. 68.

4. Department of Defense, *Soviet Military Power, 1983*, pp. 66–67; and "Soviets Develop Heavy Boosters Amid Massive Military Space Buildup," *Aviation Week and Space Technology*, vol. 122 (March 18, 1985), p. 120. See also "Jane's Analyst Says Soviets Have Lead in Space Program," *Washington Post*, June 17, 1986.

Figure 2-1. *U.S. and Soviet Space Launches, 1960–85*

Successful launches

Sources: For total launches, U.S. Department of Defense, *Soviet Military Power, 1986* (Government Printing Office), p. 52. For presumptively specialized military launches, Marcia S. Smith, *Space Activities of the United States, Soviet Union, and Other Launching Countries/Organizations: 1957–1984* (Library of Congress, Congressional Research Service, 1985), p. 68; and U.S. Joint Chiefs of Staff, *United States Military Posture, FY 1987* (GPO, 1986), p. 82.

Figure 2-2. *U.S. and Soviet Space Program Expenditures, 1965–84*

Billions of fiscal 1985 dollars

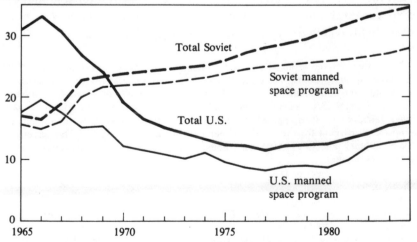

Source: *Department of Defense Appropriations for Fiscal Year 1985,* Hearings before a Subcommittee of the Senate Committee on Appropriations, 98 Cong. 2 sess. (GPO, 1984), pt. 1, p. 576.
   a. Estimated dollar cost.

Not surprisingly, given all this activity, the Soviet Union is also considered to outspend the United States: one official U.S. estimate put the Soviet space program budget for 1984 at $35 billion, virtually double the U.S. equivalent (see figure 2-2).[5]

These indices of national effort in space can give, as noted earlier, the impression that the United States has relinquished its lead in space exploitation. But more sophisticated analysis of the operational characteristics and capabilities of the superpowers' space programs gives a more accurate picture of their relative standing. As the then director of the U.S. Defense Advanced Research Projects Agency (DARPA), Robert S. Cooper, testified before Congress in 1984: "I think we clearly are ahead of the Soviets in overall space technology. . . . It largely has to do with the ability that we have to make microelectronic circuitry and to employ technologies in spacecraft that last much longer in space than Soviet spacecraft and are much smarter in many senses."[6] This becomes readily apparent when one compares the endurance and reliability, the orbital distribution and usage, and the payload capabilities of U.S. and Soviet military satellites.

Satellite Endurance and Reliability

As the U.S. Department of Defense acknowledges, the fact that the "Soviets routinely conduct about four to five times as many space launches per year as the United States . . . is necessitated primarily by the shorter system lifetimes and poorer reliability of most Soviet satellites."[7] The difference in longevity is dramatic. Soviet reconnaissance satellites, which account for nearly 60 percent of all its military space launches, stay in orbit on average only about three weeks, after which

5. "Soviets Spending $35 Billion for Space in 1984," *Soviet Aerospace* (March 5, 1984), p. 58, cited in Johnson, *Soviet Year in Space, 1984,* p. 2. The Soviet Union does not publish its space program expenditures. General Robert T. Herres, former commander in chief of the U.S. Air Force Space Command, estimates that the Soviets outspend the United States by at least $5 billion a year. Gen. Robert T. Herres, "Aerospace Defense Command: Keeping Watch on the Skies of North America," *Signal,* vol. 39 (March 1985), p. 20.

6. *Department of Defense Authorization for Appropriations for Fiscal Year 1983,* Hearings before the Senate Committee on Armed Services, 97 Cong. 2 sess. (GPO, 1982), pt. 7, p. 4625. Later in the same hearings Dr. Cooper stated that the United States had a five-to-ten-year lead over the Soviet Union in space technology. Ibid., p. 4849.

7. Department of Defense, *Soviet Military Power, 1984,* p. 46.

they are deliberately deorbited to recover and process the exposed film. In contrast, the principal U.S. photoreconnaissance satellite system—the Keyhole (KH)-11—stays in orbit as long as three years.[8] Besides carrying additional propellant to prevent orbital decay, the KH-11 achieves this longevity by transmitting images back to earth electronically, thereby avoiding the limitations imposed by consumable photographic film. Although this method was mastered by the United States in the 1960s, the Soviets have only recently begun to use the radio transmission method to return imagery from space. Similarly, U.S. communication satellites stay in orbit up to four or five times longer than their Soviet counterparts.

These asymmetries reflect, in part, different design and engineering philosophies. Instead of making radical changes with each new generation of satellites, the Soviets prefer incremental modifications to tried and trusted designs.[9] The development of Soviet launch vehicles also follows this philosophy. The workhorses of the Soviet space program continue to be the derivatives of the SS-6 ICBM first used to orbit Sputnik in 1957. Two members of this family of boosters (designated the SL-4 and SL-5 by the U.S. Defense Department) still account for more than 50 percent of all Soviet space launches.[10]

In contrast to the Soviet "assembly line" approach, U.S. satellites generally undergo numerous design changes between generations. This is especially evident when succeeding generations are built by different aerospace companies. The longer lifetimes of U.S. satellites also provide more opportunity for modifying replacements, so that often no two spacecraft are identical, even within the same production run. The Soviets, on the other hand, appear to encourage component sharing between generations of the same class of satellite, and also between satellites with different missions, such as the Molniya communication and early warning spacecraft.

8. Johnson, *Soviet Year in Space, 1983*, p. 10; Paul B. Stares, "U.S. and Soviet Military Space Programs: A Comparative Assessment," *Daedalus*, vol. 114 (Spring 1985), p. 136; and Jeffrey Richelson, "The Keyhole Satellite Program," *Journal of Strategic Studies*, vol. 7 (June 1984), pp. 137, 141.

9. For a useful discussion of Soviet design philosophy in other areas, see Joshua M. Epstein, *Measuring Military Power: The Soviet Air Threat to Europe* (Princeton University Press, 1984), pp. 43–55.

10. Some Western space experts continue to use the nomenclature introduced by the late Charles Sheldon of the Congressional Research Service, in which this family of boosters is known as the A-Class. See Johnson, *Soviet Year in Space, 1985*, p. 7.

The lower reliability of Soviet space systems also contributes to their higher launch rate. U.S. launch failures in 1986 notwithstanding, the Soviet space program consistently suffers more catastrophic malfunctions of spacecraft each year. In part this reflects the Soviets' research and development style, in which they often field premature systems to gain experience for later modification.[11] The Soviet Union insures against failure by having numerous satellites and launch vehicles available to replace those lost. The United States, on the other hand, makes the key components of its spacecraft highly redundant, so that when one part fails multiple backup systems keep the satellite in operation. The United States also deploys more spare satellites in space to take the place of those that will fail beyond recovery.[12]

Although the Soviet approach may be considered inefficient, it would have advantages in wartime by allowing them to deploy more satellites at short notice and quickly replace those lost to hostile action. Even if Soviet launch sites were damaged or destroyed, the high number of satellites would be further insurance against attack, allowing each constellation to provide at least some service over a longer period (in other words, to "degrade gracefully").[13]

Orbital Distribution and Usage

In addition to the shorter lifetimes and poorer reliability of their space systems, the Soviets often must deploy more satellites to obtain what appears to be the same level of service as (and may even be less than) their U.S. counterparts. This is partly because the United States has "learned to use space more efficiently," as one U.S. Air Force general put it.[14] But geography also influences how well the superpowers can exploit space. In particular, the equatorial geosynchronous orbit that the United States uses for communication, early warning, and signals

11. See Stephen M. Meyer, "The U.S.S.R. Use of Space," in *National Security Issues Symposium 1984: Space, National Security, and C³I* (Bedford, Mass.: Mitre Corporation, 1984), p. 22.

12. The U.S. space shuttle provides an additional hedge in being able to salvage failed satellites in certain orbits.

13. Nicholas L. Johnson, "C³ in Space: The Soviet Approach," *Signal*, vol. 40 (December 1985), p. 21.

14. Testimony of Brig. Gen. Bernard P. Randolph, *Department of Defense Authorization for Appropriations for Fiscal Year 1983*, Hearings, pt. 7, p. 4853.

intelligence gathering is more difficult for the Soviets to reach from their territory.

Launch sites close to the equator (0° latitude), such as Cape Canaveral (28.5° north), can take advantage of the earth's greater rotational speed at these latitudes to boost objects into space.[15] But since much of the Soviet Union lies above 45° latitude, including the two principal launch sites at Tyuratam (45.6° north) and Plesetsk (62.8° north), it is far harder for the Soviets to place satellites into the geosynchronous orbit over the equator. Moreover, once launched from their northern sites, Soviet satellites also have to make a greater plane change to reach the geosynchronous orbit. This necessitates consuming more fuel or sacrificing payload capacity. Although in recent years it has become more commonplace for the Soviets to deploy geosynchronous satellites, it is still much easier for them to use established low-altitude circular or highly elliptical orbits, even if such orbits may require more satellites to provide the desired level of service.

The use of these less efficient orbits remains attractive for other reasons. Due to the curvature of the earth, communication satellites placed in the geosynchronous orbit cannot satisfactorily transmit messages to the polar regions of the globe. Since key Soviet military installations are located in the far north, the Soviets rely on two separate constellations of eight satellites each that circle the earth in highly ellipitical orbits so that they spend the majority of their time over the northern hemisphere. As one satellite drops below the horizon there is always at least one rising above it to ensure continuous communication. Besides these sixteen Molniya communication satellites, the Soviet Union also operates two other constellations for military communication, totaling about twenty-seven satellites in low-altitude circular orbits.[16] In contrast, the bulk of U.S. military communication travels via approximately twelve longer lived satellites in the geosynchronous orbit and another two in orbits similar to those of the Soviet Molniya satellites.

15. See William J. Durch and Dean A. Wilkening, "Steps into Space," in William J. Durch, ed., *National Interests and the Military Use of Space* (Cambridge, Mass.: Ballinger, 1984), pp. 22, 26; and *Department of Defense Authorization and Oversight*, Hearings on Department of Defense Authorization of Appropriations for Fiscal Year 1984 before the House Committee on Armed Services, 98 Cong. 1 sess. (GPO, 1983), pt. 5, p. 449.

16. The Soviet military almost certainly makes use of communication satellites in the geosynchronous orbit as well. See sources cited in note 66.

Mission Capabilities

Another significant difference between U.S. and Soviet military satellites lies in the number of missions they can individually perform. As the former director of DARPA, Dr. Cooper, has observed:

[If] you make a comparison between . . . the military spacecraft we have and the military spacecraft they have, typically their missions are narrowly defined for their spacecraft. They are aimed at, say, one specific mission area. Typically our spacecraft look much like Christmas trees. They have a number of different missions attached to any given space platform, and as time wears on we find block changes where even additional missions get added from time to time to the same spacecraft.[17]

For example, the United States has attached communication transponders to a variety of satellites that primarily support other missions. The Navstar Global Positioning System (GPS) navigation satellites and the Defense Support Program (DSP) satellites for early warning of ballistic missile attack also carry special sensors to detect nuclear explosions. It is also likely that U.S. photoreconnaissance satellites possess equipment for gathering electronic intelligence.

In sum, the United States uses fewer, longer lasting, and more technically advanced space systems than the Soviet Union does. While the Soviets clearly have a very active military space program that duplicates the basic functions of its U.S. counterpart, it cannot be considered superior. This becomes apparent with the following more detailed examination of the military space programs of the superpowers.

The Military Applications of Satellites

The United States and Soviet Union operate on a daily basis close to 150 satellites for such military support missions as intelligence gathering, early warning of attack, arms control verification, communication, navigation, weather forecasting, and mapping. Supporting these satellites are extensive networks of ground stations that maintain and monitor their operations as well as retrieve, process, and disseminate whatever information is collected or transmitted by them. Table 2-1 gives a composite view of U.S. and Soviet satellite constellations and their

17. *Department of Defense Authorization and Oversight*, Hearings, pt. 5, p. 449.

Table 2-1. *Deployment of U.S. and Soviet Military Satellites, 1987*

	United States				Soviet Union				
Designation	Perigee × apogee (km)	Typical number of satellites in constellation	Inclination (degrees)	Period	Designation	Perigee × apogee (km)	Typical number of satellites in constellation	Inclination (degrees)	Period
Photoreconnaissance									
Keyhole (KH)-11	300 × 440	2	97	90 min	Kosmos (3d gen)	355 × 415	1	70, 73, 83	90 min
					Kosmos (4th gen)	170 × 350	1	65, 67	90 min
					Kosmos (5th gen)	180 × 270	1	65	90 min
Signals intelligence									
Chalet, Magnum	35,800 × 35,800	4(?)	0	24 hr	Kosmos	635 × 665	6	83	98 min
Jumpseat	350 × 39,200	2(?)	63	12 hr	Kosmos	850 × 855	1+	71	102 min
Ocean reconnaissance									
Whitecloud	1,100 × 1,100	8	63	107 min	RORSAT[a]	250 × 265	1-2	65	90 min
					EORSAT[a]	425 × 445	1-3	65	93 min
Ballistic missile early warning									
Defense Support Program (DSP)	35,800 × 35,800	3	0	24 hr	Kosmos	400 × 40,000	9	63	12 hr

Sources: Nicholas L. Johnson, *The Soviet Year in Space, 1986* (Colorado Springs, Colo., Teledyne Brown Engineering); Anthony Kenden, "U.S. Military Activities in Space—1986," unpublished mimeo; and U.S. National Aeronautics and Space Administration, Goddard Space Flight Center, *Satellite Situation Report*, vol. 26 (NASA, December 1986).

Category / System[a]	Altitude (km)	Number	Inclination	Period	Soviet system	Altitude (km)	Number	Inclination	Period
Communication[b]									
DSCS II, III	35,800 × 35,800	6	0	24 hr	Kosmos	790 × 810	3	74	101 min
FLTSATCOM	35,800 × 35,800	4	0	24 hr	Kosmos	1,350 × 1,550	24	74	115 min
Leasat	35,800 × 35,800	4	0	24 hr	Molniya 1	400 × 40,000	8	63	12 hr
SDS	350 × 39,200	2	63	12 hr	Molniya 3[c]	400 × 40,000	8	63	12 hr
					Raduga, Gorizont, Kosmos	35,800 × 35,800	12	0	24 hr
Navigation									
Transit-Nova	1,060 × 1,060	4–6	90	109 min	Kosmos	960 × 1,020	6	83	105 min
Navstar GPS[d]	20,000 × 20,200	18[e]	63	12 hr	Kosmos[c]	960 × 1,020	4	83	105 min
					Glonass[a]	19,000 × 19,200	9–12	65	11.3 hr
Meteorology[f]									
DMSP	810 × 830	2	99	101 min	Meteor 2	940 × 960	2–3	83	104 min
					Meteor 3	1,230 × 1,250	1–2	83	110 min
Geodesy									
Geosat	785 × 780	1	100	100 min	Kosmos	1,480 × 1,525	2	73, 83	109 min

(?) Uncertain constellation size.

a. Western acronyms.

b. DSCS = Defense Satellite Communications System; FLTSATCOM = Fleet Satellite Communications; Leasat = Leased Satellite System; SDS = Satellite Data System. For the United States, excludes the system of AFSATCOM communication transponders deployed on FLTSATCOM, SDS, and other satellites. Also excludes NATO III, Tracking and Data Relay Satellite System (TDRSS), and Lincoln Experimental Satellite (LES) 8/9 spacecraft.

c. Primarily civil satellites.

d. Also hosts nuclear detonation detector sensors (NDS).

e. When fully deployed.

f. For the United States, excludes two National Oceanic and Atmospheric Administration (NOAA) satellites.

approximate orbital parameters. What follows is a fuller description, by mission category.

Photoreconnaissance Satellites

Until 1984 the United States operated three types of photoreconnaissance satellites that were all part of the "Keyhole" (KH) program series.[18] That year the last of the KH-8 and KH-9 satellite systems apparently came to the end of their operational lives. These satellites orbited lower than any other U.S. military spacecraft (in the case of the KH-8, sometimes as low as 130 kilometers) to facilitate high-resolution photography of areas of specific interest, such as the site of a suspected arms control violation or the buildup of military forces during a crisis.[19] The exposed photographic film was periodically returned to earth for processing in special capsules. Such was the reported quality of the images that objects only six inches in diameter could be discerned.

By 1986 the only U.S. photoreconnaissance system still operational was the KH-11. These satellites orbit at somewhat higher altitudes (between 300 and 440 kilometers) and, as noted earlier, last upwards of three years. Instead of a conventional camera system, KH-11 satellites use a large telescope connected to an array of light-sensitive cells known as a charge coupled device. This filters and converts the reflected image from the earth's surface into digital electronic signals that are then transmitted by radio "in near-real time" (according to a CIA official) via two Satellite Data System (SDS) spacecraft in a highly elliptical polar orbit back to a ground station near Washington, D.C. Here the imagery data are processed and enhanced by computers, so that photos can be made available for viewing, reportedly within an hour.[20] Though not as

18. The series began in the late 1950s. See William E. Burrows, *Deep Black: Space Espionage and National Security* (Random House, 1986), pp. 23–24, 299–305; and Richelson, "Keyhole Satellite Program," pp. 121–53. Unless otherwise indicated information on U.S. photoreconnaissance satellites is from these two sources.

19. For example, KH-8 satellites appear to have been specially launched to monitor the buildup of Soviet forces along the Polish border in 1981, and Libyan forces along the Chad border in 1982. See Richelson, "Keyhole Satellite Program," p. 135. Two launches of KH-8 satellites in 1984 may have been to collect more detailed photos of the Krasnoyarsk radar site. See Craig Covault, "USAF, NASA Discuss Shuttle Use for Satellite Maintenance," *Aviation Week and Space Technology*, vol. 121 (December 17, 1984), pp. 14–16.

20. James Bamford, "America's Supersecret Eyes in Space," *New York Times Magazine* (January 13, 1985), p. 52; and George Lardner, Jr., "Satellite Unchanged from Manual Bought by Soviets, U.S. Officials Say," *Washington Post*, October 10, 1985.

good as the KH-8 satellite's, the resolution of the KH-11 imaging system is still impressive, as several photos released without authorization have indicated.[21] Typically, two KH-11 satellites are operating at any given time, although because of launch failures in August 1985 and April 1986, and furthermore delays in the deployment of the follow-on system (presumably designated the KH-12), the United States was reduced to relying on a single photoreconnaissance satellite throughout 1986 and much of 1987.[22]

The successor to the KH-11 is now scheduled to be launched from the space shuttle sometime in 1988, depending on how soon shuttle operations can resume. The KH-12 is expected to be a significant improvement over the KH-11. Besides supplying higher resolution photos, the anticipated deployment of four KH-12 satellites will enable the United States to reconnoiter specific areas of interest more quickly and with less delay between overflights than is the case today.[23] Moreover, the lifetime of these satellites is expected to be much greater than their predecessors'—probably as much as six years and maybe even longer—which will be made possible by regular refuelings and other routine maintenance by space shuttle crews.[24] The KH-12 may also incorporate infrared sensors to permit nighttime surveillance and perhaps a synthetic aperture radar (SAR)[25] to penetrate the cloud cover that can obscure areas of interest for lengthy periods.[26] If so, the resolution of these sensors will be somewhat lower than those that operate in the visible light range.

In comparison, the Soviets currently operate what appear to be three types of photoreconnaissance satellites. Though they are uniformly

21. The unauthorized release of photos from KH-11 satellites has occurred on at least two occasions. See "Soviet Strategic Bomber Photographed at Ramenskoye," *Aviation Week and Space Technology*, vol. 115 (December 14, 1981), p. 17; and "Satellite Pictures Show Soviet CVN Towering above Nikolaev Shipyard," *Jane's Defense Weekly*, vol. 2 (August 11, 1984), pp. 171–73.

22. Jack Cushman, "Space Shuttle Explosion Throws Military Programs into Disarray," *Defense Week*, vol. 7 (February 3, 1986), p. 5.

23. Charles Mohr, "Pentagon Fears Delays on Future Spy Satellites," *New York Times*, February 24, 1986.

24. James B. Schultz, "In the Shadows of Space," *Defense Electronics*, vol. 17 (April 1985), p. 81.

25. Covault, "USAF, NASA Discuss Shuttle Use," p. 14; and Burrows, *Deep Black*, p. 307.

26. Richelson, "Keyhole Satellite Program," pp. 145–46. According to one report, it took more than eighteen months to detect and photograph the Soviet phased-array radar at Pechora and more than a year to detect a similar construction near Krasnoyarsk. Covault, "USAF, NASA Discuss Shuttle Use," p. 15.

entitled Kosmos, these satellites are distinguished by Western observers according to their generational order and the estimated resolution of their camera systems.[27] At least one Soviet photoreconnaissance satellite is in orbit at any given time, with three being the average complement. Most launches are made up of the medium-resolution third-generation and high-resolution fourth-generation reconnaissance satellites. On average the third-generation craft are in orbit for fourteen days, after which the exposed film is deorbited and recovered along with the camera system. The lifetime of the fourth-generation satellites has steadily risen to an average of nearly sixty days, facilitated by the use of special capsules that periodically return the film for processing. According to a leaked but still classified General Accounting Office (GAO) appraisal, these satellites are "capable of distinguishing automobiles" from space.[28]

The Soviets have also followed the United States in developing long-duration reconnaissance satellites that reportedly use an imaging and radio-transmission system similar to that on board the KH-11. These new fifth-generation reconnaissance satellites, which apparently relay imagery via a geosynchronous communication satellite, have been able to stay operational for more than 230 days.[29] Because this system is still in its infancy, longer operational deployments can be expected in the future. Besides these dedicated satellite systems, accounts indicate the Salyut manned space stations have also been used for reconnaissance purposes.[30] If so, the new space station known as *Mir* may be employed in the same way.

27. Unless otherwise indicated the information on Soviet military space programs is from Johnson, *Soviet Year in Space*, 1981–86 issues; and *Soviet Space Programs: 1976–80*, pt. 3: *Unmanned Space Activities*, Committee Print, Senate Committee on Commerce, Science, and Transportation, 99 Cong. 1 sess. (GPO, 1985). For more information on the Soviet satellite reconnaissance program, see Philip S. Clark, "Aspects of the Soviet Photoreconnaissance Satellite Programme," *Journal of the British Interplanetary Society*, vol. 36 (1983), pp. 169–84.

28. Jack Anderson, "Space 'Peeping Toms' Are a Danger," *Washington Post*, February 12, 1985. See also *Soviet Space Programs: 1976–80*, Committee Print, pt. 3, p. 1060.

29. "USSR Boosts Reconnaissance Capabilities," *Aviation Week and Space Technology*, vol. 122 (January 21, 1985), p. 15; and Johnson, *Soviet Year in Space, 1985*, p. 18.

30. Anderson, "Space 'Peeping Toms' Are a Danger." See also U.S. Congress, Office of Technology Assessment, *Salyut: Soviet Steps toward Permanent Human Presence in Space—A Technical Memorandum*, OTA-TM-STI-14 (Washington, D.C.: GPO, 1983), p. 31.

Signals Intelligence

Since the early 1960s the superpowers have deployed satellites for signals intelligence (SIGINT) gathering.[31] These are designed for such tasks as eavesdropping on military communications, detecting the operating frequencies of enemy radars, and collecting telemetry from ballistic missile tests. The United States reportedly operates two complementary constellations of signals intelligence satellites, one deployed in the geosynchronous orbit and the other in a highly elliptical orbit over the northern part of the Soviet Union.[32] Beginning with the Rhyolite program in 1970, the geosynchronous SIGINT satellites have undergone several design changes with the Argus, Chalet, and most recently Magnum programs.[33] The other operational system, code-named Jumpseat, is presumably deployed in a highly elliptical polar orbit to collect intelligence on military activities at the Soviet Union's northernmost bases.[34] Since SIGINT satellites are the most highly classified U.S. space systems, very little is publicly known about the support infrastructure, operational life span, or even the number deployed.

Even less is known about Soviet signals intelligence satellites. During 1984 the Soviet Union evidently completed the transition from a second-generation system to a new class of much larger satellites, deployed in a

31. The standard taxonomy of satellite applications generally uses the term "electronic intelligence" (ELINT) rather than "signals intelligence." However, since the latter is a more inclusive term, covering communication intelligence (COMINT) and telemetry intelligence (TELINT) as well as electronic intelligence, it is used here.

32. While the KH-9 photoreconnaissance satellites were still operational, the United States used them to carry small subsatellites into orbit for signals intelligence gathering. Some of these may still be operational. It is unclear whether the deployment of small SIGINT subsatellites will continue using different low-altitude platforms as dispensers. See "Big Bird Satellite Is Accompanied by Electronic Ferret," *Aerospace Daily,* June 23, 1982; and Jeffrey Richelson, *The U.S. Intelligence Community* (Cambridge, Mass.: Ballinger, 1985), pp. 122–23.

33. For reference to these various programs, see Desmond Ball, "The Rhyolite Programme," Reference Paper 86 (Canberra: Australian National University, Strategic and Defence Studies Centre, November 1981); Richelson, *U.S. Intelligence Community,* pp. 120–22; "Space 'Mole' Isn't Science Fiction," *U.S. News and World Report* (October 29, 1984), p. 42; Richard Burt, "U.S. Plans New Way to Check Soviet Missile Tests," *New York Times,* June 29, 1979; Bamford, "America's Supersecret Eyes in Space"; Anthony Kenden, "Who Pays the Piper Calls the Tune," *Satellite Technology,* vol. 1 (June 1985), p. 13; and Jack Anderson, "Hiding Behind the Flag?" *Washington Post,* February 10, 1985.

34. See Seymour M. Hersh, *"The Target Is Destroyed"* (Random House, 1986), p. 4; and Richelson, *U.S. Intelligence Community,* p. 122.

constellation of six in a low-altitude circular orbit inclined 82.5° to the equator.[35] Yet another new class of SIGINT satellite made its appearance in 1984 with the launch of Kosmos 1603 into a slightly higher circular orbit but with a 71° inclination. Reported to weigh as much as 15,000 pounds, the Kosmos 1603 type is considerably larger than the third-generation SIGINT satellite, in fact among the largest unmanned military spacecraft launched by the Soviet Union.[36]

Ocean Reconnaissance

A separate class of reconnaissance satellites is used specifically for locating and tracking naval shipping. The first U.S. space program dedicated to this mission—Project Whitecloud—became operational in 1976 as part of the Navy Ocean Surveillance System (NOSS), though some earlier signals intelligence and photoreconnaissance satellites appear to have been used for this purpose.[37] Typically, each Whitecloud satellite is launched into a 1,100-kilometer circular orbit inclined 63° to the equator. Three subsatellites then separate from the main spacecraft to widen the area of coverage to about 3,200 kilometers across on each pass.[38] Each subsatellite uses millimeter-wave radio receivers and possibly some passive infrared sensors to detect radar and communication signals from surface shipping. To increase ocean coverage further, two clusters of Whitecloud satellites are usually operational at any given time in a synchronized orbital deployment.

The information gathered from these satellites is passed directly to

35. For more information on Soviet SIGINT satellites, see Johnson, *Soviet Year in Space*, 1981–86 issues; and Jack Anderson, "GAO Audits Soviet Spy Satellites," *Washington Post*, February 11, 1985.

36. "Soviets Develop Heavy Boosters Amid Massive Military Space Buildup," *Aviation Week and Space Technology*, vol. 122 (March 18, 1985), p. 120.

37. Richelson, *U.S. Intelligence Community*, pp. 140–41; and Adm. Stansfield Turner, *Secrecy and Democracy: The CIA in Transition* (Boston: Houghton Mifflin, 1985), p. 90. There have also been references to other Navy-run space-based sensors, such as Project Slow Walker. See statement of Comdr. Richard H. Truly, in *Department of Defense Authorization for Appropriations for Fiscal Year 1986*, Hearings before the Senate Committee on Armed Services, 99 Cong. 1 sess. (GPO, 1985), pt. 7, pp. 4252–58.

38. Unless otherwise indicated the information on the U.S. Whitecloud program is from "Expanded Ocean Surveillance Effort Set," *Aviation Week and Space Technology*, vol. 122 (October 22, 1984), p. 20; and Desmond Ball, "The US Naval Ocean Surveillance Information System (NOSIS)—Australia's Role," *Pacific Defence Reporter* (June 1982), p. 42.

five Naval Security Group ground stations around the world at Guam; Diego Garcia; Adak, Alaska; Winter Harbor, Maine; and Edzell, Scotland. Here the signals are processed and then transmitted to regional Fleet Ocean Surveillance Centers and then via satellite to the Navy Operational Intelligence Center (NOIC) outside Washington, D.C.[39] In return each regional fleet center receives "real-time downlink information" from U.S. satellites on the movement of Soviet naval forces in its own area.[40]

The Soviet Union operates a more elaborate though less reliable space-based ocean surveillance system, made up of passive electronic ocean reconnaissance satellites (EORSATs), which listen for and intercept radio and radar transmissions, and radar ocean reconnaissance satellites (RORSATs), which actively track their targets.[41] Both types are launched from Tyuratam by SL-11 launchers into a 65° inclined circular orbit, with the RORSATs generally at an altitude of 260 kilometers and the EORSATs at 430 kilometers. The ground tracks of the RORSATs and EORSATs appear to be synchronized so that the two detection methods can complement each other. According to Major General Carl B. Beer, deputy chief of staff for plans, U.S. Air Force Space Command, "The RORSAT satellite is used for a broad area of detection and the EORSAT gives pinpoint accuracy."[42]

When fully deployed, two satellites of each type operate in tandem, though the Soviets have managed to do this only twice, once in 1982 and

39. Richelson, *U.S. Intelligence Community*, pp. 140–41.

40. *Department of Defense Authorization for Appropriations for Fiscal Year 1985*, Hearings before the Senate Committee on Armed Services, 98 Cong. 2 sess. (GPO, 1985), pt. 8, p. 3890.

41. Unless otherwise indicated the information on the Soviet ocean reconnaissance program is from Johnson, *Soviet Year in Space*, 1981–86 issues; Nicholas L. Johnson, "Orbital Phasings of Soviet Ocean Surveillance Satellites," *Journal of Spacecraft and Rockets*, vol. 19 (March–April 1982), pp. 113–17; and *Soviet Space Programs: 1976–80*, Committee Print, pt. 3, pp. 1063–70. "EORSAT" and "RORSAT" are Western acronyms.

42. *Department of Defense Authorization for Appropriations for Fiscal Year 1986*, Hearings, pt. 7, p. 4323. The radar swath on each pass of the RORSAT has been estimated to be 400–500 kilometers. "The Soviet Military Space Program," *International Defense Review*, vol. 15, no. 2 (1982), p. 151. According to the classified GAO report referred to earlier the EORSATs can provide targeting data accurate to two kilometers. Anderson, "GAO Audits Soviet Spy Satellites." See also "Soviet Nuclear-Powered Satellite Boosts Naval Surveillance Capability," *Aviation Week and Space Technology*, vol. 123 (August 19, 1985), p. 18; and Norman Polmar and Norman Friedman, "Their Missions and Tactics," *Proceedings*, vol. 108 (October 1982), p. 43.

again in 1985. The RORSAT program in particular has been fraught with technical problems, stemming chiefly from the nuclear reactor system used to power the radar.[43] As a result, RORSAT coverage is sporadic, totaling only five months in 1986, which was one of its best years. It seems likely, therefore, that the Soviets retain their RORSATs for use only in special contingencies. In contrast, they endeavor to keep at least two EORSATs in continuous operation.

While more accurate in detecting the whereabouts of enemy shipping, the EORSATs apparently cannot transmit this information directly to targeting platforms such as ships, submarines, or aircraft but must first send it to the Soviet navy's central command center to be processed and then retransmitted to the relevant users.[44] In contrast, the RORSATs can provide "real-time tracking and targeting data to users in the vicinity of the target or non-real-time data to central control points,"[45] probably by means of a radarscope video data link (VDL) similar to that in operation on Tu-95 Bear-D reconnaissance aircraft. The resolution of the RORSAT's radar "can probably detect destroyer-size ships in good weather and aircraft-carrier-size ships or smaller ships in close proximity to each other in rough seas."[46] The latter point underscores how environmental factors—sea state and also local precipitation—can reduce the ability of radars to discriminate among objects. Poor conditions could prove a real hindrance to the accurate detection of surface shipping in ocean areas that frequently experience bad weather, such as the Norwegian Sea and the northern Pacific. The RORSAT's ability to quickly distinguish military vessels from other ships in heavily congested areas, such as the Mediterranean Sea, is also open to doubt.

Ballistic Missile Early Warning

Under the Defense Support Program the United States operates three satellites in geosynchronous orbit for detecting ballistic missile

43. The reactor is designed to separate from the main body of the satellite at the end of its mission to be boosted to a higher orbit, where its radioactive core can decay safely. On two occasions this maneuver has failed, and radioactive debris has fallen to earth following the breakup of the satellite as it reentered the atmosphere. See Craig Covault, "Soviet Nuclear Spacecraft Poses Reentry Danger," *Aviation Week and Space Technology*, vol. 118 (January 10, 1983), pp. 18–19.

44. Norman Friedman, "Soviet Naval Command and Control," *Signal*, vol. 39 (December 1984), p. 57.

45. Anderson, "GAO Audits Soviet Spy Satellites." Reportedly, targeting data can be downlinked within one orbit. See *Jane's Spaceflight Directory* (London: Jane's Publishing Co., 1984), p. 254. See also Friedman, "Soviet Naval Command and Control."

46. Anderson, "GAO Audits Soviet Spy Satellites."

launches.[47] These satellites use a focal plane array telescope with infrared sensors to detect the hot exhaust plumes of ballistic missiles during the early stages of their flight.[48] The three satellites—one over the Indian Ocean (known as DSP East) and the others over the Pacific and Atlantic Oceans (together known as DSP West)—provide constant surveillance of most of the earth's surface (see figure 2-3). Warning information is passed directly to one of two large processing stations at Nurrungar, South Australia, and Buckley Air National Guard Base, near Denver, Colorado, or to a simplified processing station at Kapaun in West Germany.[49] It is then relayed via the Defense Satellite Communications System (DSCS) or over land-submarine cable to the Data Distribution Center at Buckley ANGB. From here it is distributed to the North American Aerospace Defense Command (NORAD) headquarters in the Cheyenne Mountain Complex near Colorado Springs, Colorado; to the Strategic Air Command (SAC) headquarters at Offutt AFB, Nebraska; to the National Military Command Center in the Pentagon; and to the

47. Two spare DSP satellites may also be in orbit. See Anthony Kenden, "U.S. Military Satellites, 1983," *Journal of the British Interplanetary Society*, vol. 38 (February 1985), p. 63; and Daniel Ford, *The Button* (Simon and Schuster, 1984), p. 64. Although never officially confirmed, reports suggest the United States operates additional early warning sensors piggybacked on satellites used for other missions. See Ford, *The Button*, p. 64. An obvious candidate would be the Satellite Data System (SDS), which operates in a highly elliptical polar orbit over the Northern Hemisphere. This orbit permits coverage of the areas that are out of line of sight of the DSP satellites in geosynchronous orbit (see figure 2-3.) The former commander in chief of the U.S. Space Command, General Robert T. Herres, alluded to the problem of detecting launches in the areas not covered by the DSP satellites in a discussion of the possible deployment of mobile SS-25 missiles in the northern reaches of the Soviet Union. "Growth in Funding Yields Strategic, Tactical Benefits," *Aviation Week and Space Technology*, vol. 123 (December 9, 1985), p. 47. For a discussion of the limitations of the DSP system, see Bruce G. Blair, *Strategic Command and Control: Redefining the Nuclear Threat* (Brookings, 1985), pp. 142–43.

48. Unless otherwise indicated the information on DSP satellites is from Ford, *The Button*, pp. 58–68; Desmond Ball, "Australia and the US Defense Support Program," *Pacific Defense Reporter* (November 1982), pp. 25–47; Jack Cushman, "AF Seeks Invulnerable Warning Satellites," *Defense Week*, vol. 5 (January 16, 1984), pp. 1, 10–14; U.S. Department of the Air Force, *Supporting Data for Fiscal Year 1985 Budget Estimates, Descriptive Summaries: Research, Development, Test and Evaluation* (Dept. of the Air Force, February 1984), pp. 379–88; William M. Arkin and Richard Fieldhouse, "Nuclear Weapon Command, Control and Communications," in *World Armaments and Disarmament: SIPRI Yearbook 1984* (Taylor and Francis for the Stockholm International Peace Research Institute, 1984), pp. 470–71; and "Space Command," *Air Force Magazine*, vol. 68 (May 1985), pp. 100–02.

49. There is also a "multi-purpose facility," probably at Lowry AFB in Denver, Colorado, that serves as a backup to the two larger processing stations. See Department of the Air Force, *Supporting Data for Fiscal Year 1985*, p. 379.

Figure 2-3. *Approximate Earth Coverage of U.S. Defense Support Program Early Warning Satellites*

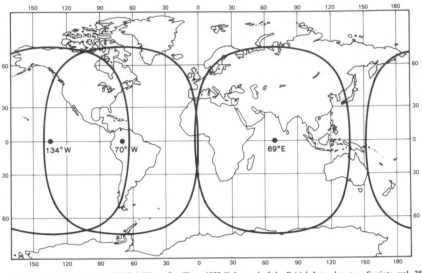

Source: Anthony Kenden, "U.S. Military Satellites, 1983," *Journal of the British Interplanetary Society*, vol. 38 (February 1985), p. 63.

Alternate National Military Command Center at Fort Ritchie in Maryland. The interval from initial detection to the receipt of the warning information can reportedly be as short as a minute.

Currently, both the performance and survivability of the DSP satellites are being improved. The sensor evolutionary development (SED) program has sharpened the satellites' ability to discriminate between launches, while the DSP upgrade program has added a second color focal plane, satellite-to-satellite laser communication cross-links, autonomous station keeping (maintaining the desired position above the earth), and a mission data message rebroadcast feature.[50] Finally, mobile ground terminals that can receive and transmit data directly to the national command authorities via DSCS satellites[51] have been procured to ensure continuity should the main processing stations be destroyed.

In contrast to the U.S. use of the geosynchronous orbit for ballistic

50. *Department of Defense Appropriations for 1987*, Hearings before a Subcommittee of the House Committee on Appropriations, 99 Cong. 2 sess. (GPO, 1986), pt. 3, pp. 668–69.

51. DSP terminals may also be fitted onto E-3A and E-4B aircraft. See Edgar Ulsamer, "The Critical R&D Challenges," *Air Force Magazine*, vol. 66 (July 1983),

missile launch detection, the Soviets maintain a constellation of nine satellites—when fully operational—in a highly elliptical Molniya orbit (400 × 40,000 kilometers) inclined 63° to the equator.[52] These equally spaced satellites permit continuous coverage of both the U.S. and Chinese ICBM fields as well as some patrol areas of U.S. ballistic-missile-carrying submarines. This orbit also allows the satellites to be in line of sight of the Soviet Union for direct transmission of data (see figure 2-4).[53] Though the Soviets employ a different orbit, presumably they too use infrared sensors for detection.

Unfortunately for the Soviets, this has been one of their least reliable space programs. Plagued with persistent malfunctions and catastrophic breakups in space, the full nine-member constellation has rarely been complete. By the end of 1984 the Soviets seemed to have finally solved the program's problems as the existing satellites were replaced with no obvious failures, but the spacecrafts' surprisingly short life spans (500 days on average) and continuing malfunctions in 1985 and 1986 raised new doubts about the system's operational readiness.

Detection of Nuclear Explosions

In the early 1960s the United States deployed a system of spacecraft known as the Vela Hotel program to detect nuclear explosions in the atmosphere. Positioned in a supersynchronous orbit, the spacecrafts' primary mission was to monitor compliance with the 1963 Limited Test Ban Treaty that prohibits nuclear testing in the atmosphere and in outer space. Though these satellites proved surprisingly durable, outliving

---

p. 19. The mobile ground terminals are reportedly deployed at Holloman AFB, New Mexico. See *Department of Defense Authorization and Oversight*, Hearings, pt. 5, p. 523.

52. Unless otherwise indicated information on the Soviet satellite early warning system is from Johnson, *Soviet Year in Space*, 1981–86 issues. There may also be rudimentary early warning sensors on Soviet Molniya communication satellites. See Stephen Meyer, "Space and Soviet Military Planning," in William J. Durch, ed., *National Interests and the Military Use of Space* (Cambridge, Mass.: Ballinger, 1984), p. 74. Another report states that the Soviets also have an early warning satellite in geosynchronous orbit. See Jim Bussert, "Soviet Air Defense Systems Show Increasing Sophistication," *Defense Electronics*, vol. 16 (May 1984), pp. 84, 86.

53. G. E. Perry, "Identification of Military Components Within the Soviet Space Programme," in Bhupendra Jasani, ed., *Outer Space—A New Dimension of the Arms Race* (London: Taylor and Francis for the Stockholm International Peace Research Institute, 1982), p. 146.

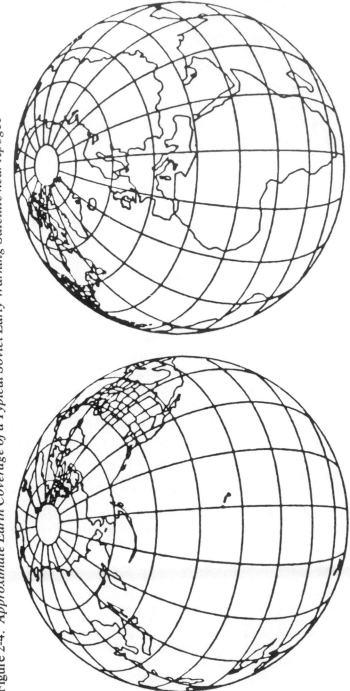

Figure 2-4. *Approximate Earth Coverage of a Typical Soviet Early Warning Satellite near Apogee*

Source: Nicholas L. Johnson, *The Soviet Year in Space, 1982* (Colorado Springs, Colo., Teledyne Brown Engineering), p. 19.

their planned life span by many years, they have now ceased operating. For some time the United States had supplemented Vela Hotel monitoring by placing nuclear detection sensors on DSP early warning satellites. Today each DSP satellite carries an Advanced Atmospheric Burst Locator to detect the visible light, X-rays, and electromagnetic pulse signals emitted by nuclear explosions.[54] A similar package of sensors—originally known as the Integrated Operational Nuclear Detection System (IONDS) and now called the Nuclear Detection System (NDS)—is being installed on the Navstar GPS navigation satellites.[55] When the full constellation of eighteen Navstar satellites becomes operational in 1990, the NDS sensors will be able to provide, in real time, information on the yield, height, and location of nuclear bursts to within 100 meters anywhere in the world.[56] The data will be sent either directly from the spacecraft to U.S. command authorities or via UHF cross-links through other Navstar satellites. All the principal U.S. command posts, including E-4B and EC-135 aircraft, will also receive NDS sensor data directly.[57]

The Soviet Union does not appear to have deployed an equivalent nuclear detection system in space, though it is conceivable that such sensors are aboard satellites deployed in Molniya-type orbits or on the new Glonass spacecraft (a Western acronym for Global Navigation Satellite System), which operate in a constellation similar to the Navstar GPS.

54. See Jack Cushman, "Defense Support Program: The Players," *Defense Week,* vol. 5 (January 16, 1984), p. 14; "Washington Roundup," *Aviation Week and Space Technology,* vol. 117 (December 6, 1982), p. 19; "Industry Observer," *Aviation Week and Space Technology,* vol. 117 (December 13, 1982), p. 13; and Desmond Ball, "Australia and the US Defence Support Program," p. 28.

55. There are also references to a W-sensor being part of the NDS package. See U.S. General Accounting Office, *Issues Concerning the Department of Defense's Global Positioning System as It Enters Production,* MASD-83-9 (GAO, 1983), p. 9; and *Department of Defense Appropriations for 1984,* Hearings before a Subcommittee of the House Committee on Appropriations, 98 Cong. 1 sess. (GPO, 1983), pt. 8, pp. 337–38. Evidence suggests that similar nuclear detection sensors have been hosted by U.S. satellites other than the DSP and Navstar GPS systems. See *Department of Energy National Security and Military Applications of Nuclear Energy Authorization Act of 1984,* Hearings of the House Committee on Armed Services, 98 Cong. 1 sess. (GPO, 1983), p. 392.

56. See *Department of Defense Authorization for Appropriations for Fiscal Year 1983,* Hearings, pt. 7, pp. 4624–25; and Charles A. Zraket, "Strategic Command, Control, Communications, and Intelligence," *Science,* vol. 224 (June 22, 1984), p. 1309.

57. Department of the Air Force, *Supporting Data for Fiscal Year 1985,* pp. 394–95.

Communication

The United States operates five distinct space-based communication systems for military purposes: the Defense Satellite Communications System (DSCS), now in a transitional stage from the DSCS II to the DSCS III program; the Fleet Satellite Communications (FLTSATCOM) System; the Satellite Data System (SDS); the Leased Satellite (Leasat) System (a replacement for the Maritime Satellite, or Marisat, program), and the Air Force Satellite Communications (AFSATCOM) System.[58] Instead of individual satellites the latter system is made up of small communication packages known as AFSATCOM transponders that are piggybacked on DSCS III, FLTSATCOM, SDS, and other satellites whose identities are classified.[59] Except for the SDS satellites, all these spacecraft can be found in the geosynchronous orbit. By the end of the 1980s the United States will have about fourteen military communication satellites (excluding spares) in operation.[60]

Compared with alternative means of long-range communication—principally cable and high-frequency (HF) radio—satellites offer significant advantages. Larger amounts of information can be transmitted in a more reliable, inexpensive, and secure fashion. HF radio transmissions typically suffer from disturbances in the ionosphere, which is used to relay the radio signals over the horizon. Also, because HF signals spread

58. For details of U.S. military communication satellites, see Department of the Air Force, "Defense Satellite Communications System," *Fact Sheet* (Dept. of the Air Force, Office of Public Affairs, March 1983); C. Richard Whelan, *Guide to Military Space Programs* (Arlington, Va.: Pasha Publications, 1984); R. J. Raggett, ed., *Jane's Communications, 1985,* 7th ed. (London: Jane's Publishing Co., 1985); Hughes Aircraft Company, "LEASAT," *Fact Sheet* (El Segundo, Calif.: Space and Communications Group, 1979); "Defense Dept. Plans New Strategies for Communications Satellites," *Aviation Week and Space Technology,* vol. 123 (December 9, 1985), pp. 49–51; and "Military Strives to Meet Growing Demand for Satellite Services," *Aviation Week and Space Technology,* vol. 123 (December 9, 1985), pp. 85–86.

59. See Harold Brown, secretary of defense, *Department of Defense Annual Report Fiscal Year 1982* (DOD, 1981), p. 122. According to one source, Defense Meteorological Satellite Program (DMSP) spacecraft are among the "classified" hosts. See Desmond Ball, "The Defense Meteorological Satellite Program (DMSP)," *Journal of the British Interplanetary Society,* vol. 39 (1986), p. 45.

60. It is hard to reach a full tally of usable military communication satellites, since some are designated from the outset as spares while others have been deliberately "switched off" near the end of their operational life to retain some capability for emergency use. The United States also has use of the constellation of three NATO III satellites, which are to be replaced by a modified British Skynet IV satellite (designated NATO IV).

out over a large area, the source of the transmissions can be compromised by direction-finding equipment. As a result, satellites have become the most favored means for long-haul communication. Currently, they utilize either the ultrahigh-frequency (UHF) bandwidth, which allows communication with mobile forces that can carry only small dish antennas, or the superhigh-frequency (SHF) bandwidth, which permits large quantities of information to be transmitted rapidly.

In the future the United States will increasingly use the extremely high frequency (EHF) bandwidth for both strategic and tactical communications, principally because EHF communications can be better protected from jamming. Beginning with the deployment of test transponders on the FLTSATCOM satellites, an entirely new class of satellites known as the Military Strategic and Tactical Relay (Milstar) System will become operational in the 1990s. Capable of operating in the UHF, SHF, and EHF bands, the Milstar constellation will consist of eight satellites, five deployed in the geosynchronous orbit and three in polar elliptical orbits. Even with the extra capacity of Milstar, the high investment in UHF equipment along with the expected demand for satellite communication will almost certainly lead to the procurement of follow-on programs to the DSCS III and FLTSATCOM systems.[61] The AFSATCOM system may also be expanded, with the deployment of single-channel transponders on the eighteen Navstar GPS satellites.[62]

A fact not generally appreciated is that the Defense Department and U.S. intelligence agencies also make extensive use of commercially owned satellites. For example, commercial satellites provide support to the network of U.S. Air Force satellite ground control stations and also the Defense Meteorological Satellite Program (DMSP).[63] As the need for military satellite communications grows almost exponentially, commercial carriers will take a larger share of the burden. In wartime the United States can be expected to make heavy use of these satellites.[64]

61. See David A. Boutacoff, "Steering a Course Toward Space," *Defense Electronics,* vol. 18 (March 1986), p. 67; and "Military Strives to Meet Growing Demand for Satellite Services," pp. 85–86.

62. Ashton B. Carter, "Satellites and Anti-satellites: The Limits of the Possible," *International Security,* vol. 10 (Spring 1986), p. 90.

63. See R. J. Raggett, ed., *Jane's Military Communications, 1982,* 3d ed. (London: Jane's Publishing Co., 1982), p. 303. See also Ball, "Defense Meteorological Satellite Program," p. 44. For a breakdown of the number of commercial communication satellite circuits leased by the Defense Department in 1982, see John J. Judge, "Commanding and Controlling C³I," *Defense Electronics,* vol. 17 (January 1985), p. 88.

64. In fact, President Carter's Directive on Space Policy (PD/NSC-37) explicitly

In the Soviet case it is considerably more difficult to single out communication satellites used primarily for military purposes from their civilian counterparts.[65] In low earth orbit there appear to be two separate Soviet constellations for communication, one made up of three satellites and another network of twenty-four satellites. Both are in roughly circular orbits tilted 74° to the equator at altitudes of about 800 and 1,500 kilometers respectively. Both also appear to operate in the UHF band and to use the "store and dump" transmission method—that is, each satellite picks up and records information and when it passes a location designated to receive it, plays back the message. Thus they are not real-time communication systems. In highly elliptical orbits the Soviets maintain, as noted earlier, a further two constellations made up of eight Molniya 1 satellites and eight Molniya 3 satellites. These apparently utilize both the UHF and SHF frequencies.

Furthermore, the Soviet Union almost certainly makes use of its satellites in the geosynchronous orbit for military communications, if only as backup. The Raduga and Gorizont systems are obvious candidates, while the Volna maritime communication satellites may also have military applications.[66] There is also the long-awaited but as yet undeployed Gals geosynchronous communication satellite system that Western analysts expect to be used primarily for military purposes.[67]

Navigation

Since the early 1960s both superpowers have recognized the value of satellites to aid navigation at sea. The present American program, known as Transit and run by the U.S. Navy, consists of between four and six satellites in a circular polar orbit at an altitude of approximately 1,000 kilometers. They supply the worldwide positional fixes needed to update

---

charged the secretary of defense with establishing "a program for identifying and integrating, as appropriate, civil and commercial resources into military operations during the national emergencies declared by the President." Quoted in Paul B. Stares, *The Militarization of Space: U.S. Policy, 1945–1984* (Ithaca, N.Y.: Cornell University Press, 1985), p. 185.

65. Unless otherwise indicated the information on Soviet satellite communications is from Johnson, *Soviet Year in Space*, 1981–86 issues.

66. See "U.S. Trends on Satcoms Being Paralleled by USSR," *Aviation Week and Space Technology*, vol. 111 (November 5, 1979), pp. 23–24; and Department of Defense, *Soviet Military Power, 1983*, p. 69.

67. See Satellite Systems Engineering, Inc., *Satellite Systems Digest* (Bethesda, Md.: Satellite System Engineering, 1979) for further information on the Gals system.

the inertial navigation systems on U.S. submarines and surface ships. By measuring the Doppler shift in radio signals from a Transit satellite passing overhead, a navigator can determine a ship's location to roughly 200 meters and sometimes nearer.[68] The Transit satellites are now being replaced by an improved version known as Nova, which should remain operational to the end of this century.

Seemingly modeled on its U.S. predecessor, the corresponding Soviet system has also undergone generational changes. Today two distinct constellations operate in orbits similar to those used by the Transit satellites but at a lower inclination to the equator (83° rather than 90°). One constellation is made up of four satellites, the other six. Sometimes referred to by Western analysts as Navsat 1 and Navsat 2, these are reportedly accurate to 200 meters and possibly 100 meters. Analysts generally agree Navsat 2 is used solely for military purposes.[69]

The United States and the Soviet Union are also fielding a completely new generation of navigation satellites. The aforementioned Navstar GPS and the Soviet Glonass system represent a significant improvement in the service provided by navigation satellites. The systems are remarkably similar in their orbital deployment if not in their construction and technical characteristics.[70] Each will travel in a circular semisynchronous orbit (about 20,000 kilometers high), so that the satellites circle the earth twice a day. The major differences are that the Navstar GPS constellation will have eighteen satellites (with three spares) equally spaced in six orbital planes at 63° inclination, while the Glonass system will probably have between nine and twelve satellites in two orbital planes.[71]

The Navstar GPS will provide navigation guidance of unprecedented accuracy, reliability, and availability to a wide range of military users. Subscribers will be able to obtain information on their precise location, whether fixed or mobile, at any time, in any place, and in any weather

---

68. K. D. McDonald, "Navigation Satellite Systems: Their Characteristics, Potential and Military Applications," in Jasani, ed., *Outer Space*, pp. 163, 165–67.

69. Anderson, "Space 'Peeping Toms' Are a Danger." In the strict sequence of generational changes since Soviet navigation satellites were first deployed, they should be classed as Navsat 2 and Navsat 3. The Soviets have also reportedly purchased 600 Transit commercial receivers from the Japanese. "Navy Expanding Its Space Command to Bolster Readiness," *Aviation Week and Space Technology*, vol. 124 (February 3, 1986), p. 57.

70. Johnson, *Soviet Year in Space, 1982*, p. 14.

71. Department of Defense, *Soviet Military Power, 1986*, p. 53.

Table 2-2. *Comparison of U.S. Navigation System Accuracies*

System	Position accuracy (meters)	Velocity accuracy (meters per second)	Time accuracy (seconds)	Range of operations	Operation
Navstar (P-code)	16 (in 3 dimensions)	0.1	.0000001 (100 nano-seconds)	Worldwide	Longitude, latitude, altitude, 24 hours, all weather
Transit satellite	200	. . .	. . .	Worldwide	Longitude, latitude, degraded performance in polar areas
LORAN	180	. . .	. . .	Regional (10% of world)	Longitude, latitude
Omega	2,200	. . .	. . .	Nearly worldwide (90% of world)	Longitude, latitude
Inertial navigation systems	1,500 maximum after 1 hour	0.8 after 2 hours	. . .	Worldwide	24 hours, all weather, degraded performance in polar areas
TACAN	400	. . .	. . .	Line of sight	3° angular error
ILS/MLS	5–10	. . .	. . .	Line of sight	Only at properly equipped airports

Source: Richard W. Blank, "The NAVSTAR Global Positioning System," *Signal,* vol. 41 (November 1986), p. 76.

to within 16 meters, and their velocity to within 0.1 meter per second. Compared with existing navigational aids such as ground-based radio transmitters (like LORAN and Omega) and even Transit, this is a radical improvement (see table 2-2). The Glonass system, according to Western analysts, will not provide the same level of service as Navstar. In particular, it will provide only two-dimensional positional data and less than 24-hour coverage. It is also estimated to be accurate only to within 100 meters.[72]

72. For comprehensive discussions of Navstar GPS, see McDonald, "Navigation Satellite System," pp. 175–80; and Richard W. Blank, "The NAVSTAR Global Positioning System," *Signal,* vol. 41 (November 1986), pp. 73–78. For more details about Glonass, see "Soviet Union Navigation Satellite System Provides Limited Worldwide Capabilities," *Defense News,* March 9, 1987, p. 3; and Department of Defense, *Soviet Military Power, 1986,* p. 53.

Meteorology

Weather satellites were among the first space systems developed by the U.S. military. Known as the Defense Meteorological Satellite Program, the capabilities of these satellites have increased significantly since the early 1960s. The current satellites, DMSP Block 5D-2, are due to be replaced by a new model, Block 5D-3, to be launched by the space shuttle in 1989. Still further in the future, the United States plans to launch a completely new system, DMSP II, in the mid-1990s. On average two satellites are traveling in a sun-synchronous 820-kilometer polar orbit. Each satellite can cover the entire earth every twelve hours, scanning a 2,560-kilometer-wide swath of the surface. One gathers meteorological data in the early morning and early evening (local time), the other during midday and mid-evening.[73]

DMSP satellites carry a battery of sensors to record atmospheric phenomena. A linescanning radiometer records visual and infrared imagery used to analyze cloud patterns. An infrared temperature-moisture sounder and a microwave sounder measure precipitation at different altitudes. And a precipitating electron spectrometer forecasts the location and intensity of the aurora borealis, data needed for calibrating radar and high-frequency communications in the northern latitudes often affected by this phenomenon. Two new sensors have been added to the latest generation of satellites: an ionosphere sounder to measure the electron distribution in the upper atmosphere, which is useful for predicting radio propagation, and a microwave imager that will be able to plot surface wind speeds, precipitation intensity, and ice formations in polar areas.[74]

DMSP meteorological data can be directly downlinked to special processing terminals or recorded and then transmitted to one of two command readout stations at Fairchild AFB, Washington, or Loring AFB, Maine.[75] Information is then relayed via a leased Hughes Westar

73. Whelan, *Guide to Military Space Programs*, pp. 84–86.

74. Department of the Air Force, Office of Public Affairs, "Defense Meteorological Satellite Program," factsheet, no date; and Department of the Navy, *Justification of Estimates for Fiscal Year 1985: Procurement* (Dept. of the Navy, 1984).

75. Department of the Air Force, "Defense Meteorological Satellite Program." Recorded data can also be recovered from the Hawaii tracking station at Kaena Point, which is part of the Air Force Satellite Control Facility (AFSCF). The command readout station at Loring AFB will close in 1989, after which its mission will be performed by the SCF at Thule, Greenland. See Department of the Air Force, *Supporting Data for Fiscal Year 1985: Research, Development, Test and Evaluation*, p. 935.

satellite to the Air Force Global Weather Central at Offutt AFB, Nebraska, and the Fleet Numerical Weather Central at Monterey, California, for further processing.[76] As a backup to DMSP the Global Weather Central is also linked directly via satellite with the Satellite Operations Control Center of the National Oceanic and Atmospheric Administration (NOAA) at Suitland, Maryland, so that it can receive weather data from NOAA's two polar-orbiting (formally Tiros) and geostationary (GOES) satellites.[77] Alternatively, DMSP ground terminals deployed worldwide can receive weather data directly from these satellites. The U.S. military makes surprisingly heavy use of NOAA spacecraft.[78]

No such distinction exists between civilian- and military-controlled weather satellites in the Soviet Meteor program. This comprises, on average, two second-generation Meteor satellites deployed in a 950-kilometer circular orbit tilted 83° to the equator, and one newer version satellite, known as Meteor 3, which is launched into a higher orbit, around 1,250 kilometers.[79] The sensors aboard the Meteor spacecraft seem similar to the DMSP satellites' and are probably comparable in performance. Over the years the Soviets have made great strides in distributing weather data to users. Earlier, three ground stations—at Obrinsk near Moscow, Novosibirsk in central Siberia, and Khabarovsk—received the data and then relayed it to the Hydrometeorological Center in Moscow for processing. Now, apparently, more than fifty receiving stations can collect information from the Meteor 2 satellites.[80] Besides the Meteor constellation, the Soviets reportedly also collect meteorological data from the Salyut manned spacecraft. In the future

76. Ball, "Defense Meteorological Satellite Program (DMSP)," p. 44; and Jerry Mayfield, "Weather Satellite Production Continues," *Aviation Week and Space Technology,* vol. 110 (June 4, 1979), pp. 47–58.

77. Thomas Karas, *The New High Ground: Systems and Weapons of Space Age War* (Simon and Schuster, 1983), p. 142; *Department of Defense Appropriations for 1984,* Hearings, pt. 4, p. 792. The DMSP's tactical terminals can also directly access data from the NOAA satellites.

78. See General Accounting Office, *Weather Satellites: User Views on the Consequences of Eliminating a Civilian Polar Orbiter,* GAO/RCED-86-11 (GAO, 1986), app. III, pp. 23–40.

79. Johnson, *Soviet Year in Space, 1984,* p. 27; and Ted W. Jensen, ed., *Space, The Next Ten Years,* A Symposium Report by the United States Space Foundation (Colorado Springs, Colo.: The Foundation, 1985), p. 61.

80. Craig Covault, "Soviets Plan Weather Satellite Advances," *Aviation Week and Space Technology,* vol. 105 (November 29, 1976), pp. 14–15; and Johnson, *Soviet Year in Space, 1981,* p. 18.

there will be the announced but not yet deployed Geostationary Operational Meteorological Satellite (GOMS).[81]

Oceanography

Since at least the early 1970s the U.S. Navy has been using satellites to acquire oceanographic data. To date, this has been carried out with sensors hosted on either DMSP or NOAA satellites.[82] By the beginning of the 1990s, the navy will be operating its own dedicated satellite program, known as the Navy–Remote Ocean Sensing System (N-ROSS).[83] Each satellite will carry sensors to detect ocean fronts and eddies, wind speeds and their direction, the age and thickness of ice field formations, and sea surface temperatures. Such information is valuable for all areas of naval operations.

In contrast, the Soviets have already deployed special satellites that use side-looking radar (SLR) and other sensors for this purpose. The SLR reportedly has a resolution of 1.5–2.0 kilometers and is used to map ice formations in the northern waters of the Soviet Union.[84]

Geodesy

Both the United States and the Soviet Union use satellites to acquire extremely precise data on the size and shape of the earth's surface and its gravitational fields. Since the 1970s the United States has apparently relied on information gathered by NASA's GEOS and Lageos satellites, although the DMSP satellites have also proved useful in this regard. In 1984 the U.S. Navy launched the Geosat spacecraft to supply new

81. Johnson, *Soviet Year in Space, 1984*, p. 27.
82. Peter A. Mitchell, "The Navy's Mission in Space," *Oceanus*, vol. 28 (Summer 1985), pp. 27–29.
83. For further information on N-ROSS, see L. Edgar Prina, "Sensors on the Seas, Satellites in Space," *Sea Power*, vol. 26 (November 1983), pp. 58–59; and "Navy Starts NROSS as Keep-It-Simple NOSS Successor," *Aerospace Daily*, vol. 131 (January 10, 1985), pp. 49–50. The navy will also use the existing oceanographic data distribution network, located at the Fleet Numerical Oceanography Center, Monterey, Calif., with other regional sites at Pearl Harbor; Guam; Rota, Spain; and Suitland, Maryland. See Department of the Navy, *Justification of Estimates for Fiscal Year 1985: Operation and Maintenance, Navy*, p. 3-48.
84. Johnson, *Soviet Year in Space, 1984*, p. 28. See also "Soviet Cosmos Spacecraft Providing Land, Sea Imagery," *Aviation Week and Space Technology*, vol. 121 (November 12, 1984), pp. 212–13.

Figure 2-5. *Projected Evolution of U.S. Military Space Programs, 1986–2000*[a]

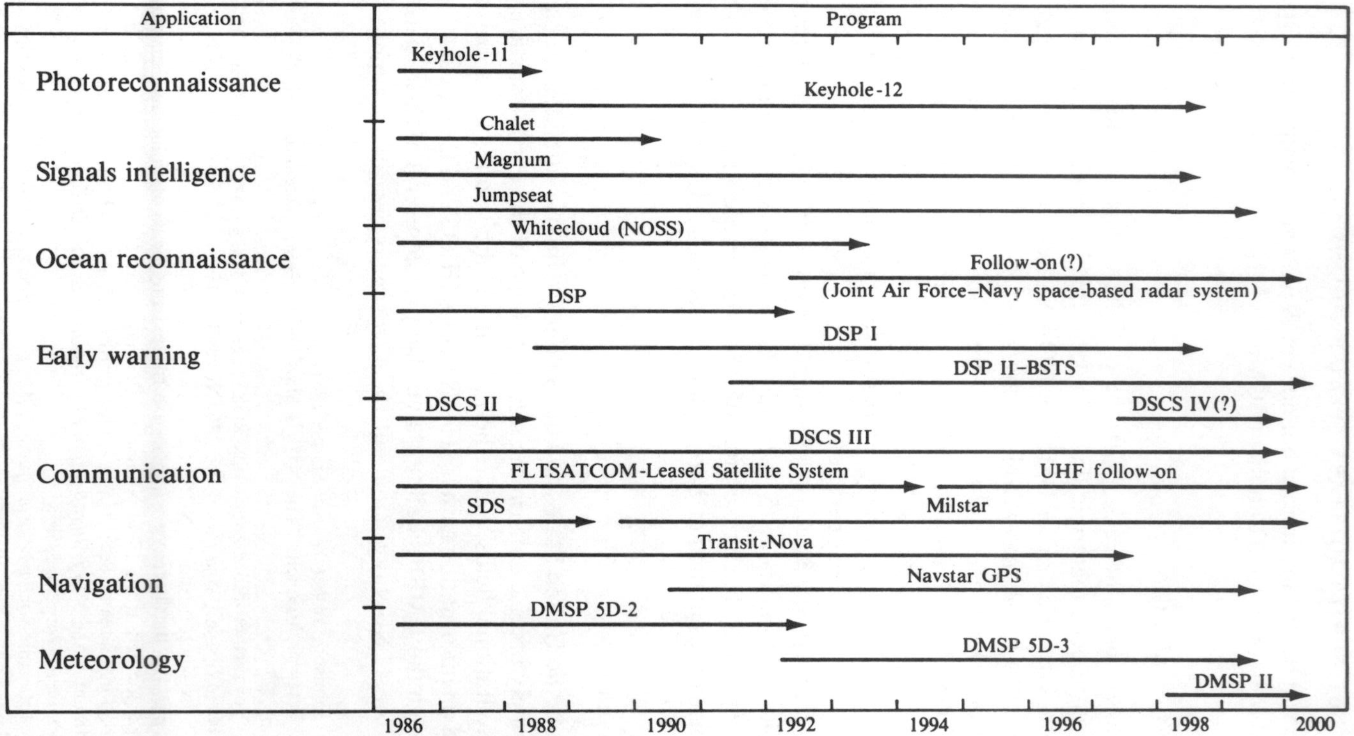

| Application | Program | | | | | | |

Photoreconnaissance
- Keyhole-11
- Keyhole-12
- Chalet
- Magnum

Signals intelligence
- Jumpseat

Ocean reconnaissance
- Whitecloud (NOSS)
- Follow-on(?)
- (Joint Air Force–Navy space-based radar system)

Early warning
- DSP
- DSP I
- DSP II–BSTS

Communication
- DSCS II
- DSCS III
- DSCS IV(?)
- FLTSATCOM-Leased Satellite System
- SDS
- UHF follow-on
- Milstar

Navigation
- Transit-Nova
- Navstar GPS

Meteorology
- DMSP 5D-2
- DMSP 5D-3
- DMSP II

1986   1988   1990   1992   1994   1996   1998   2000

Source: See text.
a. NOSS = Navy Ocean Surveillance System; DSP = Defense Support Program; BSTS = Boost Surveillance and Tracking System; DSCS = Defense Satellite Communications System; FLTSATCOM = Fleet Satellite Communications; SDS = Satellite Data System; GPS = Global Positioning System; DMSP = Defense Meteorological Satellite Program.

geodetic data for its Trident II program, which will operate from large, unsurveyed areas of the ocean.[85] The Soviet Union, in contrast, has a more active program, launching one or two geodetic satellites a year deployed in 1,490-kilometer circular orbits at 83° and 73° inclinations. Other spacecraft, such as the Salyut space station, may also provide geodetic data.[86]

Future Military Space Systems

The number of military satellites in use by the superpowers will probably not change dramatically before the mid-1990s. The likely evolution of U.S. military space programs is depicted as figure 2-5. For obvious reasons it is impossible to provide an equivalent portrait of the Soviet space program.

Beyond the mid-1990s new military applications of satellites could add significantly to the number of operational space systems. These include strategic and tactical surveillance, ballistic missile defense, air defense surveillance, satellite tracking, and submarine communication and detection. Manned space activities may also become more common.

Strategic and Tactical Surveillance

The need for more regular surveillance of military activities on earth, whether it be for arms control monitoring or to provide targeting information to strategic and tactical forces, could lead to the deployment of larger constellations of reconnaissance satellites than presently exist. The reason has to do with the nature of orbital dynamics and the relationship between altitude and the resolution of imaging systems. Currently, photoreconnaissance satellites must operate in low earth orbit to obtain high-resolution pictures. At these altitudes, however, a satellite's field of vision is limited, while the speed with which it travels over the earth's surface means that the coverage of a given area is unavoidably intermittent. Raising the altitude of the satellite increases

85. "Geosat Data to Aid Trident 2 Accuracy," *Aviation Week and Space Technology*, vol. 117 (July 19, 1982), p. 26; and "USAF Launches Geosat A Ocean Survey Satellite," *Aviation Week and Space Technology*, vol. 122 (March 18, 1985), p. 299.

86. Johnson, *Soviet Year in Space, 1984*, p. 25; and Craig Covault, "Geodetic Launches Aid Soviet Targeting," *Aviation Week and Space Technology*, vol. 104 (June 7, 1976), p. 23.

Table 2-3. *Single Satellite Coverage Requirements (Polar Orbit)*

Number of satellites		Altitude (miles)
60		300
50		400
30		600
25		800
20		1,000
12		2,000
3	Geosynchronous	23,000

Source: Patrick J. Friel, "New Directions for the U.S. Military and Civilian Space Programs," in Uri Ra'anan and Robert L. Pfaltzgraff, Jr., *International Security Dimensions of Space* (Hamden, Conn.: Archon Books, 1984), p. 124. For more sophisticated calculations of constellation size requirements, see D. C. Beste, "Design of Satellite Constellations for Optimal Continuous Coverage," *IEEE Transactions on Aerospace and Electronic Systems*, no. 3 (May 1978), pp. 466–73.

the field of vision but at the expense of reducing the resolution of the sensors unless this is also improved. The solution is either to increase the number of satellites in low earth orbit in such a way as to allow constant surveillance of the earth's surface, or to increase the field of vision by raising the altitude of the satellite's orbit. The trade-off between orbital altitude and constellation size is illustrated in table 2-3. The problem with the first option is that proliferating the number of satellites becomes prohibitively expensive, while for the second, the demands on the sensor system appear too great for current technology to satisfy. In addition, the task of processing and interpreting the vast amounts of data is enormous.

Thus constant surveillance of the earth's surface seems unlikely for the foreseeable future. However, it is conceivable that the average number of reconnaissance satellites in a constellation will be increased to improve the level of coverage.

Ballistic Missile Defense

If ballistic missile defense systems are deployed beyond current levels, space-based sensors are likely to become even more important for early warning and perhaps battle management purposes. Already the needs of the Strategic Defense Initiative are shaping the new generation of U.S. ballistic missile early warning satellites. The Boost Surveillance and Tracking System (BSTS) is scheduled to replace the DSP satellites in the 1990s.[87] Additional sensors may be deployed to track warheads in all stages of their flight rather than just the initial boost phase.

Air Defense Surveillance

For the last ten years the United States has been investigating the use of infrared sensors in space to detect and track aircraft. Under the Teal Ruby program, a prototype sensor of this type is due to be launched by the space shuttle in 1988 to conduct a yearlong proof-of-concept demonstration.[88] Although the Teal Ruby program was intended to aid in the detection of bombers, the U.S. Air Force has inevitably become interested in much smaller targets, particularly cruise missiles.[89]

Space-based radars are also under consideration for this mission. Such radars, however, require large amounts of power and are also susceptible to jamming. Furthermore, unless intermittent coverage is acceptable, the same factors that affect the feasibility of constant strategic and tactical battlefield surveillance will apply.

Satellite Tracking

Using satellites to detect and track other satellites has many advantages as a complement to ground-based space surveillance sensors. Currently, satellites have to pass within the line of sight of radars and electro-optical devices, resulting in frequent gaps in coverage.[90] Basing satellite tracking sensors in space, however, will allow constant surveillance of a much larger volume of space. The U.S. Space Surveillance and Tracking System (SSTS), which is being developed as part of the

87. For a description of the various surveillance programs being pursued under the SDI, see Department of Defense, *Report to the Congress on the Strategic Defense Initiative* (DOD, 1985), pp. 29–38.

88. Bruce A. Smith, "Tests Confirm Teal Ruby Design," *Aviation Week and Space Technology*, vol. 119 (December 26, 1983), pp. 8–9; and "Rockwell Tests Model of Teal Ruby System," *Aviation Week and Space Technology*, vol. 120 (January 23, 1984), p. 52.

89. Ibid.; "Space Sensor Planned to Detect Cruise Missiles," *Aviation Week and Space Technology*, vol. 120 (March 26, 1984), p. 16.

90. *Department of Defense Appropriations, Fiscal Year 1986*, Hearings before a Subcommittee of the Senate Committee on Appropriations, 99 Cong. 1 sess. (GPO, 1986), pt. 2, pp. 302–05.

SDI program, envisages the use of infrared sensors for this mission, but it is still unclear how soon it might become operational.[91]

Submarine Communication

The use of space-based blue-green lasers is currently under study as a medium to transmit messages to submarines. At present, submarines must rise close to the surface and expose antennas to receive and transmit messages, risking detection in the process. Because of the properties of blue-green lasers, sea water can be penetrated to many hundreds of feet. Although extremely low frequency (ELF) radio can be used to communicate with deeply submerged submarines, it suffers from a very low data rate. In contrast, lasers can transmit information in short bursts up to several kilobits a second.[92] Aircraft have already been used as platforms to test the feasibility of such lasers with encouraging results. As a consequence, the U.S. Navy is actively considering the deployment of blue-green lasers aboard satellites for communicating with submarines and other submerged systems, such as mines and acoustic arrays.[93]

Submarine Detection

Both the United States and the Soviet Union have also begun investigations on the use of surveillance satellites for detecting the whereabouts of submarines.[94] On the Soviet side, it was reported that the Salyut 7 manned space station used a synthetic aperture radar (SAR) in 1984 to track the wakes of Soviet Delta-class ballistic-missile-carrying submarines operating off the USSR's Pacific coast.[95] Likewise, the U.S. Navy studied data collected from a synthetic aperture radar during

91. David J. Lynch, "Star Wars Satellite Put on Hold for Now," *Defense Week*, vol. 6 (November 12, 1985), pp. 1, 11.

92. "Submarine Communications via Laser," *Defense Electronics*, vol. 17 (January 1985), p. 97. See also Jack Cushman, "How Navy's Blue Laser Works," *Defense Week*, vol. 6 (January 14, 1985), p. 5.

93. Jack Cushman, "DOD Scores Dramatic Gain in Laser Links with Ballistic Subs," *Defense Week*, vol. 5 (October 22, 1984), pp. 1, 18.

94. For a useful discussion of the problem of detecting submarines from space, see Donald C. Daniel, "Antisubmarine Warfare in the Nuclear Age," *Orbis*, vol. 28 (Fall 1984), pp. 543–45.

95. Edgar Ulsamer, "Penetrating the Sea Sanctuary," *Air Force Magazine*, vol. 67 (September 1984), p. 29; and "Soviet Test Sub Detection from Space," *Military Space*, August 20, 1984, p. 1.

NASA's SEASAT mission in 1978 for the same reasons.[96] Navy officials, however, remain pessimistic about the likelihood of an early breakthrough in this area.[97]

Manned Space Systems

The use of manned systems to perform military missions in space has traditionally been considered a poor alternative to the greater cost effectiveness of automated systems. These can perform all the functions considered beneficial to the support of military forces without the burden of having to sustain a manned presence in space. Although this observation remains true, the U.S. Air Force in association with NASA is in the early stages of developing a National Aerospace Plane that can lift off from existing runways and operate in outer space. Among the military missions identified for such craft are strategic bombing, strategic reconnaissance, and in-orbit inspection and interception.[98] The Pentagon may also use the manned space station under development by NASA for some military experiments.

Conclusion

The United States and the Soviet Union use space for very similar military purposes but accomplish these missions in significantly different ways. The United States tends to rely on a small number of highly sophisticated and long-lasting satellites that often perform more than one function. The Soviets, in contrast, build simpler satellites that are usually dedicated to a single mission. Moreover, they are generally

96. *Department of Defense Authorization for Appropriations for Fiscal Year 1985*, Hearings, pt. 7, pp. 3413–14. See also Frank Elliott, "New Ways to Track Submarines," *Navy News and Undersea Technology* (December 5, 1986), p. 1.

97. Walter Andrews, "Soviet Ability to Target Subs Is Denied," *Washington Times*, August 17, 1984. See also *Department of Defense Appropriations for 1984*, Hearings, pt. 8, p. 431; and "Shuttle Flight Yields Data on Hiding Subs," *Washington Post*, March 22, 1985.

98. For details of this project, see Alton K. Marsh, "USAF Studies Transatmosphere Vehicle," *Aviation Week and Space Technology*, vol. 119 (November 7, 1983), pp. 44–45; Clarence A. Robinson, Jr., "USAF Spurs Spaceplane Research," *Aviation Week and Space Technology*, vol. 120 (March 26, 1984), pp. 16–18; and Craig Covault, "DARPA Studying Manned Space Cruiser," *Aviation Week and Space Technology*, vol. 120 (March 26, 1984), pp. 20–21.

deployed in larger constellations and are shorter lived than their U.S. counterparts, which means that they must be replaced much more frequently for the same level of service.

Unless one fully understands the reasons for these differences, such as different design philosophies, engineering traditions, and geography, simple numerical comparisons of space activity can be fundamentally misleading. The United States continues to lead the Soviet Union in the development and exploitation of military space technology. As Secretary of the Air Force Edward C. Aldridge, Jr., stated in the spring of 1987, "From the standpoint of the national security and defense uses of space, the United States is far ahead of whatever country thinks it is in second place. And the United States is not slowing down."[99] Nevertheless, the larger size of Soviet constellations and the USSR's ability to launch replacements rapidly has made the Soviet Union's military space program more resilient than that of the United States. Should hostilities break out in space the United States would be at a comparative disadvantage because of its greater dependency on a smaller number of satellites and, moreover, its inability to replace them at short notice if they are lost to enemy action. The significance of this conclusion becomes more evident in the next chapter, which examines the value of military satellites to the superpowers.

99. Edward C. Aldridge, Jr., "The Myths of Militarization of Space," *International Security*, vol. 11 (Spring 1987), p. 155.

CHAPTER THREE

The Value
of Military Satellites

THE survey of U.S. and Soviet space programs in the preceding chapter details what each side is doing in space. This chapter examines how those space assets contribute to the national security and military effectiveness of the superpowers on earth. For without a clear picture of the current and future value of military satellites, no decisionmaker can prudently judge what is at stake in the debate over antisatellite weapons. Only by understanding the role that satellites play in preserving the armed peace between the superpowers is it possible to judge how their potential vulnerability could undermine it. Similarly, only by understanding the role of satellites in wartime is it possible to judge whether the reasons advanced for developing ASAT weapons are sound. Finally, only by judging the *relative* value of satellites to the superpowers it is possible to conclude whether one side has any more to lose in the event of hostilities.

Assessing the Importance of Satellites

According to statements by American officials, the United States is now heavily dependent on the services of military satellites. How dependent is a matter of some disagreement. During his tenure as undersecretary of the U.S. Air Force, Edward C. Aldridge, Jr., stated that "US satellites have become essential to national security and must be safeguarded."[1] Likewise, George Keyworth III, a former science adviser to President Ronald Reagan, has argued that "even in a very limited war, we would have an absolutely critical dependence on space today."[2] A report from the congressional Office of Technology Assessment, however, dissents from this viewpoint: "Space systems are used extensively for military support, but satellites do not now fill a crucial, indispensable, and irreplaceable role. Many functions now carried out in space can be performed by other means."[3]

Similar differences of opinion exist over the relative dependency of the superpowers on space systems. The U.S. Joint Chiefs of Staff in their fiscal 1987 military posture statement reported that "both the United States and the Soviet Union depend on space systems for operational support, the United States more so than the Soviet Union."[4] Yet when asked to comment on this, Secretary of Defense Caspar W. Weinberger replied: "It is not clear that we depend more heavily. We depend on it very heavily. They depend on satellites to a great extent, too."[5]

How can these conflicting appraisals be evaluated? In making judgments about "value" and "dependency," it is essential to draw a distinction between the importance of the mission that a satellite supports and the importance of the satellite to executing that mission. The former depends largely on contextual factors; many satellites have peacetime missions, such as arms control treaty monitoring and early warning of hostile activities, that are critically important yet largely irrelevant once war begins. Similarly, the type of conflict in which the superpowers could become engaged, whether it is a war between third world client states or a full-scale nuclear exchange between themselves, would also determine the usefulness and therefore value of certain satellites. How

---

1. Quoted in Robert C. Toth, "Military Shuttle in Key Part of Pentagon Plan," *Los Angeles Times*, January 20, 1985.

2. Quoted in Robert A. Kittle, "Space-War Era—It's Already Here," *U.S. News and World Report* (December 17, 1984), p. 30.

3. U.S. Congress, Office of Technology Assessment, *Arms Control in Space: Workshop Proceedings*, OTA-BP-ISC-28 (Government Printing Office, 1984), p. 11.

4. U.S. Joint Chiefs of Staff, *United States Military Posture, FY 1987* (GPO, 1986), p. 81.

5. *Department of Defense Authorization for Appropriations for Fiscal Year 1985*, Hearings before the Senate Committee on Armed Services, 98 Cong. 2 sess. (GPO, 1984), pt. 1, p. 87. For similar assessments see also John Pike, "Anti-Satellite Weapons," *F.A.S. Public Interest Report*, vol. 36 (November 1983), p. 2; and Nicholas L. Johnson, "C³ in Space: The Soviet Approach," *Signal*, vol. 40 (December 1985), p. 21.

each superpower intends to fight a war is another factor influencing the value of its space assets. The combatants' operational plans may demand different services from their satellites.

The importance of a satellite to the mission is contingent not only on whether alternative means are available but also on how efficiently the auxiliary systems can perform the task. To a large extent, each superpower can decide how dependent it wishes to be on a given space system for a specific mission. Provision can be made for additional backup satellites, either pre-positioned in space or deployed ready for launch. Nonsatellite alternatives can also be procured and maintained to further increase the level of redundancy. Even so, contextual factors can again determine the importance of satellites. In particular, the location of a conflict can increase or decrease the reliance on satellite services. For example, the use of satellites for communication and intelligence gathering is likely to be much higher when the conflict is in a remote part of the world than when it is close to one's national borders. Auxiliary systems such as reconnaissance aircraft that rely on the support of host nations in remote areas are also subject to political factors that could impede operations. Even when alternative means are available, these may be more vulnerable to wartime attrition, thereby raising the value of satellites over the duration of the conflict.

The level of dependency on space systems is not therefore a static condition. Simply stated, not all satellites are important all of the time. The factors identified here that determine the value of space systems become more apparent in the following discussion of the missions of military satellites in peacetime, in a conventional war, and in a nuclear conflict.

Peacetime Missions

The peacetime uses of military satellites can be divided into five principal missions: intelligence gathering, arms control monitoring, war planning, crisis management, and early warning of attack. As will become clear, the same satellites are often used for more than one mission.

—*Intelligence gathering.* Reconnaissance satellites, particularly those that return visual evidence, have become without doubt the most reliable and productive source of military intelligence for both superpowers. Not only is highly detailed imagery available from satellites on a more regular basis (cloud cover permitting)[6] than from other intelligence sources, but the evidence of military activities that they present is considerably less ambiguous than the product of other national technical means and especially human intelligence sources. The information supplied by photoreconnaissance and signals intelligence (SIGINT) satellites has become invaluable for defense planning in general and weapon procurement in particular. For example, defense planners can evaluate the strengths and weaknesses of opposing weapon systems and design their countermeasures accordingly. Theoretically at least, this prevents wasteful expenditures on unnecessary or outmoded weaponry.

—*Arms control monitoring.* The process of monitoring compliance with arms control agreements is virtually identical to that of intelligence gathering. The only real difference is that the reconnaissance assets may be tasked to concentrate on specific areas or events to meet the verification requirements of a particular accord. Thus, if a violation is suspected, coverage by photoreconnaissance satellites is likely to increase to collect more evidence. SIGINT satellites have also proved to be particularly useful aids to verification. For example, the collection and analysis of telemetry signals from flight tests of ballistic missiles can indicate the likely range, payload, throw weight, accuracy, and number of warheads carried by a new system.[7]

Although the Soviet Union does not appear to have an equivalent system, the United States uses the nuclear explosion detection sensors aboard its Defense Support Program (DSP) satellites (and, in the future, will use those aboard its Navstar GPS satellites) for monitoring compliance with the Limited Test Ban Treaty and the Nuclear Non-Proliferation Treaty.

—*War planning.* Photoreconnaissance satellites are the principal source of intelligence for the strategic targeting plans of the superpowers.[8] Without precise information on the location of potential aimpoints

6. Meteorological satellites are useful for planning photoreconnaissance missions to forestall taking pictures of clouded areas. See Desmond Ball, "The Defense Meteorological Satellite Program (DMSP)," *Journal of the British Interplanetary Society*, vol. 39 (1986), p. 45.

7. See Desmond Ball, "The Rhyolite Programme," Reference Paper 86 (Canberra: Australian National University, Strategic and Defence Studies Centre, November 1981), pp. 19–22; and Farooq Hussain, *The Future of Arms Control—Part IV: The Impact of Weapons Test Restrictions,* Adelphi Papers 165 (London: International Institute for Strategic Studies, 1981), p. 42.

8. Jeffrey Richelson, "The Keyhole Satellite Program," *Journal of Strategic Studies*, vol. 7 (June 1984), p. 144.

such as missile silos and command centers, counterforce targeting options simply would not be available.[9] Satellites also contribute directly to the accuracy of strategic nuclear delivery systems. The accurate mapping of the earth's surface carried out by geodetic satellites is invaluable for targeting intercontinental ballistic missiles (ICBMs) and submarine-launched ballistic missiles (SLBMs).[10] One estimate is that the accuracy of the Trident II SLBM will increase as much as 10 percent for certain potential launch areas through the use of the U.S. Navy's Geosat satellite.[11] Similarly, the U.S. strategic cruise missiles now entering service rely on guidance information originally derived from satellite imagery that has been converted into digital format for storage in the on-board computer. Once launched and over land, the cruise missile will be able to correlate radar altimeter readings with the stored data.[12]

Both superpowers also use SIGINT satellites to draw up the "electronic order of battle" of their adversary. Besides acquiring information on the whereabouts of radar systems (particularly the mobile variety) for direct targeting in wartime, the characteristics of radar signals—their frequency, strength, pulse length, and pulse rate—are plotted for electronic countermeasures (ECM) such as jamming and "spoofing."[13] This allows bomber and strategic reconnaissance aircraft to plan their penetration routes into enemy airspace and suppress the defenses they encounter.[14]

9. Thomas Karas, *The New High Ground: Systems and Weapons of Space Age War* (Simon and Schuster, 1983), p. 109.

10. Desmond Ball, "Geodetic Satellites," Reference Paper 125 (Canberra: Australian National University, Strategic and Defence Studies Centre, October 1984).

11. "Geosat Data to Aid Trident 2 Accuracy," *Aviation Week and Space Technology*, vol. 117 (July 19, 1982), p. 26.

12. "Mapping Agency to Expand Digital Use," *Aviation Week and Space Technology*, vol. 121 (July 16, 1984), p. 52; James B. Schultz, "Cruise Missile Deployment Marked by System Upgrades and Operational Tests," *Defense Electronics*, vol. 16 (May 1984), p. 52; and John C. Toomay, "Technical Characteristics," in Richard K. Betts, ed., *Cruise Missiles: Technology, Strategy, Politics* (Brookings, 1981), p. 39.

13. Ball, "Rhyolite Programme," pp. 16–18.

14. It was for this mission that the Soviet Union accused the United States of using signals intelligence (SIGINT) satellites in coordination with the incursion of the Korean airliner KAL 007 into Soviet airspace in September 1983. Serge Schmemann, "Soviet Cites Role of U.S. Satellite," *New York Times*, September 20, 1983. See also P. Q. Mann, "Reassessing the Sakhalin Incident," *Defense Attaché*, no. 3 (1984), pp. 41–56; and "Soviet Union Offers Proof KAL 007 Was on Spy Mission," *Defense Electronics*, vol. 16 (March 1984), pp. 20–21.

—*Crisis management*. Reconnaissance satellites are especially useful for monitoring events or conflicts that threaten superpower stability. Certainly they are invaluable when alternative surveillance methods—principally aircraft—are difficult to use for geographical or logistical reasons, or if they are likely to be politically inflammatory or militarily hazardous. The Soviets in particular have come to rely on these satellites for observing third world conflicts, as evidenced by the frequency of launches during specific crises and the manipulation of satellite ground tracks to increase the coverage of key areas of interest.[15]

With their advantages for long-distance communication, satellite links have become important aids to international crisis management. Admiral James D. Watkins has recalled that while acting as chairman of the Joint Chiefs of Staff during the U.S. peacekeeping operations in Lebanon, "I communicated from my quarters, in the middle of the night, with our Marine peacekeepers on the ground in their foxholes near the Beirut airport. This proved to me the incredible value of our capabilities in space for immediate command and control, linkages so vital to the decisionmaking process."[16] Another recent illustration is the Gulf of Sidra incident of October 1981, when U.S. Navy aircraft destroyed two Libyan fighters. Information on the incident was back to the White House in less than a minute and subsequent events were monitored virtually as they occurred.[17]

The U.S. Diplomatic Telecommunications Service relies heavily on Defense Satellite Communications System (DSCS) spacecraft for connecting the State Department with its embassies and consulates abroad. At a higher level, NATO has developed its own satellite communication system linking alliance capitals and military command centers to permit multilateral consultations in a serious crisis.[18] Similarly, satellite communication was the obvious choice for modernizing the U.S.-Soviet hot line that is known officially as the Direct Communications Link.[19]

15. Recent examples have been the Iran-Iraq war, the Libyan withdrawal from Chad, and the U.S. invasion of Grenada.

16. Quoted in L. Edgar Prina, "Signal Flags to Satellites," *Sea Power*, vol. 26 (December 1983), p. 45.

17. Ibid., p. 45.

18. See Sir John Anderson, "The Evolution of NATO's New Integrated Communications System," *NATO's Fifteen Nations* (Special issue 2, 1980), pp. 26–30; Larry K. Wentz and Gope D. Hingorani, "Outlook for NATO Communications," *Signal*, vol. 37 (December 1982), pp. 53–59; and I. Mason-Smith, "NATO SATCOM—A Synopsis of Its Technological Evolution," *NATO's Fifteen Nations*, vol. 26 (October–November 1981), pp. 28–32.

19. This now consists of a leased circuit through an Intelsat IV satellite with ground

—*Early warning*. Among the first and still most critical tasks carried out by satellites is to provide strategic and tactical early warning of attack. Strategic warning refers to indications that an attack is being prepared, while tactical warning refers to evidence that one is either imminent or under way.

In a serious crisis involving the United States and the Soviet Union, reconnaissance satellites are likely to provide the earliest indications that military operations are being planned. The dispersal of bombers and theater nuclear forces from their peacetime bases, the "flushing" of ballistic missile submarines from port, and the general mobilization of conventional forces are classic strategic warning indicators. SIGINT satellites complement their photoreconnaissance cousins in warning of heightened or unusual military activity. An increase in signals traffic to a sensitive area, the formation of new tactical communication nets, the call signs of new military units, changes in the radio frequencies used by frontline troops, and, of course, the interception of attack orders can all indicate preparations for war.[20] Signals intelligence may in some cases provide the only source of strategic warning, as photographic evidence may be unavailable for climatic or other reasons.

The principal function of the ballistic missile early warning satellites is to provide positive evidence that an attack has started—in other words, tactical warning. In the case of an ICBM attack, these satellites may give as much as twenty-five minutes' warning time before the missiles reach their targets, while with submarine-launched and inter-mediate-range ballistic missiles, the time may be considerably less depending on the location of the launch. The role and value of ballistic missile early warning satellites will be discussed more fully in the section dealing with nuclear operations.

In addition to these five principal missions, satellites provide general support for peacetime military operations. This includes weather fore-casting, navigation, and communications. For example, a frequently cited statistic is that more than 70 percent of all long-haul U.S. military

stations in Etam, West Virginia, and Moscow, and another circuit through a Soviet Stationar satellite with its ground stations at Vladimir in central Russia and Fort Detrick, Maryland. See Desmond Ball, *Can Nuclear War Be Controlled?* Adelphi Papers 169 (London: International Institute for Strategic Studies, 1981), p. 22; and "Text of the 1963 Hot Line Agreement with 1971 and 1984 Amendments," in Barry M. Blechman, ed., *Preventing Nuclear War: A Realistic Approach* (Bloomington: Indiana University Press, 1985), pp. 189–91.

20. William J. Broad, "Experts Say Satellite Can Detect Soviet War Steps," *New York Times*, January 25, 1985.

communication goes via satellite.[21] While in peacetime a great deal of this traffic is made up of such routine, nonurgent messages as inventory stock requests and personnel information, a major proportion is for the U.S. intelligence community, which takes advantage of high-capacity communication satellites, especially those using the superhigh-frequency (SHF) band such as the DSCS II and III systems, to shift large amounts of raw data from points all over the globe to the United States for processing.[22]

Several general conclusions emerge about the relative superpower dependency on satellites in peacetime. Given the closed nature of Soviet society, the United States is plainly more dependent on reconnaissance satellites for intelligence gathering and arms control verification. No comparable alternatives are available for penetrating the veil of secrecy that envelops the Eastern bloc. This asymmetry should not be exaggerated, however. The Soviets also need photoreconnaissance satellites for observing activities in China, for strategic targeting purposes, and for corroborating intelligence obtained from other sources. They may be able to collect vast quantities of information from the U.S. press and from congressional hearings, but there are still highly classified U.S. military installations and research facilities that can be inspected only from space. Moreover, the Soviets have on balance a greater dependence on photoreconnaissance satellites for monitoring activities in remote parts of the world. American forces, in comparison, have more alternative means at their disposal, such as SR-71 and TR-1 reconnaissance aircraft, that can operate far from the continental United States with inflight refueling or from numerous bases around the world.[23] Although

21. Quoted in Richard Halloran, "U.S. Plans Big Spending Increase for Military Operations in Space," *New York Times,* October 17, 1982.

22. The CIA is reported to operate its own covert satellite system for communicating with agents or emplaced sensors abroad. See Desmond Ball, "CIA Covert Communications Satellites," Reference Paper 100 (Canberra: Australian National University, Strategic and Defence Studies Centre, October 1981); and Dusko Doder, "Soviet Jailed as Alleged Spy for CIA," *Washington Post,* August 23, 1983. The KGB uses communication satellites for the same purpose. See *Soviet Space Programs: 1976–80,* pt. 3: *Unmanned Space Activities,* Committee Print, Senate Committee on Commerce, Science, and Transportation, 99 Cong. 1 sess. (GPO, 1985), p. 1088.

23. The SR-71 has an unrefueled range of more than 3,000 miles and can reportedly photograph an area of 100,000 square miles at an altitude of 80,000 feet in one hour. For more information on the SR-71, see Jay Miller, *Lockheed SR-71* (A-12/YF-12/D-21) (Arlington, Tex.: Aerofax Inc., 1985), pp. 4–5; and Robert R. Ropelewski, "SR-71 Impressive in High-Speed Regime," *Aviation Week and Space Technology,* vol. 114

the Soviets also have long-range reconnaissance aircraft, these planes are generally considered inferior to their U.S. counterparts, and they do not have access to as many foreign bases. This is true of U.S. and Soviet SIGINT systems as well.[24]

Conventional War Missions

Support of conventional force operations is the area where military space systems have had the most impact in recent years. It is also the area that shows the greatest promise for expansion in the future. Though modern warfare can no longer be neatly separated into ground, air, and maritime operations, it is useful for analytical purposes to discuss the growing contribution of satellite services to conventional warfare in these three areas.

Ground Operations

Ground forces have probably been the last of the armed services to benefit from satellite support. This is now changing as reconnaissance, communication, and navigation satellites begin to play a larger role in aiding land operations.

In wartime, the contribution of reconnaissance satellites has always been limited by the unavoidable delay in repeating the overflight of a specific area (due to the rotation of the earth under a satellite's orbit)

(May 18, 1981), pp. 47–56. The TR-1 reportedly can cover 263,014 square miles an hour from an altitude of 65,000 feet. See Col. William V. Kennedy and others, *Intelligence Warfare* (New York: Crescent Books, 1983), p. 142; and "TR-1s Provide High-Altitude Reconnaissance and Surveillance," *Aviation Week and Space Technology*, vol. 123 (August 5, 1985), pp. 59–62. Both the SR-71 and TR-1 use synthetic aperture radars that permit stand-off reconnaissance at night and in any weather. See speech by Donald C. Latham, *Signal*, vol. 39 (August 1985), p. 40. One advantage of the TR-1 over the SR-71 is that it can downlink information almost instantaneously, while the SR-71 has to return to base. See *Department of Defense Appropriations for 1986*, Hearings before a Subcommittee of the House Committee on Appropriations, 99 Cong. 1 sess. (GPO, 1985), pt. 2, p. 377.

24. For more information on alternative U.S. and Soviet SIGINT systems, see Kennedy and others, *Intelligence Warfare*, pp. 152–65; and more specifically Martin Streetly, "US Airborne ELINT Systems—Part 3: The Boeing RC-135 Family," *Jane's Defence Weekly*, vol. 3 (March 16, 1985), pp. 460–65; and Martin Streetly, "US Airborne ELINT Systems—Part 4: The Lockheed SR-71A," *Jane's Defence Weekly*, vol. 3 (April 13, 1985), pp. 634–35.

and the time needed to process and transmit tactically relevant intelligence to field commanders. As Admiral Wesley McDonald, the commander of U.S. forces during the Grenada invasion, pointed out after the operation, "We have designed and are continuing to design systems which collect intelligence in great volume and in near-real time, but I am concerned as to whether we are designing into these systems the communications capability to get that data to the tactical commander in a usable fashion and in a timely manner." The admiral went on to lament: "What good is sophisticated satellite imagery sitting in Washington, D.C., or Norfolk, Va., when the field commander who needs it is on the ground in Grenada, on a ship off Lebanon, or in some even more remote corner of the world?"[25]

At least one of the superpowers is endeavoring to change this situation. As the former director of the U.S. Defense Advanced Research Projects Agency (DARPA), Robert S. Cooper, has stated: "A key goal of DoD programs in the past seven or eight years has been to make intelligence information from satellites also available to field commanders in real-time."[26] The most important of these programs is known as TENCAP, for Tactical Exploitation of National Capabilities.[27] Each service including the Marine Corps is procuring special receiver and processing equipment, sometimes called "fusion centers," to receive satellite imagery and signals intelligence. Satellite photos were apparently used to direct the U.S. naval bombardment of Lebanon in 1983. According to one report:

> New Marine Corps target acquisition radars were able to backtrack incoming artillery rounds and locate enemy gun positions to within about 30 meters. When those data were correlated with satellite imagery, the positions were quickly targeted to within about 13 meters accuracy—well within the lethal radius of the battleship *New Jersey*'s 16-in guns.[28]

25. "McDonald Reviews C3I during Grenada Operation," *Aerospace Daily*, December 16, 1983.
26. Robert S. Cooper, "No Sanctuary: A Defense Perspective on Space," *Issues in Science and Technology*, vol. 11 (Spring 1986), p. 43.
27. "Army, Intel Officials Note TENCAP Uses," *Military Space* (October 29, 1984), p. 1. See also "Eye in the Sky for the Grunts on the Ground," *Defense Week*, vol. 6 (November 4, 1985), p. 11; and *Department of Defense Appropriations for 1987*, Hearings before a Subcommittee of the House Committee on Appropriations, 99 Cong. 2 sess. (GPO, 1986), pt. 3, pp. 680–81.
28. Deborah G. Meyer, "DoD Likely to Spend $250 Billion on C³I through 1990," *Armed Forces Journal International*, vol. 122 (February 1985), p. 75. Unfortunately, the accuracy of the *New Jersey*'s guns did not match up to the targeting data it had received.

The new generation of U.S. photoreconnaissance satellites due to become operational by the end of the 1980s will probably be able to downlink imagery directly to senior field commanders without today's time delays. As a result, satellites will make a larger contribution to battlefield intelligence gathering and, with it, the targeting of enemy forces. However, although local commanders will receive intermittent "snapshots" of the battlefield, *constant* real-time surveillance of events, for reasons discussed in chapter 2, will not be available for the foreseeable future.

It is difficult to judge how fast the Soviets are moving in the same direction. Although they have developed a space-based ocean reconnaissance system as a naval tactical targeting aid (see below), their use of digital transmission links to hasten the flow of imagery from photoreconnaissance satellites is relatively new. It seems fair to assume, therefore, that while the Soviets can be expected to make greater use of reconnaissance satellites for tactical purposes, they still lag behind the United States in this regard.

The advent of small transportable satellite communication terminals and even man-pack-sized radio transceivers has permitted an unprecedented degree of control over military operations. This is particularly true for operations in areas not well served by alternative means. To quote again from Admiral Wesley McDonald's report of the 1983 U.S. invasion of Grenada: "Satellite communications were used in most cases all the way from the company level to the JCS. . . . We had several satellite channels assigned, so we made extensive use of man-pack satellite terminals. . . . I don't think I will surprise anyone when I say that in this type of operation, satellite connectivity is absolutely essential."[29]

While the tactical use of communication satellites by U.S. forces is becoming quite common, the adoption of small portable or easily transportable terminals by Soviet ground forces does not seem so widespread, no doubt reflecting technical inferiorities and to some extent Soviet command style.[30] Nevertheless, the Soviets obviously recognize the benefits of satellite communication as indicated by the effort they

29. "McDonald Reviews C3I during Grenada Operation," *Aerospace Daily,* December 16, 1983.

30. Stephen M. Meyer, "Space and Soviet Military Planning," in William J. Durch, ed., *National Interests and the Military Use of Space* (Cambridge, Mass.: Ballinger, 1984), p. 72.

expend maintaining their various constellations in orbit for this purpose.[31] As a consequence, the use of communication satellites by Soviet forces is becoming more evident, with terminals present at army group and divisional headquarters.[32]

When the Navstar Global Positioning System (GPS) becomes fully operational, U.S. ground troops will for the first time make use of navigation satellites that have hitherto been used almost exclusively by naval forces. Besides allowing ground forces to navigate better, particularly in desert and jungle areas, it should also significantly improve the accuracy and coordination of artillery barrages, air-to-ground attacks, and parachute supply drops. Since each of the relevant users will be operating from common time and position data supplied by Navstar, the chances of error should diminish dramatically.[33]

Air Operations

For the same reasons that apply to the land battle, the added intelligence input from reconnaissance satellites will be particularly useful for planning ground attack and long-range interdiction strikes from the air. Meteorological satellites have already proved their worth in operations like these. The receipt of timely and accurate weather information is critical for air operations. It enables military commanders to decide whether to postpone a mission, what route to take, when and where to strike a particular target, from what altitude, and sometimes even what type of ordnance to use.[34] During the war in Southeast Asia, weather satellites proved their worth for the first time.[35] As Air Force General William Momyer stated:

31. The store-dump low-altitude communication satellites are often identified as tactical-theater communication systems.
32. Charles Dick, "Soviet C³ Philosophy: The Challenge of Contemporary Warfare," *Signal*, vol. 39 (December 1984), p. 49; and James C. Bussert, "Soviet Military Communications in the 1980's," *Defense Electronics*, vol. 15 (October 1983), p. 139. The Soviets have reportedly deployed satellite terminals in Bagran, Afghanistan, and close to the SA-5 air defense missile batteries that they control in Syria. See Jon L. Boyes, "Scanning Soviet C³," *Signal*, vol. 39 (December 1984), pp. 15–16; and Meyer, "Space and Soviet Military Planning," p. 71.
33. Richard W. Blank, "The NAVSTAR Global Positioning System," *Signal*, vol. 41 (November 1986), p. 78.
34. Maj. Thomas L. Sack, USAF, "Air Weather Service as a Force Intensifier," *Air Force Magazine*, vol. 63 (November 1980), p. 110.
35. See Henry W. Brandli, "The Use of Meteorological Satellites in Southeast Asia

As far as I am concerned, this weather picture is probably the greatest innovation of the war. I depend on it in conjunction with the traditional forecast as a basic means of making my decisions as to whether to launch or not to launch a strike. . . . The [DMSP] satellite is something no commander has ever had before in a war.[36]

The U.S. Air Force and Marines are procuring new transportable and rapidly deployable terminals to make Defense Meteorological Satellite Program (DMSP) weather data available wherever American forces are sent in sizable numbers. The Harris MK IV terminal, which can be airlifted by C-130 transport planes, then off-loaded, assembled, and made operational by a three-man crew in less than six hours, receives both hard and soft copy data and allows retransmission of soft copy over battlefield telephone lines to other tactical commanders.[37] The Soviets no doubt find meteorological satellites equally useful for the same reasons.

The latest, and arguably most valuable, contribution of satellites to U.S. air operations will come with the full deployment of the Navstar GPS system. Since 1977 the U.S. Air Force at its Yuma Proving Ground in Arizona has been exploring the applications of the Navstar system, with impressive results. Using six satellites simulating the full constellation, helicopters have made blind landings within several feet of the designated spot, jet fighters have rendezvoused with tanker aircraft for refueling without the help of other navigational aids, cargo aircraft have parachuted supplies within thirty to forty feet of a ground marker, and fighter-bombers have delivered conventional "iron bombs" to their target with the precision of "smart" munitions.[38] In wartime, the impact of Navstar GPS is expected to be dramatic. The efficiency of bombing operations in terms of the quantity of munitions and the number of sorties required to perform a given mission is likely to improve signifi-

Operations," *Aerospace Historian*, vol. 29 (September 1982), pp. 172–75. Britain reportedly also relied on U.S. meteorological satellites to pick the optimum time to conduct its amphibious assault on the Falkland Islands. See Defense Marketing Services Inc., "NOAA," *DMS Market Intelligence Report* (Greenwich, Conn., 1984).

36. Quoted in Desmond Ball, "Code 417, The Defense Meteorological Satellite Program (DMSP)," draft of paper prepared at the Strategic and Defence Studies Centre, Australian National University, Canberra, Australia, December 1984.

37. James B. Schultz, "Air Force Budget Emphasizes Research and Development," *Defense Electronics*, vol. 16 (September 1984), p. 74.

38. *Department of Defense Authorization for Appropriations for Fiscal Year 1981*, Hearings before the Senate Committee on Armed Services, 96 Cong. 2 sess. (GPO, 1980), pt. 5, p. 2674. See also Karas, *New High Ground*, chap. 5.

cantly. For example, some predict that for close air support operations and long-range interdiction of ground targets, the "kill probabilities" could improve by several orders of magnitude.[39] Navstar receivers are already being fitted to F-111 long-range bombers, F-16 fighters, and tanker aircraft.

Scant information is available on how the Soviet Union intends to use its Glonass navigation system in wartime, but given the similarities with Navstar, one can expect many of the same applications.

The majority of the present applications of satellites for air operations relate to ground attack missions. In the future it is conceivable that spacecraft will be used to support air defense operations. Just as AWACS aircraft today warn of attacks and coordinate interceptor aircraft, so spacecraft could become the ultimate battle management platform for air defense. As discussed in the preceding chapter, the use of space-based radars and infrared sensors for this purpose is already being investigated in the United States. General Lawrence A. Skantze, commander of Air Force Systems Command, has graphically depicted the benefits of such a system: "Information [from the space sensors] could be passed through AWACS to our fighters. We could then more selectively scramble our fighters to splash incoming targets."[40] Though attractive, space-based air defense sensors are unlikely to be available before the late 1990s. Major questions of cost effectiveness and vulnerability still need to be resolved.

Naval Operations

Arguably, naval forces have been the greatest beneficiaries of military satellite support. Ocean reconnaissance, communication, navigation, and meteorological satellites all contribute in important ways to maritime operations.

For well over a decade the United States and the Soviet Union have employed satellites for ocean reconnaissance. The United States appears

39. K. D. McDonald, "Navigation Satellite Systems: Their Characteristics, Potential and Military Applications," in Bhupendra Jasani, ed., *Outer Space—A New Dimension of the Arms Race* (London: Taylor and Francis for the Stockholm International Peace Research Institute, 1982), p. 178. For other examples, see David A. Boutacoff, "Navstar Forecast: Cloudy Now, Clearing Later," *Defense Electronics*, vol. 18 (May 1986), p. 99.

40. Quoted in Edgar Ulsamer, "What's Up in Space," *Air Force Magazine*, vol. 69 (February 1986), p. 48.

to use its space-based ocean reconnaissance system for general intelligence gathering on the worldwide deployment of naval forces. In contrast, the Soviet ocean reconnaissance system appears specifically designed to support the primary mission of the Soviet navy in wartime, which is to prevent U.S. naval forces, especially carrier battle groups and attack submarines, from coming within striking range of the Soviet homeland and in particular the bastions for its ballistic-missile-carrying submarines in the Barents Sea and the Sea of Okhotsk.[41] The Soviet RORSAT and EORSAT satellites would provide early warning of the movement of U.S. naval forces in the principal avenues of approach to the Soviet submarine bastions, information that could then be used to target those surface ships.

Despite the operational shortcomings of both the EORSATs and RORSATs (discussed in chapter 2), the Soviets clearly believe that these satellites will play an active role in wartime. As the director of U.S. naval intelligence, Rear Admiral John Butts, reported to Congress: "The new generation of ships and submarines entering the Soviet fleet are equipped to receive surveillance and targeting data directly from satellites and we believe their navy will rely increasingly on such data in the years ahead."[42] Long-range attacks by *Backfire* bombers armed with stand-off cruise missiles are another option that the Soviets have apparently exercised.[43] Furthermore, attacks on U.S. carrier battle groups by land-based intermediate-range ballistic missiles cannot be ruled out, certainly in nuclear contingencies.[44]

41. On the wartime missions of the Soviet navy, see U.S. Department of Defense, *Soviet Military Power, 1985* (GPO), pp. 91–92; Michael MccGwire, "Naval Power and Soviet Global Strategy," *International Security*, vol. 3 (Spring 1979), pp. 134–89; and Louise Hodgden, "Satellites at Sea: Space and Naval Warfare," *Naval War College Review*, vol. 32 (July–August 1984), pp. 31–45.

42. *Department of Defense Authorization for Appropriations for Fiscal Year 1986*, Hearings before the Senate Committee on Armed Services, 99 Cong. 1 sess. (GPO, 1986), pt. 8, p. 4366.

43. Hodgden, "Satellites at Sea," p. 40; Paul Bracken, *The Command and Control of Nuclear Forces* (Yale University Press, 1983), p. 153.

44. See Robert P. Berman and John C. Baker, *Soviet Strategic Forces: Requirements and Responses* (Brookings, 1982), p. 55. Berman and Baker state that "within ninety minutes of detection, enemy combat vessels or high-value convoys on the open seas could be struck by ballistic missiles fired from either sea or land." Ibid., p. 163. Such attacks, however, would not be easy to execute given the inevitable delays in processing the intelligence, changing the missile's guidance system, and reaching the target. The potential for midcourse targeting updates could make this more feasible in the future, however.

Although ocean reconnaissance satellites do not appear to play such an active role in U.S. naval operations, communication satellites, by contrast, have become virtually indispensable. According to one report the U.S. Navy now relies on satellites for relaying 95 percent of all its messages.[45] Terminals for using the FLTSATCOM and Leasat spacecraft are fitted to all of the navy's major surface ships, submarines, P-3C Orion aircraft, and shore stations around the world.[46] These are interconnected through the fleet's Naval Tactical Data System (NTDS), which encompasses a variety of information exchange subsystems designed to support specific naval missions.[47]

One critical area that has benefited enormously from satellite communication is antisubmarine warfare. The rapid collection, collation, and dissemination of ASW-relevant information from sensors around the world has immensely facilitated the task of tracking Soviet submarines. Information obtained from such diverse sources as reconnaissance satellites, the Sound Surveillance System (SOSUS), P-3C Orion aircraft, and other sensors is integrated and processed by regional shore-based U.S. ASW Operations Centers (see figure 3-1) and then distributed to naval forces via the FLTSATCOM network.[48] The U.S. Navy's new mobile version of SOSUS, the Surface Towed-Array Sensor System (SURTASS) deployed from T-AGOS ships, makes use of the higher capacity DSCS system to transmit the data it collects.[49]

45. Prina, "Signal Flags to Satellites," p. 47. An estimate of 85 percent is cited by Vice Admiral Gordon Nagler in "Space: Air Force and Navy Outlook," *Signal*, vol. 38 (January 1984), p. 24.

46. "Navy Space Expansion Requires Dedicated Satellites," *Defense Electronics*, vol. 13 (July 1981), p. 81.

47. They include the Common User Digital Information Exchange System (CUDIXS), which handles all the hard copy fleet broadcast messages, the Submarine Satellite Information Exchange System (SSIXS), the Antisubmarine Warfare Information Exchange System (ASWIXS), now subsumed within the Officer in Tactical Command Information Exchange System (OTCIXS), and the Tactical Intelligence System (TACINTEL). See "U.S. Navy Strategic and Tactical C³I for the 80s," *Signal*, vol. 37 (September 1982), p. 17.

48. This system is apparently part of the Classic Wizard program. See Louise Hodgden, "Satellites at Sea: Space and Naval Warfare," in Durch, ed., *National Interests and the Military Use of Space*, p. 123. See also Joel S. Wit, "Advances in Antisubmarine Warfare," *Scientific American*, vol. 224 (February 1981), p. 35.

49. See U.S. Department of the Navy, *Justification of Estimates for Fiscal Year 1985: Operation and Maintenance* (Dept. of the Navy, February 1984), p. 3-11. The T-AGOS ships will send their data to ground terminals in Northwest, Virginia; Fort Detrick, Maryland; and Clark Air Base, the Philippines. From here the data are passed

Figure 3-1. *Earth Coverage of U.S. Fleet Satellite Communications System, with Sites of U.S. Navy Antisubmarine Operations Centers*

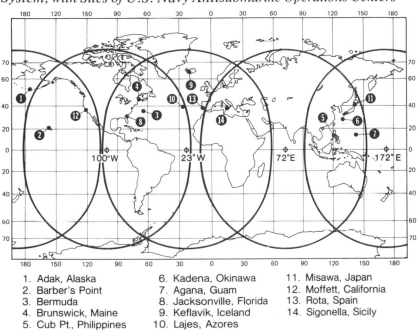

1. Adak, Alaska	6. Kadena, Okinawa	11. Misawa, Japan
2. Barber's Point	7. Agana, Guam	12. Moffett, California
3. Bermuda	8. Jacksonville, Florida	13. Rota, Spain
4. Brunswick, Maine	9. Keflavik, Iceland	14. Sigonella, Sicily
5. Cub Pt., Philippines	10. Lajes, Azores	

Source: Based on "Navy Expansion Requires Dedicated Satellites," *Defense Electronics,* vol. 13 (July 1981), p. 79.

To deliver up-to-date intelligence for surface operations, the U.S. Navy is setting up its own fusion centers, known as Tactical Flag Command Centers, aboard aircraft carriers, which will receive targeting data via satellite. As part of the TENCAP program mentioned earlier, other major naval ships will also be fitted with Fleet Imagery Support Terminals (FISTs) to receive processed imagery from ashore.[50]

For many of the same reasons, the Soviet navy also has exploited the advantages of satellites for maritime communication. Although the extent to which satellite user equipment has been deployed throughout the Soviet fleet is unclear from the public record, it is known that certain warships and auxiliaries have been fitted with "Big Ball" and "Punch Bowl" satellite communication antennas to serve as command centers

---

to the navy's ocean processing facilities at either Dam Neck, Virginia, or Ford Island, Hawaii.

50. Ted W. Jensen, ed., *Space, The Next Ten Years*, A Symposium Report by the United States Space Foundation (Colorado Springs, Colo.: The Foundation, 1985), p. 61.

afloat. These include two converted Sverdlov-class cruisers, the *Zhdanov* (Black Sea Fleet) and *Admiral Senyavin* (Pacific Fleet); four Kiev-class aircraft carriers; two Kirov battle cruisers; and some submarine tenders.[51] Also, two Golf-class submarines and possibly one or more Hotel-class submarines have been converted into communication centers. Soviet nuclear ballistic-missile-carrying submarines (SSBNs) and nuclear attack submarines (SSNs) are also known to employ ultrahigh-frequency (UHF) satellite communication terminals.[52]

Not surprisingly naval forces, particularly submarines, have also been the principal beneficiaries of navigation satellites. With Navstar, the U.S. Navy expects to expand its usage considerably. As with ground and air operations, the provision of common positioning information to a variety of weapons platforms—ASW aircraft, helicopters, surface ships, and amphibious forces—is expected to dramatically improve the coordination and therefore efficiency of such key missions as sonarbuoy and mine emplacement, mine clearing, and amphibious deployments, as well as the full range of naval air operations.[53]

Finally, naval forces are among the largest subscribers to satellite-derived meteorological reports. Timely and precise forecasts, particularly when they relate to adverse weather, are absolutely essential for naval operations. For U.S. forces, the majority of weather reports will continue to be transmitted by communication satellites from the Fleet Numerical Weather Central in Monterey, California, although the navy is also fitting DMSP terminals aboard its major aircraft carriers to receive weather data directly. Presumably, the Soviet navy derives similar benefits from the Meteor satellites, though the extent to which surface ships can receive data directly from these spacecraft is unclear.

Of equal importance to naval operations is the data supplied by oceanographic satellites. As noted in chapter 2, the U.S. Navy is developing its own space system specifically for this purpose: the Navy–

51. Jim Bussert, "Wartime Needs Give Direction to Soviet C^{3}I Technology," *Defense Electronics*, vol. 17 (May 1985), pp. 154–55; and Norman Polmar, "Soviet C^3: An Overview," *Signal*, vol. 39 (December 1984), p. 29. See also Norman Friedman, "Soviet Naval Command and Control," *Signal*, vol. 39 (December 1984), p. 58. Admiral Sergey G. Gorshkov is reported to have directed the Soviet navy's worldwide exercise *Okean 75* from one of these command ships.

52. See Capt. W. J. Ruhe, USN (ret.), "Soviet Submarine C^3," *Signal*, vol. 39 (December 1984), p. 65.

53. See L. Edgar Prina, "A Constellation of Capabilities," *Seapower*, vol. 30 (February 1987), pp. 8, 10.

Remote Ocean Sensing System. Though N-ROSS will be useful for a multitude of naval missions, it is in the area of ASW and counter-ASW operations that the most benefit will be gained. Information supplied by N-ROSS will help naval commanders make sonar range predictions, select weapon settings, and choose the right spacing and depth for sonarbuoys and towed arrays. Wind speed measurements will help in the prediction of ambient noise and improve the accuracy of sonar readings, while information on the thickness of the ice caps can help determine likely enemy surfacing locations. Alternatively, the same information can be used by submarines to evade detection—for instance, ocean eddies are ideal places to hide.[54] Again, the existence of Soviet oceanographic satellites indicates that their navy finds these data useful for similar reasons.

In the future, the use of reconnaissance satellites for naval air defense and over-the-horizon targeting is likely to increase, certainly by the U.S. Navy. Still further in the distance is the possibility of subsurface surveillance for submarines, although as discussed earlier, tremendous technological obstacles still need to be overcome.

Regardless of the prospects for space-based detection of submarines, satellites will increasingly be used to collect data from terrestrial-based ASW sensors for processing and dissemination. A glimpse of the shape of things to come was given in 1985, when DARPA sponsored the launch of an experimental satellite, known as GLOMR (for global low-orbiting message relay), to test the ability of small communication satellites to collect raw data from passive sensors such as sonarbuoys and relay the information to ground stations or ships for processing.[55] Thus, whether or not the oceans become "transparent" from space, the importance of satellites for ASW operations will grow.

Judgments about the relative superpower dependency on satellite services in a conventional war are, for the reasons discussed at the beginning of this chapter, difficult to make. While none of the services provided by satellites in wartime are unique, satellites can in certain cases provide significant additional capabilities to the non-space-based alternatives at the disposal of the United States or the Soviet Union. These additional means may also be more vulnerable and, depending on the location of the conflict, not readily available.

54. Ibid., p. 13.
55. Craig Covault, "Spacelab 3 Mission to Launch University, Defense Spacecraft," *Aviation Week and Space Technology,* vol. 122 (April 15, 1985), pp. 14–16.

In a NATO–Warsaw Pact conflict in central Europe, the level of redundancy for both superpowers would be high. The battlefield commanders of both sides would probably rely more on the intelligence-gathering assets under their direct control—ground-based SIGINT systems, reconnaissance aircraft, and, increasingly, remotely piloted vehicles—than on satellites.[56] Beyond the immediate zone of engagement, however, reconnaissance satellites would be particularly useful for identifying the movement of men and materiel to the front, information that would be valuable for planning long-range attacks. For NATO, with its new strategy of targeting successive echelons of advancing Soviet forces, known as Follow-on Forces Attack (FOFA), satellites would become even more important, especially as the transmission of imagery to local commanders is speeded up. Long-range reconnaissance aircraft could also perform this mission, but with the likelihood of high attrition. Over a prolonged conflict, the reliance on reconnaissance satellites could increase as ground and aerial systems were lost to enemy action.

For communication, navigation, and weather forecasting, NATO and the Warsaw Pact are again not totally reliant on space systems. Given the geographic separation of the United States from its allies, however, NATO is, on balance, more dependent on satellite communication. The Navstar GPS is also likely to be employed by a larger community of users for more military missions than its Soviet counterpart.[57] Furthermore, as one analyst has argued:

> Soviet military capabilities would not suffer for the lack of space-based navigation. In the context of the air-land battle in the [European] theater, the Soviet Air Force has provided for a wide range of ground control points on the battlefield and in the rear areas, and radio locator beacons are also deployed.[58]

In conflicts away from the European theater, the level of dependency is likely to increase for both sides as the availability of alternative assets declines. The relative position, however, will still depend on where the war is being fought. In areas that are close to the Soviet homeland such as Southwest Asia, the United States is likely to be more reliant on

56. Meyer, "Space and Soviet Military Planning," p. 68. See also Kennedy and others, *Intelligence Warfare*, pp. 141–65.

57. Twenty thousand receiver sets are being provided for U.S. forces, in addition to those for NATO. See U.S. General Accounting Office, *Issues Concerning the Department of Defense's Global Positioning System as It Enters Production*, GAO/MASAD-83-9 (GAO, 1983), p. 14.

58. Meyer, "Space and Soviet Military Planning," pp. 76–77.

satellite services, particularly for communication, navigation, and weather forecasting. But when both superpowers are fighting at a distance from their homelands, the relative dependency is likely to reverse itself. This is especially true for intelligence gathering systems, as noted in a leaked but still classified General Accounting Office (GAO) report: "As the Soviet Union projects its forces further from its borders, or into a denied area, such as China, it becomes increasingly dependent on this type of [reconnaissance satellite]."[59] In contrast, for the same reasons that apply in peacetime crisis monitoring, the United States will probably have more alternative reconnaissance assets at its disposal in remote parts of the world than will the Soviet Union.

For maritime operations, the U.S. Navy is clearly more dependent on space systems. As noted earlier, communication satellites are responsible for relaying virtually all the U.S. fleet's messages. Not only has the alternative high-frequency (HF) network contracted, so that certain areas of the globe such as parts of the South Pacific, the South Atlantic, and the Indian Ocean reportedly cannot be covered satisfactorily, but also the level of experience in operating HF systems has diminished.[60] Similarly, the United States is likely to become increasingly dependent on space-based navigation aids. For one thing, since Navstar will provide worldwide service, it will create a dependency on satellite systems in those areas not now served by other radio navigation aids, such as Omega and LORAN-C.[61] For another, these alternative systems are scheduled to be phased out of service in the 1990s, after which reliance on Navstar will inevitably grow.[62]

The Soviet navy—certainly the surface fleet—is likely to be deployed in home waters during a major conflict, which should lower its reliance on satellite support. For example, while ocean reconnaissance satellites

59. Jack Anderson, "Space 'Peeping Toms' Are a Danger," *Washington Post*, February 12, 1985.

60. Jensen, ed., *Space, The Next Ten Years*, p. 59. Also, according to Vice Admiral Gordon Nagler, "We have become so dependent on satellites for our day-to-day communications to the fleet that we really don't have as much expertise as I would like . . . in keeping a high-frequency circuit in [operation]." Prina, "Signal Flags to Satellites," p. 47.

61. For information on the coverage of existing systems, see table 2-2 above; and John Bell, "A Dozen Ways to Keep on the Straight and Narrow," *New Scientist*, vol. 104 (October 11, 1984), p. 47.

62. *Hearings on Military Posture and Department of Defense Authorization for Appropriations for Fiscal Year 1983*, Hearings before the House Committee on Armed Services, 97 Cong. 2 sess. (GPO, 1982), pt. 5, p. 593.

appear to be valued highly by the Soviet navy, it is by no means dependent on them. The Soviet ocean surveillance system is made up of an extensive network of sensors including trawlers fitted with eavesdropping equipment, special auxiliary general intelligence ships (AGIs), submarines, long-range aircraft, and high-frequency/direction-finding (HF/DF) stations based on land.[63] These are likely to be more readily available in maritime areas close to the Soviet land mass. The same applies to navigation and communication support.

Nuclear Operations

One way to assess the value of satellites in a nuclear war is to examine their probable roles in a preemptive first strike, a retaliatory second strike, and a protracted conflict. They can also aid tactical nuclear operations.

—*In a first strike*. Photoreconnaissance and signals intelligence satellites would provide a great deal of information for planning a coordinated first strike against an opponent's strategic forces. The most susceptible to being detected and thus targeted from space are ICBM silos, bombers, SSBNs in port, and fixed command and control (C^2) centers. Even mobile C^2 centers could be located and targeted by SIGINT satellites.[64] Planners would rely on meteorological satellites to provide up-to-date information on the weather over the target area. Since the accuracy of ballistic missile warheads can be adversely affected by wind and precipitation, timely information would be critical for modifying their guidance systems.[65] Bomber crews would also need to take into account the weather en route to their targets.

Similarly, navigation satellites would indirectly contribute to the accuracy of the attacks. If ballistic-missile-carrying submarines were

63. Norman Polmar and Norman Friedman, "Their Missions and Tactics," *Proceedings*, vol. 108 (October, 1982), pp. 42–44. For more information on U.S. and allied ocean surveillance systems, see Kennedy and others, *Intelligence Warfare*, pp. 166–91; and more specifically Martin Streetly, "US Airborne ELINT Systems—Part 1: The US Navy," *Jane's Defence Weekly*, vol. 3 (January 12, 1985), pp. 69–70.

64. Daniel Ford, *The Button: The Pentagon's Strategic Command and Control System* (Simon and Schuster, 1985), p. 164; and Bruce G. Blair, *Strategic Command and Control: Redefining the Nuclear Threat* (Brookings, 1985), p. 159.

65. Ball, *Can Nuclear War Be Controlled?* p. 19. The targeting data on the Minuteman missiles are changed every twenty-four hours to accommodate weather conditions over the target areas.

engaged, they would obtain last-minute position fixes from satellites to update their inertial navigation systems. Such fixes provide the reference points to adjust the guidance systems of the SLBMs. The accuracy of the new generation of U.S. sea-based strategic forces, however, is unlikely to improve markedly from the presence of Navstar GPS. The Trident D-5 missile, for example, has a star-tracking system for mid-course guidance, while the submarine-launched cruise missiles use terrain-matching radar. Although the United States has considered fitting Navstar GPS receivers to its strategic missiles, the idea has so far been rejected for fear that the satellites could be rendered inoperable or that the radio links could be subjected to jamming and disruption by nuclear blasts.[66] However, receivers have been added to B-52, FB-111, and B-1 bomber and tanker aircraft, which should improve their performance in wartime.[67]

Valuable though satellites would be in supporting a damage-limiting first strike (that is, one that limited the enemy's capacity to retaliate), they would not make it possible to execute a fully disabling attack. Deployed submarines remain undetectable from space and dispersed mobile ICBMs will be extremely difficult to find. Although the United States and almost certainly the Soviet Union are investigating ways to locate and continuously track, in real time, land-based mobile strategic targets, success is still long way off. How far off is a matter of some debate. Secretary of the Air Force Edward C. Aldridge, Jr., believes that the U.S. effort will yield "positive results within 8 to 10 years," but other experts, including the Defense Science Board and Air Force Science Advisory Board, are reportedly skeptical of this timetable.[68] Besides increasing satellite constellation size requirements (see the

66. James B. Schultz, "Navstar GPS Offers Mid-Course Guidance Improvements to Cruise Missiles," *Defense Electronics*, vol. 16 (May 1984), p. 68; and Clarence A. Robinson, Jr., "Parallel Programs Advance Small ICBM," *Aviation Week and Space Technology*, vol. 120 (March 5, 1984), p. 17. In 1979 and again in 1980, Navstar GPS receivers were fitted on Minuteman II missiles and launched from Vandenberg AFB to assess Navstar's potential use for ballistic missile guidance. The results indicated that significant improvements in accuracy could be achieved. Similar experiments were carried out with cruise missiles. See Schultz, p. 70; and Walter Andrews, "New Satellite System Found Right on Target," *Washington Times*, April 25, 1983.

67. *Department of Defense Appropriations for 1984*, Hearings before a Subcommittee of the House Committee on Appropriations, 98 Cong. 1 sess. (GPO, 1983), pt. 8, pp. 394–95; and Karas, *New High Ground*, p. 135.

68. R. Jeffrey Smith, "Proposal to Ban Mobile Missiles Favors Targeting over Arms Control," *Science*, vol. 233 (August 22, 1986), p. 831.

discussion of "Strategic and Tactical Surveillance" in chapter 2), the imaging and data-processing demands would also be immense; targets must be discriminated from the background "clutter" virtually instantaneously, a difficult task even without Soviet active and passive deception measures. In short, the prospects for constant real-time surveillance of mobile strategic targets before the twenty-first century do not look promising.

—*In a second strike*. Satellites improve the chances that either superpower could retaliate effectively after suffering a first strike. The earliest confirmation of such an attack would, as noted earlier, be supplied by each side's early warning satellites.[69] This warning would provide the option to launch a retaliatory strike before the arrival of the attacking warheads. At the very least, vulnerable strategic forces like bombers, tankers, and airborne command posts could be sent aloft to avoid immediate destruction. The early warning satellites—at least the DSP system—would also be able to determine the general size of the attack and detect the approximate launch sites, which would in turn provide clues as to the types of missiles used.[70] This knowledge could be useful for helping decisionmakers discern the purpose of the attack, especially if it is a relatively limited strike, and for deciding on the most prudent response.[71] Locating the source of the attack would also give the national command authorities information to target the adversary's remaining ICBM forces.[72]

The space-based U.S. Nuclear Detection System (NDS) would complement the data supplied by the DSP early warning satellites in important ways. Though the decision time would be slim, the NDS sensors could,

69. The Soviet over-the-horizon (OTH) radar systems can actually provide warning almost simultaneously with the satellites, although they are not considered to be so precise. See Department of Defense, *Soviet Military Power, 1985*, p. 45. For more information on current and planned U.S. and Soviet early warning radars, see Thomas K. Longstreth, John E. Pike, and John B. Rhinelander, *The Impact of U.S. and Soviet Ballistic Missile Defense Programs on the ABM Treaty*, 3d ed. (Washington, D.C.: National Campaign to Save the ABM Treaty, 1985).

70. Ford, *The Button*, p. 62. The current DSP satellites are not able to pinpoint the exact silos or the likely aimpoints of the attacking missiles. Blair, *Strategic Command and Control*, p. 223.

71. See Ford, *The Button*, p. 62; and Ashton B. Carter, "The Command and Control of Nuclear War," *Scientific American*, vol. 252 (January 1985), p. 35.

72. The ability to rapidly reprogram the guidance systems of ICBMs and other strategic forces is obviously critical to this kind of retargeting. This is reportedly being improved in the U.S. case. See "Fast Targeting for Minuteman," *Defense Week*, vol. 6 (March 18, 1985), p. 5.

for example, "record the detonation of Soviet SLBMs on U.S. territory some 10 to 20 minutes before the expected arrival of the more accurate 'silo killing' Soviet ICBMs. The U.S. leadership would have additional information to use in making the dangerous decision of whether to save the threatened ICBMs by launching them promptly."[73] It would "also aid commanders in identifying areas that have escaped destruction so that they could direct bombers, tankers, and command post aircraft to them."[74]

Finally, communication satellites would be used to set the second strike in motion. In the U.S. case, there are AFSATCOM terminals to receive launch orders (the Emergency Action Message) aboard all the airborne command posts (EC-135, E-4B, and the navy's TACAMO aircraft), on B-52, FB-111, and B-1 bombers, on KC-10 tankers, and at all SAC command posts and missile launch control centers (LCCs).[75] In the future, the Milstar system will bear the burden of strategic command and control both during and after the attack. Soviet strategic forces are presumably connected in a similar way.

—*In a protracted conflict.* For obvious reasons, assessing the role of satellites over the course of an intercontinental nuclear war becomes increasingly hypothetical. Conceivably, many of the same functions described above would be repeated for successive nuclear exchanges. Thus early warning satellites would detect follow-on strikes for as long as there were means to receive and process their data. Communication satellites would be used to control surviving strategic forces and relay damage assessment reports and targeting information from photoreconnaissance satellites. The United States is in fact deploying a fleet of trucks equipped with satellite terminals to operate as mobile command posts in a protracted nuclear war.[76] These and other command posts will also receive data from the NDS sensors, which would make it easier to plan subsequent strikes against the Soviet Union. As General Bernard P. Randolph, director of the U.S. Air Force's space systems and command, control, and communication research, testified: "When we

73. Carter, "Command and Control," p. 35.
74. Blair, *Strategic Command and Control*, p. 273.
75. Under the ICBM superhigh-frequency satellite terminal (ISST) program, Minuteman silos will also be fitted with receive-only SHF terminals. See Gen. Larry D. Welch, USAF, "Strategic C³: The Tie That Binds," *Signal*, vol. 40 (March 1986), p. 28.
76. See Richard Whitmire, "U.S. Builds Command Post Juggernauts," *San Bernardino Sun*, April 1, 1985.

try to destroy hard targets in the Soviet Union, we are able [with NDS] to demonstrate or to understand our success in destroying those hard targets, and therefore, [we do] not have to go back and restrike those targets, and we can retarget in near real time.[77] Furthermore, according to air force budget documents, NDS data could be a "major information component during negotiations to terminate a nuclear conflict."[78] Communication satellites might also conceivably play a role in the war termination discussions.

—*Tactical nuclear operations.* For the conduct of tactical nuclear operations, satellites would also play a useful role. Information from the nuclear explosion detection sensors in space would be able to confirm the use of tactical nuclear weapons outside U.S. territory and perhaps prevent hasty decisions based on erroneous information. Weather forecasts from meteorological satellites would also help gauge the likely pattern of fallout from the use of battlefield nuclear weapons. Furthermore, communication satellites are the most direct and reliable means of authorizing the release of such weapons. This is reflected in the fact that all the U.S. nuclear weapon storage sites worldwide are linked by the AFSATCOM system.[79] A special satellite communications net known as Flaming Arrow is also being deployed for U.S. forces in the European theater.[80]

Important though satellites have become to the conduct of nuclear operations, neither superpower is dependent on their services for basic retaliation. In particular, since both sides possess invulnerable ballistic-missile-carrying submarines, neither side is dependent on satellite-derived tactical warning to carry out a second strike. And both have deemed it prudent to deploy a variety of systems that duplicate the main functions of the most important satellites. For example, the United States and the Soviet Union have ground-based radars that would detect

77. *Department of Defense Authorization for Appropriations for Fiscal Year 1983*, Hearings before the Senate Committee on Appropriations, 97 Cong. 2 sess. (GPO, 1982), pt. 7, p. 4625. See also Colin S. Gray, *American Military Space Policy: Information Systems, Weapon Systems and Arms Control* (Cambridge, Mass.: Abt Books, 1982), p. 28; and Desmond Ball, *Targeting for Strategic Deterrence*, Adelphi Papers 185, (London: International Institute for Strategic Studies, 1982), pp. 34–36.

78. U.S. Department of the Air Force, *Supporting Data for Fiscal Year 1985, Budget Estimates, Descriptive Summaries: Research, Development, Test and Evaluation* (Dept. of the Air Force, February 1984), p. 393.

79. *Department of Defense Appropriations for 1984*, Hearings, pt. 8, pp. 383–84.

80. Jack Cushman, "New Arms and Archaic C³ Units," *Defense Week*, vol. 4 (December 19, 1983), pp. 4–5. This is in addition to the HF-based Regency Net system.

the launch of a ballistic missile roughly five minutes after the early warning satellites had reported the event. Each side also has numerous other ways for communicating with strategic forces. Nevertheless, satellites give each side additional confidence that it could retaliate effectively after a surprise attack. For the Soviet Union, with a higher proportion of its strategic arsenal made up of fixed land-based ICBMs, the extra warning time a satellite could supply might be highly valuable, especially if, as some Western analysts believe, it has adopted a launch-on-warning posture to compensate for this vulnerability.[81] Although the United States does not rely so heavily as the USSR on land-based missiles to ensure retaliation, its strategic bomber force and particularly its airborne command posts, which are vital to the wartime control of U.S. nuclear forces, would profit considerably from tactical warning to escape attack.[82]

Compared with the Soviet Union, the United States also appears more interested in the use of satellites for postattack assessments and retargeting, as evidenced by its proliferation of spaceborne nuclear explosion detection sensors. The advent of land-based mobile theater and strategic forces will encourage the further use of reconnaissance satellites for this purpose.[83] In contrast, some Western analysts contend, there is no evidence of a Soviet inclination to use satellites in this way.[84]

81. See Raymond L. Garthoff, "Mutual Deterrence and Strategic Arms Limitation in Soviet Policy," *International Security*, vol. 3 (Summer 1978), pp. 129–31; and Stephen M. Meyer, "Soviet Perspectives on the Paths to Nuclear War," in Graham T. Allison, Albert Carnesale, and Joseph S. Nye, Jr., eds., *Hawks, Doves, and Owls: An Agenda for Avoiding Nuclear War* (W.W. Norton, 1985), pp. 173-74. Some have also argued that the United States is operationally geared to launch on warning. Officially this is denied, but there is some circumstantial evidence as well as statements by responsible officials to support the contention. See R. J. Smith, "A Worrisome Shift in Nuclear Strategy," *Science*, vol. 232 (June 6, 1986), p. 1187.

82. See Blair, *Strategic Command and Control*, pp. 180, 188. Indeed, Blair argues that "reliance on tactical and strategic warning has grown so that both are essential to the control of retaliatory forces." Ibid., p. 210. The Soviet bomber forces and airborne command posts would presumably benefit in the same way.

83. As Lt. Gen. Richard Saxer, director of the U.S. Defense Nuclear Agency, testified to Congress: "With the advent of Soviet and Warsaw Pact mobile systems, an area of overriding concern is having the ability for U.S. planners to perform near-real-time targeting of these mobile assets." Quoted in "Fast Targeting for Minuteman," p. 5.

84. Meyer, "Space and Soviet Military Planning," p. 68. Soviet references—albeit fragmentary—to "withholding" nuclear forces and maintaining a strategic reserve, whether ballistic-missile-carrying submarines or mobile ICBMs, suggest that postattack assessment may be more important to the Soviets than is often credited. For a brief

Conclusion

In peacetime satellites perform many stabilizing and benign functions. They reduce the likelihood of misunderstandings between the superpowers, provide a crucial tool for monitoring arms control agreements, and help guard against surprise attack. Although satellites also make it possible for both sides to target strategic forces with great precision, a completely successful first strike is still not feasible. Satellites are not, therefore, a threat to strategic stability nor are they likely to become one in the near future. The deployment of new, more extensive and intrusive forms of surveillance that could undermine the security of each side's deterrent forces is not likely to occur before the twenty-first century at the earliest.

Benign though satellites may be in peacetime, their role can change dramatically in wartime. Many have become force multipliers in that they directly enhance the effectiveness of the weapon systems and combatants. For this reason they are valued by one's own forces and feared in the hands of an adversary. How much they are valued and how much of a threat they pose is, as discussed earlier, largely determined by a range of contextual factors—particularly the level and locale of the conflict. Although both superpowers would benefit considerably from their military satellites during a conflict, in the places where U.S. and Soviet forces are most likely to clash, such as central Europe or Southwest Asia, it is the United States that on balance would benefit most from satellite support. It has more to lose, therefore, if denied that support. How such attacks on satellites might be carried out and also thwarted are the subjects of the following chapter.

---

discussion of this topic, see Ball, *Can Nuclear War Be Controlled?* pp. 32–34; and Jan S. Breemer, "The Soviet Navy's SSBN Bastions: Evidence, Inference, and Alternative Scenarios," *RUSI Journal*, vol. 130 (March 1985), pp. 19–21.

CHAPTER FOUR

The Threat to Space Systems

THE NEED TO counter the threat posed by the Soviet Union's operational antisatellite system remains the principal rationale for the U.S. ASAT program. Unless the United States deploys a commensurate antisatellite capability, it is argued, the Soviets will be able to attack U.S. space assets with impunity. Furthermore, the presence of the Soviet interceptor and of so-called "residual" ASAT capabilities (weapons that can be used against satellites though they were not designed to do so) are cited as the main reasons that an ASAT ban would not be practicable or even desirable.

In response, the supporters of space arms control argue that the Soviet ASAT threat has been overrated and, moreover, the superior U.S. system under development will only encourage the Soviet Union to field more advanced antisatellite weapons in the future. They argue, furthermore, that a variety of unilateral satellite survivability measures can reduce the threat from both the Soviet Union's ASAT and whatever residual capabilities it may possess.

This chapter examines these competing arguments in closer detail. It assesses the current and planned antisatellite capabilities of the superpowers and compares them with the weapon systems that could be fielded in the absence of arms control. A necessary prerequisite is an understanding of the generic threats to space systems and the counter-measures that can be employed to increase their survivability.

Generic Threats and Countermeasures

Satellites are just one, albeit the most obvious, part of a space system. To function successfully a satellite must be in regular communication with ground stations, which help maintain its orbit, support its mission, and ultimately receive whatever information it collects or relays. An antisatellite act in the broadest sense, therefore, can be anything that disrupts or destroys a part of the space system, whether it be the satellite, the communication links, or the ground stations. These are sometimes referred to as the orbital segment, the link segment, and the ground segment, respectively.[1] Although public discussion of the ASAT issue has focused almost solely on the weapons designed specifically to attack satellites, the threats to the other parts of space system are equally important. Each is discussed in turn.

The Orbital Segment

Though built to withstand the rigors of launch and the barrenness of space, satellites are still relatively fragile objects constructed of light-weight materials and packed full of sensitive electronic components. To disable a satellite does not require that it be destroyed completely, merely that the vital subsystems that keep it functioning be sufficiently damaged to put it out of service.[2] This can be accomplished with three classes of weapon systems: those using nuclear, kinetic, or directed energy as the means of disablement. These are discussed in the order of their effectiveness and availability for use today.

A nuclear device can be lofted into space or the upper atmosphere by any ballistic missile with sufficient thrust and detonated at an appropriate time and place. Since space is a vacuum, satellites would be affected not by the blast from an explosion but rather by the nuclear radiation, which would travel many thousands of kilometers unimpeded by the atmosphere. Depending on a satellite's proximity to the explosion, the radiation would damage it through thermomechanical shock, ionization burnout, or a system-generated electromagnetic pulse (SGEMP). Thermomechanical shock occurs when the satellite becomes overheated after absorbing X-rays from the explosion, although this is likely to be preceded by ionization burnout, in which X-rays penetrate the thin skin

1. George F. Jelen, "Space System Vulnerabilities and Countermeasures," in William J. Durch, ed., *National Interests and the Military Use of Space* (Cambridge, Mass.: Ballinger, 1984), p. 89.

2. For a good introduction to the workings of a satellite, see J. A. Vandenkerckhove, "Technology of Earth Satellites," in David Fishlock, ed., *A Guide to Earth Satellites* (London: McDonald, 1971), pp. 15–16.

of a spacecraft to damage its electronic components.[3] Within a few hundred kilometers of the detonation these two phenomena will be lethal to unshielded satellites. At greater distances (more than 1,000 kilometers) damage will occur largely as a result of SGEMP. SGEMP is essentially a positive photoelectric current generated after the X-rays have stripped electrons from the surface of the satellite. The resultant electrical charge can spread throughout the satellite, causing the malfunction and burnout of electronic parts.

Even satellites not within direct line of sight of a nuclear explosion can later suffer damage from radiation trapped within the earth's magnetic field. Known as the Argus effect, it was first observed in 1958 when the United States detonated in space three low-yield nuclear devices in a test program of the same name. The effects of trapped radiation were again graphically demonstrated in 1962 when another U.S. high-altitude nuclear test (code-name Starfish Prime) inadvertently damaged six satellites.[4]

Kinetic energy weapons, in contrast, are guided or unguided projectiles that disable their targets by the mechanical shock of impact. Because satellites are already traveling at enormous speeds (about four or five kilometers a second in low earth orbit), a collision with even a tiny object can be catastrophic. A variety of devices can be used, ranging from conventional fragmentation charges that explode near the target to more sophisticated homing vehicles that smash into it. Another method, which is currently being studied for antimissile applications but which has equal relevance for attacking satellites, is the electromagnetically propelled, hypervelocity "railgun."

Directed-energy weaponry is the generic term for lasers, particle beam weapons, and high-powered radio-frequency generators. Lasers are coherent beams of electromagnetic radiation (that is, beams in which all the electromagnetic waves oscillate in step). They can be created in numerous ways with different characteristics.[5] Depending on the power

3. The discussion of the effect of nuclear explosions on satellites is from Bruce G. Blair, *Strategic Command and Control: Redefining the Nuclear Threat* (Brookings, 1985), pp. 205–06, 327–31; and Joseph S. Tirado, "Rad-Tolerant ICs Are Available Off the Shelf," *Defense Electronics,* vol. 16 (November 1984), p. 58.

4. For more information on the Argus tests, see Paul B. Stares, *The Militarization of Space: U.S. Policy, 1945–1984* (Ithaca, N.Y.: Cornell University Press, 1985), pp. 107–08.

5. For useful discussions of lasers, see Dean A. Wilkening, "Space-Based Weapons," in Durch, *National Interests and the Military Use of Space,* p. 141; and U.S. Congress,

of the beam, a laser could damage a satellite by overheating its surface, by "blinding" key on-board sensors, or by puncturing the outer surface of the spacecraft to expose internal equipment.

Particle beam weapons in essence consist of large accelerators that propel charged or neutral particles at great speeds to their target. Given the earth's magnetic fields, a *charged* particle beam would bend in space and thus not be a practical weapon system. However, a *neutral* particle beam would not suffer from this problem. Unlike a laser, a particle beam could immediately penetrate the surface of a satellite and disable its internal components through thermal and radiation damage.[6]

A high-powered radio-frequency weapon such as a microwave generator could also be used to overload and damage electronic equipment on satellites. At lower power levels, temporary interference or jamming would be the most likely effect.[7]

The weapon systems used to disable satellites can be further distinguished by their approach to the target. A ground-based interceptor can be launched into space so that it arrives at the same place and at the same time as the passing target satellite. This is generally known as the direct-ascent method. Alternatively the ASAT can be placed into the same orbit as its prey, so that it can stalk and eventually intercept it. This is known as the co-orbital method. Variations can be employed. For example, the interceptor can be maneuvered into an orbit that temporarily matches the target's or passes close enough to it for its guidance system and kill mechanism to be effective. A space-based system can be positioned within striking range of its prey, or it can be put into an orbit that allows it to be quickly brought within range when required. Those employing an explosive charge are commonly referred to as "space mines."

Depending on how they are deployed and used, there are operational tradeoffs to each of these methods of disabling satellites. In theory at least, any ballistic missile with the requisite reach, such as an ICBM, SLBM, or IRBM, can be used as an ASAT weapon, whether it is fitted with a nuclear or conventional warhead. Similarly, antiballistic missiles

Office of Technology Assessment, *Ballistic Missile Defense Technologies* (Washington, D.C.: Government Printing Office, 1985), pp. 147–53.

6. Office of Technology Assessment, *Ballistic Missile Defense Technologies*, pp. 153–55. See also Wilkening, "Space-Based Weapons," p. 152.

7. Office of Technology Assessment, *Anti-Satellite Weapons, Countermeasures, and Arms Control* (Washington, D.C.: GPO, 1985), pp. 66–67.

(ABMs) capable of intercepting warheads outside the atmosphere (exo-atmospheric missiles) have, by definition, the same potential. Due to the wide radius of destruction of a nuclear explosion in space, nuclear weapons are an effective and cheap way of carrying out an ASAT attack. However, they are not ideal for discrete attacks because of the risk of collateral damage to friendly satellites and, if used against targets in low orbit, the possible disruption of communications on earth. Short of a nuclear war, their use would also risk escalating a conflict.

Conversely, while conventional kinetic energy weapons are more discriminating than nuclear weapons, they require accurate pre-attack targeting information and would in most cases involve the use of sophisticated guidance and fuzing mechanisms to execute the attack. Depending on the type of kinetic energy weapon, a propulsion system with enough fuel to maneuver close to the target satellite, especially one capable of evasive action, would also be required. And space-based ASATs would need a responsive command and control system to carry out an attack. For conventionally armed space mines, prolonged shadowing of their prey is a difficult task, especially if it is to be performed covertly.

Directed-energy weapons can be deployed within the atmosphere on land, ships, and aircraft, or alternatively in outer space. Again there are operational tradeoffs involved with each basing mode. Though ground-based lasers would not suffer from the size constraints of orbiting systems, their effectiveness can be seriously attenuated by such atmospheric conditions as clouds and precipitation. Basing such weapons in space would eliminate this problem but create new challenges for their design, maintenance, command and control, and last but not least, survivability.

Conceivably, satellites could also be interfered with by manned spacecraft or even captured by reusable launch vehicles like the U.S. space shuttle. The attractiveness of such operations will most likely be tempered by the prospect of satellites being booby-trapped as a precaution against retrieval. The risk of losing an expensive and difficult-to-replace manned or reusable space vehicle would probably deter attacks of this kind.

Although no single survivability measure provides insurance against all the threats outlined here, the vulnerability of the orbital segment can be reduced in numerous ways. These can be grouped into three categories: initial *precautionary* measures that make an ASAT attack more difficult, *defensive* measures that allow the satellite to avoid or survive an attack, and *redundancy* measures to maintain satellite services after the loss of the primary systems.[8] Like the weapons that can threaten them, satellite survivability measures also have operational tradeoffs.

If it can be achieved without unduly compromising the vulnerable satellite's mission, the simplest precautionary measure is to raise the orbit beyond the reach of the immediate threat. Though this change would not safeguard the satellite entirely, it could help protect it from ground-based direct-ascent ASAT devices. For example, moving a satellite to the geosynchronous orbit would add between three and six hours to the flight time of an ASAT system using a standard rocket booster.[9] The delay would give the satellite controllers an extra margin of warning time and increase the opportunity for evasive maneuvers. Raising the altitude of high-value spacecraft might also take them out of the lethal range of some directed-energy weapons. Another elementary measure is to space satellites sufficiently far apart to prevent a single nuclear explosion from disabling more than one at a time.

Since an ASAT weapon of any type first has to find its target, another precautionary survivability measure is to reduce the likelihood of detection. Satellites could be designed with low radar cross sections, for example by replacing large solar panels with small nuclear generators. They could also incorporate other "stealth" technologies such as radar-absorbing materials and paints to mask them from targeting sensors.[10] This tactic would be especially effective for hiding spare satellites in high-altitude orbits, where objects are generally hard to identify. It would also complicate and delay the targeting of satellites in lower orbits following deliberate maneuvers in anticipation of an ASAT attack.

Beyond these first-order survivability precautions are the defensive countermeasures that help protect a satellite against attack. Some satellites have already been equipped with radar and laser illumination sensors to warn of an attack and with special emergency propulsion

---

8. For comprehensive discussions of satellite survivability measures see Jelen, "Space System Vulnerabilities and Countermeasures"; Col. Robert B. Giffen, USAF, *US Space System Survivability: Strategic Alternatives for the 1990s,* National Security Affairs Monograph 82-4 (Washington, D.C.: National Defense University Press, 1982); and Office of Technology Assessment, *Anti-Satellite Weapons,* pp. 76–86.

9. Giffen, *US Space System Survivability,* p. 38.

10. For further information on generic "stealth" techniques, see Alex Weiss, "Stealth: The Invisible Aircraft?" *International Defense Review,* vol. 17 (July 1984), pp. 972–73.

systems that permit evasive maneuvers. Furthermore, satellites can try to directly counter an imminent attack with decoys, radar-jamming devices, and infrared flares to deceive or deflect the ASAT's guidance system or warhead.[11] The logical extension of these "active" countermeasures to thwart an ASAT attack is to give the satellite its own capability to shoot back. Specially designed defensive satellites for escort duty are another, albeit expensive, option.

Although little can be done to protect a satellite from a nuclear weapon detonated in close proximity, it is possible to harden space systems to withstand the effects of long-range prompt and delayed radiation.[12] The outer surface of the satellite can be constructed of special metals and other materials to reduce conductivity to SGEMP. The inner electrical components can be shielded by protective enclosures known as Faraday cages. Similarly, cables can be wrapped in copper foil or materials of lower atomic number to reduce the available electrons. Lastly, the electronic components themselves can be made resistant to large electrical surges and other radiation effects. Thus a combination of sufficient orbital spacing and appropriate hardening can significantly reduce the vulnerability of satellites to nuclear attack.

Satellites can similarly be designed to withstand the thermal effect of lasers. Special ablative materials such as those using graphite derivatives are among the methods now under study. Sensitive optical systems can be shielded by special shutters or filters that operate on warning of laser illumination.[13] Some of the techniques for hardening against nuclear effects would also help protect satellites from particle beam weapons, but it is unclear how effective these would be against sustained or repeated attacks.

Increasing satellite redundancy is a third route to ensuring their

11. For more details see Lt. Col. Richard E. Fitts, ed., *The Strategy of the Electromagnetic Conflict* (Los Altos, Calif.: Peninsula Publishing, 1980), pp. 175–78.

12. Details of hardening measures are from William B. Scott, "Radiation Hardening Found Effective," *Aviation Week and Space Technology*, vol. 116 (March 15, 1982), p. 73; V. Josephson, *Huron King and Satellite Hardening*, Aerospace Report TOR-0081 (6403-01)-3 (El Segundo, Calif.: Aerospace Corp., 1981); Tirado, "Rad-Tolerant ICs Are Available Off the Shelf," pp. 56–65; and D. Howard Phillips, "Space-Hardened Microelectronics Bring New Advances," *Military Electronics/Countermeasures*, vol. 8 (August 1982), pp. 76–78. See also Marion A. Rose, "Nuclear Hardening of Weapon Systems," *Defense Electronics*, vol. 11 (September 1979), pp. 43–53; and Cedric R. Braun, "Rad Hardening Poses Problems in Large Systems," *Defense Electronics*, vol. 14 (October 1982), pp. 177–82.

13. Giffen, *US Space System Survivability*, p. 36.

services in wartime. Spare satellites can be pre-positioned in space to replace those lost to enemy action. Redundancy of this kind is not cheap, however, and the benefits may be short-lived against an adversary armed with a rapidly retargetable multishot ASAT system.[14] A variation of this strategy is to proliferate critical sensors and communication equipment among a range of host satellites for use in an emergency. Alternatively, disabled satellites could be replaced from the ground using special emergency launch facilities. One idea is to use ICBMs in hardened silos or even SLBMs to launch small, relatively crude satellites to provide the minimum necessary service in wartime. The net effect of these measures would be to force the attacker to expend more resources countering an increased number of hardened or redundant targets and also to lengthen the period—perhaps by a vital margin—in which the orbital segment remains serviceable.

The Link Segment

A satellite is next to worthless if it cannot receive or send information. Satellites rely on communication from ground stations (known as the uplink) at the very least for vital station-keeping commands and often for mission-related messages. As one expert points out:

> Many satellites require constant monitoring and intervention to turn systems on and off, to direct maneuvers, to maintain stable pointing attitudes, to function properly in the earth's shadow, to keep proper spin rates, etc. The command and control demands may be so high that the satellite will fail catastrophically within a few hours . . . without help from ground controllers.[15]

Reconnaissance satellites, for example, often must be commanded to concentrate on certain areas of interest and be told when to activate their sensors. Likewise the antennas and signal-processing equipment aboard communication satellites have to be carefully managed to ensure message reception and the most efficient allocation of channel capacity.[16]

The communication link from the satellite (known as the downlink) is just as important. Typically, it comprises mission-related information

---

14. Desmond Ball, *Can Nuclear War Be Controlled?* Adelphi Papers 169 (London: International Institute for Strategic Studies, 1981), p. 20; and Office of Technology Assessment, *Anti-Satellite Weapons*, pp. 81–83.

15. Giffen, *US Space System Survivability*, p. 17.

16. See Marc I. Spellman, "ECM and Satellite Communication Network Control," *Signal*, vol. 38 (April 1984), pp. 63–68.

(for example, digitally encoded reconnaissance data, navigation radio signals, communications, weather pictures), telemetry on the state of the satellite's health (for example, temperature levels, battery power, fuel consumption, attitude), and also identification and tracking signals.[17] Besides the uplinks and downlinks, satellites sometimes communicate via other satellites—that is, through cross-links. These are used either to speed the transmission of information to the user or reduce the dependence on overseas ground stations.

The communication links to and from a satellite can be deliberately disrupted or interfered with in various ways. For example, a nuclear explosion in the upper atmosphere would cause the twin phenomena of signal absorption and scintillation. Absorption could "black out" communications for up to an hour over a region a few hundred kilometers in diameter, while scintillation could cause severe disruption for much longer periods and over an even larger area.[18]

Communication links can be targeted in a more discriminating manner by electronic countermeasures (ECM), principally jamming and spoofing. Jamming essentially entails transmitting a competing signal with sufficient power to an enemy receiver so as to drown out the meaningful reception of other signals.[19] It can be directed at the entire frequency bandwidth of the target signal (barrage jamming) or at specific channels (spot jamming).[20] Jamming requires that the competing signal be within the line of sight of the target receiver. Since communication satellites in the geosynchronous orbit have enormous geographical "footprints," their uplinks (particularly those employing ultrahigh-frequency, or UHF, signals) are especially vulnerable to jamming. In comparison, communication satellites in low altitude circular orbits are not so exposed.[21]

Spoofing entails feeding false commands and information to a satellite, either to impede its mission or to render it inoperable. For example, the sensors, thermal controls, or propulsion systems aboard a satellite could

17. Jelen, "Space System Vulnerabilities and Countermeasures," p. 99.
18. See Blair, *Strategic Command and Control*, pp. 203–04; and Office of Technology Assessment, *MX Missile Basing* (GPO, 1981), pp. 280–82.
19. Jelen, "Space System Vulnerabilities and Countermeasures," p. 101.
20. Robert Bernhard, "Electronic Countermeasures," *IEEE Spectrum*, vol. 19 (October 1982), p. 61.
21. Office of Technology Assessment, *MX Missile Basing*, pp. 280–81. See also Ashton B. Carter, "Communication Technologies and Vulnerabilities," in Ashton B. Carter, John D. Steinbruner, and Charles A. Zraket, eds., *Managing Nuclear Operations* (Brookings, 1987), pp. 260–63.

be tampered with to degrade its performance or to shorten its operational life.[22] Spoofing is perhaps the most discreet and undetectable way of interfering with satellites.

Again, countermeasures are available to thwart threats of this kind. One precaution is to make satellites more autonomous to reduce their reliance on command uplinks and with it the opportunities for jamming and spoofing. The disruptive effects of nuclear blasts on communications can be diminished by moving to higher frequencies, particularly to the extremely high frequency (EHF) band. At these frequencies, disruption from scintillation and absorption would last only a few minutes.[23] The relatively wide EHF band also provides more opportunities to employ a variety of antijamming techniques such as spreading messages over the entire bandwidth (direct-sequence pseudonoise techniques) or randomly changing the transmission frequency (frequency hopping) in a way known only to the satellite and the friendly ground stations. Alternatively, signals can be compressed and transmitted in short, rapid bursts. Satellite antennas can also be designed to "null out" electronic interference and still receive messages.[24] Encryption and authentication procedures such as entry codes are the standard methods for combating spoofing and unauthorized usage.

The Ground Segment

The ground segment of a space system typically consists of launch facilities, command and control (C^2) centers (including airborne platforms), and tracking stations. Dependency on the ground segment varies considerably between different types of satellites. For example, a low-altitude reconnaissance satellite demands regular attention from tracking facilities and command and control centers because of the daily perturbations of its orbit. These satellites also require special facilities to recover and process the collected imaging or signals intelligence data. A

22. Giffen, US Space System Vulnerability, p. 26.

23. Office of Technology Assessment, MX Missile Basing, p. 281.

24. For a comprehensive discussion of antijamming techniques and strategies, see Jelen, "Space System Vulnerabilities and Countermeasures," pp. 103–07; Carter, "Communications Technologies and Vulnerabilities," in Carter and others, eds., Managing Nuclear Operations, pp. 260–63; and E. Biglieri, "System Aspects in Military Satellite Communications," in Bhupendra Jasani, ed., Outer Space—A New Dimension of the Arms Race (London: Taylor and Francis for the Stockholm International Peace Research Institute, 1982), pp. 190–96.

communication satellite in a geostationary orbit, on the other hand, relies less heavily on ground support.

All parts of the ground segment are vulnerable to sabotage, terrorist activity, and direct military attack. Tighter security measures can help reduce the likelihood of the first two, while hardening the facilities to withstand at least the collateral effects of nuclear blast can prolong their operation in wartime. Ultimately, redundancy through the procurement of mobile and hardened land-based or airborne back-up systems provides the best insurance against attack. Satellite launch facilities, however, are hardest to duplicate, although, as noted earlier, some hardened ICBM silos and missile-launching submarines could be configured for this role.

A complementary strategy is to work from the opposite direction and reduce the dependence on the ground segment. Satellites can be made more autonomous through better diagnostic, self-maintenance, and on-board processing capabilities.[25] Satellite cross-linking would also help bypass damaged or destroyed ground stations, while satellite spares in orbit would reduce the need for survivable launch facilities.

Survivability Planning

As with the various methods of attacking a satellite, there are operational tradeoffs to the different space system survivability measures. For example, some antijamming techniques can severely restrict communication channel capacity and flexibility. Besides the added expense, hardening a satellite and equipping it with decoys can exact major weight penalties. Similarly, on-board fuel for emergency maneuvering takes up space that could be used for other purposes. Deploying spare satellites in space is also costly and may not add significantly to an attacker's task, yet the alternative—relying on ground-based spares—requires a responsive and survivable launch capability, which in certain types of conflict will be difficult to ensure.

With these operational tradeoffs in mind, space system survivability planning should be shaped by several guiding principles. First, protective measures tend to work synergistically. Increasing ground-segment redundancy and satellite autonomy is a case in point; other examples can

25. See B. G. Evans, "Satellite Onboard Processing," *Electronics and Power,* vol. 30 (July 1984), pp. 533–36.

Table 4-1. *Threats to Space Systems and Associated Countermeasures*

Threat	Associated countermeasure	
	Specific	General
Orbital segment		
Nuclear-armed ballistic missiles (ICBMs, IRBMs, SLBMs, ABMs)	Radiation hardening (for example, shielding for system-generated electromagnetic pulse)	Raise orbit beyond range of threat. Reduce likelihood of detection or targeting. Satellite spares. Hosting
Kinetic energy weapons (homing vehicles, fragmentation charges, others)	Warning sensors, emergency maneuvering systems, decoys, electronic countermeasures, shootback systems	Same
Directed-energy weapons (lasers, particle beam weapons, others)	Warning sensors, reflective coatings, laser hardening or shielding, radiation hardening, shootback systems	Same
Link segment		
Nuclear effects (scintillation, absorption)	Higher frequencies (for example, EHF)	Greater satellite autonomy
Electronic countermeasures	Antijamming techniques (antenna nulling, frequency hopping, others)	Same
Spoofing	Authentication procedures, encryption	Same
Ground segment		
Sabotage, terrorist attack	Increased security precautions	Proliferation of ground sites (for example, mobile facilities). Greater satellite autonomy. Cross-linking and internetting
Direct military attack (nuclear or conventional)	Hardening (electromagnetic pulse shielding)	

Source: See text.

be found in table 4-1. Second, the space system is only as survivable as its weakest link. It is pointless to protect one part of the system while leaving the others comparatively vulnerable.[26] Third, satellite survivability measures should be kept in proportion to the value of the satellite's mission. Some satellites are more important than others in time of war and should be protected accordingly. Fourth, satellite survivability measures should be kept in proportion to the threat. Hardening satellites against, say, nuclear effects is only meaningful up to a certain threshold,

26. John Pike, "Anti-Satellite Weapons," *F.A.S Public Interest Report,* vol. 36 (November 1983), p. 12.

after which it is better to rely on reconstitutable spares or non-space-based alternatives.

As a general rule, ensuring survivability will become harder and costlier as ASAT weapons become more numerous and sophisticated. The U.S. Department of Defense has estimated that survivability measures can add between 30 and 40 percent to the final cost of the spacecraft.[27] Threats can also materialize after the design of the satellite has been made final, with the result that it becomes vulnerable long before the end of its operational life.[28] This fact makes satellite survivability planning particularly difficult as long as the ASAT threat remains unconstrained.

Soviet ASAT Capabilities and U.S. Vulnerabilities

The Soviet Union possesses the only specifically designed or "dedicated" antisatellite weapon system in operational service today. In addition, the Soviets have at their disposal a range of nondedicated, or "residual," ASAT capabilities that could also be used against U.S. space systems.

Dedicated Systems

The Soviet ASAT system has been described as a co-orbital, or more accurately co-planar, interceptor that is launched into space by a large liquid-fueled SL-11 booster.[29] After the system achieves orbit, ground controllers maneuver the interceptor vehicle so that after either one or

27. *Department of Defense Appropriations for 1987*, Hearings before a Subcommittee of the House Committee on Appropriations, 99 Cong. 2 sess. (GPO, 1986), pt. 5, p. 415.

28. Charles W. Cook, "The U.S. Air Force Space Program," in *National Security Issues Symposium 1984: Space, National Security, and C³I* (Bedford, Mass.: Mitre Corp., 1984), p. 41.

29. The SL-11 designation is from the nomenclature used by the U.S. Department of Defense. It is essentially a modified SS-9 ICBM. In a somewhat puzzling interview with a West German paper, Col. Gen. Nikolai Chervov, a member of the General Staff of the Soviet armed forces, denied the existence of a co-orbital Soviet ASAT system but admitted to the possession of direct-ascent "antisatellite missiles" that had been successfully tested against "imaginary points outside the atmosphere." See "Soviet General Says USSR Possesses ASAT System," in Foreign Broadcast Information Service, *Daily Report: Soviet Union* (May 30, 1985), p. AA5.

Table 4-2. Soviet Antisatellite Tests, 1968–82

Test number	Date	Target (Kosmos number)	Target orbit (km)			Interceptor	Intercept orbit (km)			Attempted intercept altitude (km)	Mission type (revolutions)	Probable outcome
			Inclination	Perigee	Apogee		Inclination	Perigee	Apogee			
Phase I												
1	Oct. 20, 1968	K248	62.25	475	542	K249	62.23	502	1,639	525	2	Failure
2	Nov. 1, 1968	K248	62.25	473	543	K252	62.34	535?	1,640(?)	535	2	Success
3	Oct. 23, 1970	K373	62.93	473	543	K374	62.96	530	1,053	530	2	Failure
4	Oct. 30, 1970	K373	62.92	466	555	K375	62.86	565	994	535	2	Success
5	Feb. 25, 1971	K394	65.84	572	614	K397	65.76	575?	1,000(?)	585	2	Success
6	Apr. 4, 1971	K400	65.82	982	1,006	K404	65.74	802	1,009	1,005	2	Success
7	Dec. 3, 1971	K459	65.83	222	259	K462	65.88	231	2,654	230	2	Success
Phase II												
8	Feb. 16, 1976	K803	65.85	547	621	K804	65.86	561	618	575	1	Failure
9	Apr. 13, 1976	K803	65.86	549	621	K814	65.9(?)	556?	615(?)	590	1	Success
10	Jul. 21, 1976	K839	65.88	983	2,097	K843	n.a.	n.a.	n.a.	1,630(?)	2	Failure[a]
11	Dec. 27, 1976	K880	65.85	559	617	K886	65.85	532	1,266	570	2	Failure[b]
12	May 23, 1977	K909	65.87	993	2,104	K910	65.86	465?	1,775(?)	1,710	1	Failure
13	June 17, 1977	K909	65.87	991	2,106	K918	65.9(?)	245?	1,630(?)	1,575(?)	1	Success[c]
14	Oct. 26, 1977	K959	65.83	144	834	K961	65.8(?)	125?	302(?)	150	2	Success
15	Dec. 21, 1977	K967	65.83	963	1,004	K970	65.85	949	1,148	995	2	Failure[b]
16	May 19, 1978	K967	65.83	963	1,004	K1009	65.87	965	1,362	985	2	Failure[b]
17	Apr. 18, 1980	K1171	65.85	966	1,010	K1174	65.83	362	1,025	1,000	2	Failure[b]
18	Feb. 2, 1981	K1241	65.82	975	1,011	K1243	65.82	296	1,015	1,005	2	Failure[b]
19	Mar. 14, 1981	K1241	65.82	976	1,011	K1258	65.83	301	1,024	1,005	2	Success
20	June 18, 1982	K1375	65.84	979	1,012	K1379	65.84	537	1,019	1,005	2	Failure[b]

Source: Nicholas L. Johnson, *The Soviet Year in Space, 1983* (Colorado Springs, Colo., Teledyne Brown Engineering), p. 39.
n.a. Not available.
(?) Uncertain.
a. Apparently failed to enter intercept orbit.
b. Reportedly used new optical sensor.
c. Conflicting data exist for intercept orbit.

Figure 4-1. *Soviet ASAT Co-orbital Interception Technique*

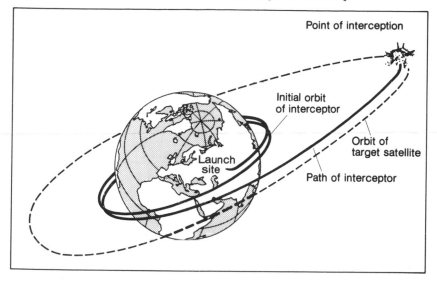

two revolutions of the earth it passes sufficiently near the target satellite for its own guidance system to take over. When in range an explosive charge aboard the interceptor is detonated, sending a cloud of shrapnel at high speed to destroy the target.[30]

Western observers generally agree that the Soviet Union has tested its ASAT system against satellite targets on twenty occasions since October 1968. There have been no tests since June 1982. (See table 4-2.) In each case the interceptor has been launched from Tyuratam and the target satellites (since 1971) from Plesctsk. All the intercepts have occurred at roughly the same orbital inclination, ranging between 62° and 66°, and no higher than approximately 1,700 kilometers. Although this does not mean that only satellites at those inclinations are vulnerable, the Soviet ASAT does have to be launched into the same orbital plane as the target—hence its classification as a co-planar intercept system.[31] (See figure 4-1.) Thus it must wait for the earth's rotation to bring the launch site under the orbital path of the target satellite. Since satellites

30. The interceptor is reported to be fifteen to twenty feet long and five feet in diameter, with a weight of about 2.5 tons. Unless otherwise indicated the discussion of the Soviet ASAT system is from Stares, *Militarization of Space,* pp. 135–56, 187–89.

31. See William J. Durch, "Anti-Satellite Weapons, Arms Control Options, and the Military Use of Space," prepared for the U.S. Arms Control and Disarmament Agency (July 1984), p. 12.

Table 4-3. *Success Rate of the Soviet ASAT Test Program,*
by Guidance System, 1968–82

Type	Number of tests	Success rate
All tests	20	.45
Radar guided	14	.64
Two revolutions	10	.70
One revolution	4	.50
Infrared guided	6	.00

Source: See text.

in low earth orbit pass over Tyuratam only twice a day, the average wait to intercept a specific satellite will be six hours.[32]

Once the ASAT is launched, the time taken to execute the attack will depend on the number of orbits around the earth that the interceptor makes. Most of the test intercepts have occurred after two revolutions, or about three and a half hours. Since 1976 a much faster approach after just one revolution has been demonstrated, cutting the elapsed time by half.

The Soviet ASAT test program has had a mixed record of success. From table 4-2 it can be calculated that 70 percent of the tests between 1968 and 1971 were considered a success by Western analysts, but the rate plummeted to a dismal 30 percent between 1976 and 1982, evidently because the Soviets began to test a new guidance system. Whereas before 1976 the interceptor had relied solely on radar to guide it toward the target, half the tests since then have reportedly involved the use of an optical infrared guidance system.[33] This appears to have failed on every attempt. Table 4-3 gives a more detailed breakdown of the record of the Soviet ASAT test program according to guidance system used and the number of revolutions taken to approach the target.

The official U.S. assessment of the Soviet ASAT system has changed significantly since the 1970s, when it became an object of concern to U.S. defense planners. In 1977, when Harold Brown, then secretary of defense, first acknowledged that the Soviet Union possessed an "operational capability" to destroy some U.S. satellites in space, he described the threat as only "somewhat troublesome."[34] Two years later, during

32. Richard L. Garwin, Kurt Gottfried, Donald L. Hafner, "Antisatellite Weapons," *Scientific American*, vol. 250 (June 1984), p. 49.

33. Nicholas L. Johnson, *The Soviet Year in Space, 1981* (Colorado Springs, Colo., Teledyne Brown Engineering), p. 26.

34. Bernard Weinraub, "Brown Says Soviets Can Fell Satellites," *New York Times*, October 5, 1977.

the Senate hearings on the SALT II treaty, Brown's low opinion of the Soviet ASAT was echoed by the then air force chief of staff, General Lew Allen:

> The system that they have tested so far has the potential of being effective against our low-altitude satellites. It was tested in that kind of mode, and it has had some successful tests. On the other hand, it is difficult to assign it a very high degree of credibility because it has not been a uniformly successful program.

Furthermore, noted the general:

> They have the systems that are more or less at the ready. It is not a very quick reacting system. The systems that are at the ready are located in the missile test areas. So, I think our general opinion is that we give it a very questionable operational capability for a few launches. In other words, it is a threat that we are worried about, but they have not had a test program that would cause us to believe it is a very credible threat.[35]

The Reagan administration, however, has painted a considerably different picture of the Soviet ASAT's operational readiness and effectiveness. For example, the 1984 edition of *Soviet Military Power* stated that at Tyuratam "two launch pads and storage space for additional interceptors and launch vehicles are available. Several interceptors could be launched *each* day from *each* of the pads."[36] Moreover, in a probable effort to counter unofficial assessments that downplayed Soviet ASAT capabilities, the 1986 edition stated: "Given the complexity of launch, target tracking, and radar-guided intercept, the Soviet ASAT system is far from primitive. Soviet ASAT tests have been largely successful, indicating an operational system fully capable of performing its mission."[37]

What can be made of these contrasting assessments? While it is not possible to evaluate the readiness of the Soviet ASAT system from unclassified sources, it is possible to reach some conclusions about its potential threat to U.S. satellites from what is publicly known. At a minimum one can list the U.S. satellites that are theoretically in range

35. *The SALT II Treaty*, Hearings before the Senate Committee on Foreign Relations, 96 Cong. 1 sess. (GPO, 1979), pt. 1, pp. 423–24.

36. U.S. Department of Defense, *Soviet Military Power, 1984* (GPO), pp. 34–35 (emphasis added). Interestingly, the following year's edition dropped the reference to the number of launch pads at Tyuratam and stated only that "several interceptors could be launched each day." Department of Defense, *Soviet Military Power, 1985*, p. 56.

37. Department of Defense, *Soviet Military Power, 1986*, p. 49.

Table 4-4. *U.S. Military Satellites within Reach of the Soviet ASAT System*[a]

Application	Designation	Number of targets
Photoreconnaissance	Keyhole (KH)-11, 12[b]	2–4
Ocean reconnaissance	Whitecloud	8
Navigation	Transit-Nova	4–6
Meteorology	Defense Meteorological Support Program	2
Total		20

Source: Extrapolated from table 2-1.
a. Excludes space shuttle and satellite spares.
b. KH-12 not yet deployed.

of the interceptor. Although there have apparently been no attempted intercepts above 1,710 kilometers, the U.S. Department of Defense credits the Soviet ASAT with being able to reach targets at "more than 5000 kms."[38] Assuming that its effective altitude reach is not more than double the Defense Department's estimate, a survey of U.S. military satellites shows that about twenty are currently exposed to attack, excluding spares and the space shuttle (see table 4-4). This is less than half the total complement of U.S. military satellites. Although the Satellite Data System (SDS) communication and Jumpseat SIGINT satellites pass within Soviet ASAT range during the perigee of their highly elliptical orbits, this occurs in the Southern Hemisphere and thus puts them out of line of sight of Soviet ground controllers maneuvering the interceptor. The satellites also travel at too great a relative speed for an interception to be feasible.[39] During the next ten years the number of vulnerable U.S. satellites will probably remain about the same. By the mid to late 1990s, the high-altitude Navstar GPS will have replaced the low-altitude Transit-Nova constellation, but new low-altitude U.S. systems for various surveillance tasks (see chapter 2) may have been deployed by then. In addition to the Defense Department satellites, the Soviets may want to target U.S. civilian-operated space systems that

38. Department of Defense, *Soviet Military Power, 1985*, p. 56. For a useful discussion of how the orbital inclination of the target can affect the altitude reach of the Soviet ASAT, see Durch, "Anti-Satellite Weapons," pp. 12–13.

39. Ashton B. Carter, "Satellites and Anti-Satellites: The Limits of the Possible," *International Security*, vol. 10 (Spring 1986), p. 74.

also serve military users, like the National Oceanic and Atmospheric Administration's meteorological satellites, and non-U.S. reconnaissance spacecraft like the French Spot satellite and its successors.

The U.S. satellites shown in table 4-4 are all theoretically vulnerable, but how easy would it be for the Soviets to carry out a campaign against them in wartime? How long would it take for the Soviets to disable all or a significant part of the target set? Assessments of this kind require difficult judgments about a whole range of variables, some of which even the Soviets can only estimate. The number of interceptors and compatible launch pads available for antisatellite operations have to be estimated, as does the rate at which they can be serviced and used. Though the Soviets have on at least two occasions conducted tests of their ASAT system in conjunction with other military exercises, they have yet to carry out multiple ASAT launches to simulate the likely conditions of wartime use.[40] The rate at which the Soviet ASAT system can be used is not just governed by the availability of ready lauch pads but also, as discussed above, by the orbital phasing of the target satellites. The interceptor may have to remain idle for a significant period until a launch opportunity presents itself. However, the best moment for an attack may not always coincide with an operationally ready launch pad. The Soviet ASAT is also dependent on ground-based surveillance radars and battle management systems to supply timely targeting data and post-attack damage assessments. Once the ASAT has been launched, another set of factors will determine its success. In addition to the various rocket stages functioning properly, the guidance system has to lock on to the target and the kill mechanism detonate at the appropriate moment. Test data give some indication of the system's operational reliability, but they cannot reflect fully the stress of wartime use.

Despite the analytical uncertainty inherent in such exercises, it is still useful to go beyond listing which U.S. satellites are vulnerable to the Soviet ASAT system and estimate how effective it would be in wartime. A standard method to compensate for the lack of hard information is to assign a range of plausible values for the probability that each intercept attempt would succeed. This is usually defined as the single-shot probability of kill (*SSPK*). In this case it is the compound probability of the

40. The two occasions were in 1976 and 1982. See "Russia's Killer Satellites," *Foreign Report*, January 14, 1981, p. 2; and Johnson, *Soviet Year in Space, 1982*, p. 25.

booster, guidance system, and kill mechanism all functioning successfully.[41] A range of *SSPK* values can then be used to estimate in the
following way the number of interceptors needed to disable a given set
of target satellites.

Assuming that a certain number (*n*) of independent launchings or
shots are made against each target satellite and the probability of kill
(*SSPK*) is the same for each shot, then the overall probability of kill
(*OPK*) with *n* shots (OPK_n) will be

(1) $OPK_n = 1 - (1 - SSPK)^n.$

In turn, the overall probability of any given target surviving *n* shots
directed at it (OPS_n) is given by

(2) $OPS_n = (1 - SSPK)^n.$

Taking the natural logarithm of both sides of equation 2, we can solve
for the number of shots, *n*, required to attain a given *OPS*.[42]

(3) $$n = \frac{\ln(OPS)}{\ln(1 - SSPK)}.$$

This equation can in turn be used to estimate the number of launchings,
or shots, needed to destroy a given set of target satellites with a specified
level of confidence, or put differently, overall probability of survival.
Furthermore, by adding a time factor, in this case the number of feasible
shots each day, we can also estimate how long it would take to complete
the campaign.

Although it is important to recognize that wartime performance often
falls short of the results achieved in peacetime,[43] the data on the Soviet
ASAT test program shown in table 4-3 provide a useful range of
hypothetical *SSPK* values. A plausible "best-case" figure for the Soviets
would be .75, which is higher than the most successful portions of the
test program to date. This would also be assuming that the individual
components of the overall *SSPK* value, that is, the probability of the

41. The standard definition of the single-shot probability of kill does not normally
involve compounding the reliability of the booster, guidance system, and so forth.
Strictly speaking, "terminal kill probability" (TKP) is the correct term.

42. I am indebted to Joshua M. Epstein for developing this model. For a similar
analysis of analogous problems, see I. Anureev and others, *Application of Mathematical
Methods in Military Affairs*, translated from the Russian by the U.S. Army Foreign
Science and Technology Center, Charlottesville, Va., 1973, pp. 31–32.

43. For historical examples see Joshua M. Epstein, *Measuring Military Power: The
Soviet Air Threat to Europe* (Princeton University Press, 1984), pp. 148–49.

booster, guidance system, and warhead all functioning successfully, is greater than .90. A useful middle range *SSPK* value is .65, which approximates the success achieved by the tests of the radar-guided interceptor. The lowest *SSPK* value used here is .45, which represents the success rate achieved in the test program as a whole.

If we assume that the Soviet Union will want to disable each U.S. satellite it attacks with 95 percent confidence—that is, with each satellite having an overall probability of survival (*OPS*) of .05—we can estimate, using equation 3, how many shots per target (interceptor launches per satellite) will be needed to guarantee this effectiveness criterion with each of the *SSPK* values chosen above. Also, assuming, as the U.S. Department of Defense believes, that the Soviets can launch several interceptors daily from each of their two dedicated launch pads—say between two and six shots maximum—we can further estimate how long it would take them to complete ASAT campaigns against various numbers of U.S. satellites (target sets). In this case four arbitrary target sets—of 3, 6, 12, and 24 satellites—have been chosen. The largest set represents the full complement of U.S. satellites (plus some spares) currently vulnerable to the Soviet ASAT system, while the other sets could be made up from a single category of satellites or from combinations thereof. For example, a target set of 6 might comprise the constellation of Transit navigation satellites, or a combination of photoreconnaissance and weather satellites. It should be noted, however, that a constellation need not be completely disabled to undermine its operational usefulness. Thus destroying four out of six Transit satellites might be sufficient. Table 4-5 shows the number of shots and table 4-6 the number of days needed to complete an ASAT campaign according to these variables.

If the Soviets were to attempt a "sky-sweeping" attack against the largest target set of U.S. military satellites (24) then we can see from table 4-6 that under best-case *SSPK* assumptions for the USSR it would take more than a week allowing six shots a day and nearly two weeks with four shots a day. With lower *SSPK* values the sky-sweeping campaign would take even longer, up to a month. Faced with such a lengthy campaign, it seems fair to assume that the Soviets would be more discriminating and target only the most critical U.S. satellites. From the table we can see that assuming medium to high values for the ASAT's *SSPK* and four to six shots a day, it would take only a few days to disable the smaller target sets.[44]

44. These estimates change somewhat if the initial Soviet effectiveness criterion for

Table 4-5. *Estimates of Soviet ASAT Shots Required to Disable a Range of U.S. Satellite Target Sets, by Probability of Kill*[a]

Launch shots per target set

Single-shot probability of kill	Target set				
	1 satellite	*3 satellites*	*6 satellites*	*12 satellites*	*24 satellites*
High (.75)	2	6	13	26	52
Moderate (.65)	3	9	17	34	68
Low (.45)	5	15	30	60	120

Source: Author's calculations as explained in text. Figures are rounded.
a. Assumes Soviet ASAT operations are 95 percent effective (U.S. satellites have an overall probability of survival of .05). Total shots are obtained by multiplying the *pre-rounded* number of shots required per target (see equation 3 in text) by the number of satellites in the target set.

Table 4-6. *Estimates of Days Required to Disable a Range of U.S. Satellite Target Sets, by Probability of Kill*[a]

Days per target set

Single-shot probability of kill	Target set			
	3 satellites	*6 satellites*	*12 satellites*	*24 satellites*
At six shots a day				
High (.75)	1.1	2.2	4.3	8.6
Moderate (.65)	1.4	2.8	5.7	11.4
Low (.45)	2.5	5.0	10.0	20.0
At four shots a day				
High (.75)	1.6	3.2	6.5	13.0
Moderate (.65)	2.1	4.3	8.6	17.1
Low (.45)	3.8	7.5	15.0	30.1
At two shots a day				
High (.75)	3.2	6.5	13.0	25.9
Moderate (.65)	4.3	8.6	17.1	34.2
Low (.45)	7.6	15.0	30.1	60.1

Source: Same as table 4-5.
a. Assumes Soviet ASAT operations are 95 percent effective (U.S. satellites have an overall probability of survival of .05).

These calculations, however, ignore other operational factors that could significantly affect the length of an ASAT campaign. In addition to the time taken to refurbish the launch pads, the on-site fueling facilities would have to be restocked and interceptors and boosters brought from distant storage to replace those used. And these calculations do not take

each attack is relaxed. For example, if the specified overall probability of kill (*OPK*) is lowered from .95 to .75 (that is, an *OPS* of .25 instead of .05) the time taken to conduct

into account U.S. countermeasures, either to improve the survivability of its satellites (by stealth, evasive maneuvers, decoys, and so on), or to reduce the pace of Soviet ASAT operations (by attacks on space surveillance radars and launch sites). The latter, of course, are only relevant if superpower hostilities have escalated to attacks on the Soviet homeland.

On balance then, the Soviet ASAT system in its current configuration suffers from significant operational constraints, particularly in terms of the types of U.S. satellites it can realistically threaten and the pace at which it could conduct an ASAT campaign. As two officers of the Central Intelligence Agency concluded in testimony before Congress in 1985: "While the Soviets seek to be able to deny enemy use of space in wartime, current Soviet antisatellite capabilities are limited and fall short of meeting this apparent requirement."[45] Nevertheless, the Soviet interceptor could be employed selectively against a few key U.S. spacecraft (such as the reconnaissance systems) in low earth orbit. Unless the appropriate countermeasures are taken, the success of such attacks could have a serious effect on U.S. military operations in certain wartime contingencies. These are discussed more fully in chapter 6.

---

an ASAT campaign is considerably shorter. However, considering what may be at stake in an ASAT attack, the higher probability that the target survives may be too great for contingency planning purposes. Increasing the Soviet launch rate (shots each day) also reduces estimates of the time needed to conduct similar ASAT campaigns using this analysis. Besides the absence of evidence that the Soviets could conduct such high-intensity operations, there is still the constraint imposed by the orbital phasing of the target satellites.

A more general criticism of this approach to estimating the likely operational effectiveness of the Soviet ASAT system is that it assumes the full expenditure of a predetermined number of shots for each satellite target to ensure its destruction with a given level of confidence. In practice, targets may be disabled with fewer shots, allowing the use of unexpended shots against other targets. This reallocation is, of course, only possible if a damage assessment can be made after each attempted intercept. The campaign, therefore, could conceivably be briefer than prudent assumptions allow. Since we are dealing with probabilities, it could last longer. The model also assumes that each ASAT engagement has an independent probability of success, whereas the learning experience of combat operations could progressively improve the single-shot kill probability of successive shots. This improvement would likewise shorten the campaign, but again it cannot be assumed beforehand.

45. Testimony of Robert M. Gates and Lawrence K. Gershwin, in *Soviet Strategic Force Developments,* Joint Hearing before the Subcommittee on Strategic and Theater Nuclear Forces of the Senate Armed Services Committee and the Subcommittee on Defense of the Senate Committee on Appropriations, 99 Cong. 1 sess. (GPO, 1986), p. 18.

Residual ASAT Capabilities

In addition to its dedicated ASAT weapon system the Soviet Union possesses some weapon systems built for other purposes that can, theoretically at least, be used against U.S. satellites.

ANTIBALLISTIC MISSILE SYSTEMS. High on the Pentagon's list of accredited Soviet residual ASAT capabilities is the system of sixty-four nuclear-armed antiballistic missile interceptors code-named Galosh that are deployed around Moscow. This system, which is currently being upgraded with new battle management radars and an improved version of the Galosh interceptor (designated SH-04), is designed to intercept attacking warheads outside of the earth's atmosphere.[46] Because of this, an antisatellite capability is attributed to it. While the SH-04 interceptors can probably reach targets as high as several hundred kilometers above the earth, the radiation from their nuclear warheads would affect satellites well beyond this altitude.

Though their potential use as ASAT weapons is undeniable, it is, however, implausible short of a nuclear war for several reasons. As discussed earlier, the detonation of nuclear weapons above the atmosphere would not only be highly escalatory, but also likely to damage friendly satellites and disrupt communications in the area below the explosion. Also, using the Galosh antiballistic missiles in this manner reduces the number available for the protection of Moscow, which is, after all, their primary mission.

LONG-RANGE BALLISTIC MISSILES. In theory, any Soviet long-range ballistic missile (ICBM, SLBM, or IRBM) could be modified to attack U.S. satellites by reprogramming the missile's guidance logic and changing the fuzing on the warhead to detonate at a given point in space. While these changes would not be difficult, using ballistic missiles in this way has the same drawbacks—radiation damage to friendly satellites and disrupted communications—as nuclear-armed ABM interceptors,

46. For a comprehensive account of Soviet ABM capabilities, see Sayre Stevens, "The Soviet BMD Program," in Ashton B. Carter and David N. Schwartz, eds., *Ballistic Missile Defense* (Brookings, 1984), pp. 182–220. The modernization of the Moscow ABM system also includes the deployment of silo-based interceptors (designated SH-08 and code-named Gazelle) that are designed to intercept warheads within the atmosphere. See Department of Defense, *Soviet Military Power, 1985*, p. 48. A combined total of 100 launchers of both types is expected to be deployed. This number is permitted by the 1974 protocol to the 1972 ABM treaty. The treaty also allows for another fifteen interceptors to be stored for test purposes at the Sary Shagan proving ground.

although against higher altitude (semisynchronous and geosynchronous) targets the amount of collateral damage would probably not be so great.

DIRECTED-ENERGY WEAPONS. In 1984 the U.S. Department of Defense declared for the first time that "the Soviets have two ground-based test lasers that could be used against satellites."[47] Both are at the Sary Shagan proving ground. Another report cites a completely new laser facility under construction at Dushanbe in the Tadzhik Socialist People's Republic near the Afghanistan border.[48] Without more information (particularly on their wavelength, mirror size, and power output), it is hard to make a detailed assessment of the current and potential operational effectiveness of these laser systems. The Defense Department's assessment that they could be used to interfere with the sensors on some low-altitude U.S. satellites appears plausible, but anything more seems doubtful. As discussed earlier, ground-based lasers need clear weather to operate effectively, and targeted satellites must pass within their line of sight and at not too great a slant angle to avoid undue atmospheric distortion and attenuation of the beam. Moreover, to disable targets positioned at higher altitudes would require ground-based lasers of much greater power than those available today.[49]

ELECTRONIC COUNTERMEASURES. In 1978 Air Force General Alton Slay

47. Department of Defense, *Soviet Military Power, 1984*, p. 35.

48. Tom Diaz, "Soviets Lead in Laser Beam Weapons for Space Shield," *Washington Times*, February 10, 1986. See also Thomas K. Longstreth, John E. Pike, and John B. Rhinelander, *The Impact of U.S. and Soviet Ballistic Missile Defense Programs on the ABM Treaty*, 3d ed. (Washington, D.C.: National Campaign to Save the ABM Treaty, 1985), p. 22; Roger P. Main, "The USSR and Laser Weaponry: The View from Outside," *Defense Systems Review*, vol. 3 (March 1985), pp. 67–80; and William J. Broad, "Experts Say Soviet Has Conducted Space Tests on Anti-Missile Weapons," *New York Times*, October 15, 1986.

49. See Donald L. Hafner, "Potential Negotiating Measures for ASAT Arms Control," in Joseph S. Nye, Jr., ed., *Seeking Stability in Space* (University Press of America, forthcoming). Using the example of a deuterium fluoride (DF) laser with a two-meter mirror and a sustained power output of two megawatts (roughly equivalent to current U.S. capabilities), Hafner calculates that the "energy deposited on a geosynchronous satellite by such a laser would be only 0.04 W/cm², or less than one-third the energy deposited on the satellite by the sun (0.14 W/cm²). The energy deposited on a satellite such as Navstar, at 20,000 km altitude, would be only 0.12 W/cm², still less than the solar flux." He goes on to argue that "such low levels of illumination could kill only if the laser dwelled long enough to build up heat on a satellite that was extraordinarily sensitive to overheating. Even then it might be hard to confirm that the satellite had been damaged. Getting quick, high confidence kills by burning through the skin of high-altitude satellites will require illumination levels hundreds or thousands of times higher than currently achievable."

declared that "the Soviet Union has electronic warfare facilities which could be employed against certain U.S. satellites."[50] Similar statements have also appeared in the annual publication *Soviet Military Power*. Although no incidents of deliberate interference with U.S. satellites have been officially acknowledged, any radio transmitter broadcasting from the right position with the requisite power and at the appropriate frequency could interfere with a satellite's communication links. Given the large footprints of most U.S. military communication satellites, such high-powered jammers need not be located on Soviet territory. "Jamming sources might include shipborne facilities, ground-based facilities in places like Cuba, or jammers covertly operated inside U.S. territory."[51]

SOVIET SPACE VEHICLES. Because of their demonstrated maneuvering and docking capabilities, the unmanned Progress space vehicles that are used to resupply the Salyut space station are sometimes categorized as potential ASAT devices. However, since the Progress vehicle relies on a transponder system to dock with cooperative targets, its use as an ASAT weapon is at best limited and more likely nonexistent.[52]

Collectively, Soviet dedicated and residual ASAT capabilities pose a broad range of threats to U.S. space operations. At one end of the spectrum is the potential use of electronic countermeasures and low-powered lasers, while at the other there is the possibility of nuclear attacks using modified ICBMs and antiballistic missiles. Lying in the middle is the dedicated satellite interceptor. Each method has its operational shortcomings, however. ECM and laser systems at current levels of development do not give the Soviets the ability to execute rapid, high-confidence "kills" in space, especially if the United States takes basic precautionary steps to reduce the vulnerability of its satellites to threats like these. Using nuclear-armed ballistic missiles would provide a higher confidence ASAT capability but, as discussed earlier, this approach entails the significant risk of unwelcome collateral damage, and if used in a conventional conflict, the sobering prospect of the war escalating to a nuclear conflict. Using the Soviet satellite interceptor would avoid these problems, but in its present configuration, it is limited

50. *Department of Defense Appropriations for Fiscal Year 1979*, Hearings before a Subcommittee of the Senate Committee on Appropriations, 95 Cong. 2 sess. (GPO, 1978), pt. 5, p. 407.

51. Blair, *Strategic Command and Control*, p. 205.

52. Johnson, *Soviet Year in Space, 1984*, pp. 37–38.

to attacking satellites in low earth orbit. Again, with appropriate countermeasures such as warning sensors, emergency maneuvering systems, and decoys, this threat can be reduced. Appendix A provides a more detailed account of the vulnerability of the individual U.S. space systems and their associated ground facilities.

U.S. ASAT Capabilities and Soviet Vulnerabilities

The United States at present has no dedicated antisatellite system in operation, although the U.S. Air Force hopes to deploy one by the early 1990s. This system is discussed below along with U.S. residual ASAT capabilities, which in many respects duplicate those available to the Soviet Union.

Planned Dedicated Systems

Since 1977 the United States has been developing an air-launched missile with a heat-seeking warhead to intercept Soviet satellites in low earth orbit. Known officially as the Air-Launched Miniature Vehicle (ALMV), it consists of a terminal homing warhead that is boosted into space by a two-stage rocket made up of a modified first stage of the Short-Range Attack Missile (SRAM) and the ALTAIR III booster taken from the Scout launch vehicle. The warhead, or Miniature Vehicle (MV), is an extremely complex and sophisticated device consisting of eight cryogenically cooled infrared telescopes, a laser gyro, and sixty-four small computer-controlled rockets used for final course adjustments before colliding with the target. All this is packed into a twelve-by-thirteen-inch casing. After being guided to and released near the target, the Miniature Vehicle homes in on the heat emitted by the satellite and rams into it with sufficient force to destroy it.[53]

The F-15 fighter has been chosen as the launch platform for the ALMV, with each aircraft capable of carrying one missile. In time of

53. For more details on how the ALMV works, see Craig Covault, "Antisatellite Weapon Design Advances," *Aviation Week and Space Technology*, vol. 112 (June 16, 1980), pp. 243–47; Bruce A. Smith, "Vought Tests Small Antisatellite System," *Aviation Week and Space Technology*, vol. 115 (November 9, 1981), pp. 24–25; Eric Raiten, "Technologies for Conventional Anti-Satellite Weapons," in Kosta Tsipis and Penny Janeway, eds., *Review of U.S. Military Research and Development, 1984* (London: Pergamon Brasseys, 1984), pp. 51–57.

Figure 4-2. U.S. ASAT Mission Profile

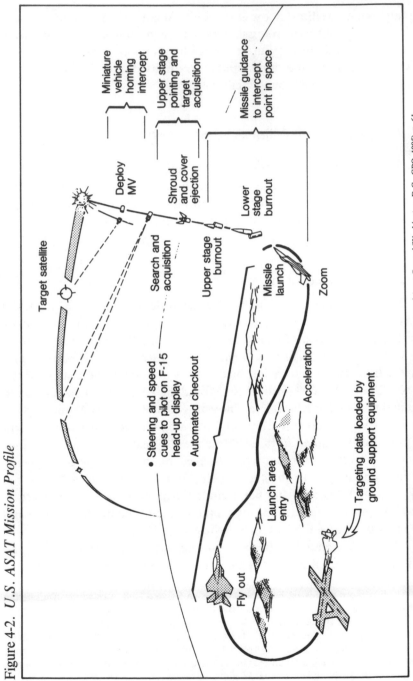

Target satellite

Deploy
MV

} Miniature
vehicle
homing
intercept

Shroud
and cover
ejection

} Upper stage
pointing and
target
acquisition

Lower
stage
burnout

} Missile guidance
to intercept
point in space

Upper stage
burnout

Search and
acquisition

Missile
launch

Zoom

• Steering and speed
  cues to pilot on F-15
  head-up display

• Automated checkout

Acceleration

Launch area
entry

Fly out

Targeting data loaded by
ground support equipment

Source: U.S. Congress, Office of Technology Assessment, *Anti-Satellite Weapons, Countermeasures, and Arms Control* (Washington, D.C.: GPO, 1985), p. 61.

war ASAT operations will be controlled from the Space Defense Operations Center (SPADOC) at the North American Aerospace Defense Command (NORAD) in the Cheyenne Mountain Complex near Colorado Springs, Colorado. Once a decision had been taken by the national command authorities to attack a Soviet satellite, SPADOC would provide target attack coordinates to the ASAT Control Center at the F-15's air base. The targeting instructions would then be loaded into the ALMV's on-board computer, which in turn would give flight instructions to the pilot through the head-up display instruments in the cockpit. The F-15 would then fly to a predetermined launch "box" and enter it according to a flight profile that optimizes either the missile's altitude or range.[54] At the appropriate moment, determined by the on-board computer, the missile would be launched to intercept the satellite. A high-frequency radio data link has been fitted to the aircraft's wing tip to receive last-minute launch corrections or instructions to abort the mission.[55] The sequence of events is illustrated in figure 4-2. After the engagement, space surveillance sensors would help NORAD determine whether the attack was successful and, if required, prepare for further ASAT operations.

The U.S. Air Force had originally planned to purchase 112 ALMVs and modify 40 dual-purpose air defense F-15 aircraft to perform the ASAT mission.[56] It was also envisaged that the F-15s would operate from two airbases: Langley Air Force Base near Norfolk, Virginia, and McChord Air Force Base near Tacoma, Washington. But as a result of a reassessment carried out by the air force in 1986 and announced in March 1987, the planned U.S. ASAT force has been drastically cut to

54. Maj. Gen. Bruce K. Brown, USAF, "New Initiatives and Technology Thrusts," paper presented to Electronics Industries Association Conference, April 1983. See also Keith F. Mordoff, "Test ASAT Launched Autonomously from USAF F-15 Carrier Aircraft," *Aviation Week and Space Technology*, vol. 123 (October 7, 1986), pp. 18–19.

55. Office of Technology Assessment, *Anti-Satellite Weapons*, p. 59. Given the speed at which the target is traveling and the need for precise timing of the launch, it is unclear from public sources whether major retargeting of the missile's guidance system could take place after the F-15 has taken off. According to Major General Brown, "The pilot will have a keyboard in the cockpit to enter modest corrections." Brown, "New Initiatives and Technology Thrusts," p. 167.

56. *Department of Defense Authorization of Appropriations for Fiscal Year 1984*, Hearings before the House Committee on Armed Services, 98 Cong. 1 sess. (GPO, 1983), pt. 5, p. 310; and *Department of Defense Appropriations for 1986*, Hearings before a Subcommittee of the House Committee on Appropriations, 99 Cong. 1 sess. (GPO, 1985), pt. 2, p. 431.

just 18 converted F-15s and 35 missiles that will all be based at Langley AFB.[57]

Several factors were responsible for the reassessment of the U.S. ASAT program. Foremost has been the program's escalating cost. Originally priced at roughly $1.4 billion in 1980, the estimated price of the unrevised program had rocketed to $5.3 billion by 1986. Even with the latest restructuring, in March 1987, the final cost is expected to be $4.3 billion.[58]

The cost overrun can be largely traced to technical problems in getting the chosen design to work as planned.[59] The air force clearly underestimated the difficulty of building an air-launched homing hit-to-kill missile system.[60] On top of these problems, Congress has also imposed constraints on the testing of the system, which the air force claims added to its rising cost.[61] For fiscal 1985, Congress mandated that no more than three tests against a target in space could take place, and then only after the president had certified that the United States was endeavoring in good faith to negotiate an ASAT arms control agreement with the Soviet Union.[62] The next year it prohibited *all* testing against objects in space, a ban it later extended into fiscal 1987.[63] A total of five tests have been carried out to date in a planned program of twelve (see table 4-7). If the testing moratorium is lifted for fiscal 1988, the air force calculates that an initial operating capability (IOC) can be reached in the early 1990s.[64]

Understandably, details of the expected performance characteristics

57. David C. Morrison, "New ASAT Weapons, Old Worries," *National Journal*, vol. 19 (March 21, 1987), p. 707.

58. Ibid. See also David J. Lynch, "Cutbacks Don't Halt ASAT Cost Rise," *Defense Week*, vol. 7 (March 31, 1986), p. 2; *Department of Defense Appropriations for 1986*, Hearings, pt. 2, p. 431; and U.S. General Accounting Office, *Status of the U.S. Antisatellite Program*, GAO/NSIAD 85-104 (June 14, 1985).

59. See Wayne Biddle, "Antisatellite Weapon Facing Delays and Sharp Cost Increases," *New York Times*, May 16, 1985; and Wayne Biddle, "Antisatellite Weapon Is Reported Sent Back to Its Maker for Repairs," *New York Times*, July 10, 1985.

60. Former Secretary of the Air Force Verne Orr admitted to Congress: "This, I am told, is one of the most complex problems we have tackled." Quoted in Wayne Biddle, "Drawing a Bead on a Target in Space," *New York Times*, August 25, 1985.

61. General Accounting Office, *Status of the U.S. Antisatellite Program*, p. 3.

62. There were other requirements also. For the full text of the certification provision, see *Congressional Record*, daily edition (May 24, 1985), p. S7174.

63. *Making Continuing Appropriations for Fiscal Year 1987*, Conference Report 99-1005, House of Representatives, 99 Cong. 2 sess. (GPO, 1986), p. 186.

64. Department of Defense news briefing by Brig. Gen. Robert Rankine, USAF, director, space systems and command, control, and communications, March 10, 1987.

Table 4-7. *U.S. ALMV Antisatellite Tests, 1984–86*

Date	Description	Outcome
January 21, 1984	Missile tested without Miniature Vehicle	Success
November 13, 1984	Directed at a star with Miniature Vehicle	Failure
September 13, 1985	Directed at Solwind satellite	Success
August 22, 1986	Directed at a star	Success
September 29, 1986	Directed at a star	Success

Sources: Fred Hiatt, "U.S. Tests Satellite Destroyer," *Washington Post*, January 22, 1984; "Telemetry Data Shows U.S. Anti-Satellite 'Performed Well,' " *Defense Electronics*, vol. 16 (February 1984), p. 30; "Air Force Tests Antisatellite Payload," *Aviation Week and Space Technology*, vol. 121 (November 19, 1984), p. 28; Arthur F. Manfredi, Jr., Cosmo DiMaggio, and Marcia Smith, "ASATS: Antisatellite Weapon Systems" (Congressional Research Service, Science Policy Research Division, 1986), p. 7; "ASAT System Tested," *Aviation Week and Space Technology*, vol. 125 (September 1, 1986), p. 45; "News Digest," *Aviation Week and Space Technology*, vol. 125 (October 6, 1986), p. 30.

of the U.S. ASAT system remain classified. Perhaps the most important undisclosed fact is the maximum altitude reach of the ALMV. This is obviously useful for determining which Soviet satellites would be vulnerable to attack. Though it was designed from the first to intercept targets in low earth orbit, the ALMV's capabilities have nevertheless been criticized both outside and apparently also within the air force.

In 1983 the General Accounting Office (GAO) highlighted the ALMV's inability to meet the stated ASAT requirements of the U.S. Joint Chiefs of Staff, which consists of a "prioritized target list" of Soviet satellites that are to be attacked in wartime.[65] When the list was drawn up in 1978, the JCS target set totaled 82 current and projected Soviet satellites, divided about equally between those in high- and low-altitude orbits. By 1981, when the JCS ASAT target list was revised, the projected total had grown to 175, with 82 spacecraft in low earth orbit.[66] According to leaked portions of the GAO report, however, the ALMV as currently configured would be able to attack only 30 percent of the these 175 targets.[67] The Defense Department responded by arguing that the JCS

65. General Accounting Office, *U.S. Antisatellite Program Needs a Fresh Look*, Unclassified Report by the Comptroller General of the United States, GAO/C-MASAD-83-5 (January 27, 1983), p. i. See also *Department of Defense Appropriations for 1980, Hearings before a Subcommittee of the House Committee on Appropriations*, 96 Cong. 1 sess. (GPO, 1979), pt. 6, p. 682.

66. Clarence A. Robinson, Jr., "USAF Will Begin Antisatellite Testing," *Aviation Week and Space Technology*, vol. 119 (December 19, 1983), p. 21. See also Jack Anderson, "Space Wars," *Washington Post*, August 16, 1981.

67. Robinson, "USAF Will Begin Antisatellite Testing."

target list represented a "fiscally unconstrained" statement of requirements, and that given the exorbitant cost of building a system capable
of attacking the entire target set, the Defense Department and the air
force had decided "to apply available resources to only a subset of the
JCS requirement."[68]

The U.S. Air Force has also not been happy with the ALMV's
capabilities. The former air force deputy chief of staff for planning at
Space Command is on record as saying that the F-15 ASAT is "fine,
necessary and needed, but has one limitation. The altitude it reaches is
not all that great."[69] This was later confirmed, albeit implicitly, when
the air force announced in March 1987 that it intends to study ways to
upgrade the altitude reach of the ALMV, either by improving the thrust
capability of the lower stage booster, or by fitting the upper stage and
the Miniature Vehicle to a ground-based Pershing II missile.[70]

From circumstantial information it is possible to get a more specific
idea of the maximum altitude reach of the ALMV as presently configured.
Since the missile successfully intercepted a defunct satellite at an altitude
of 525 kilometers, this is at least its minimum capability. The Instrumented Test Vehicles launched on December 13, 1985, to serve as targets
in the ASAT program pass the Western Test Range off California, where
all the testing has taken place, at roughly 720–740 kilometers.[71] At the
press conference in March 1987 announcing the restructured program,
Brigadier General Robert R. Rankine, the director of space systems and
command, control and communications for the U.S. Air Force, indicated
that the altitude enhancement would take the MV "to about twice the
level that we're capable of today." Later he also admitted that the
Pershing II can "get to about the altitude to which the Soviets have

68. Department of Defense Appropriations for 1984, Hearings before a Subcommittee
of the House Committee on Appropriations, 98 Cong. 1 sess. (GPO, 1983), pt. 8, p.
501.

69. Quoted in Edward H. Kolcum, "Dispute Grows over Shift of USAF Shuttle
Payloads," Aviation Week and Space Technology, vol. 120 (April 30, 1984), p. 25.

70. Office of the Assistant Secretary of Defense, Public Affairs, "Secretary of
Defense Announces Details of Restructured Anti-Satellite Program," news release 100-
87, Washington, D.C., March 10, 1987.

71. Both figures were calculated using data supplied by NASA. The Instrumented
Test Vehicles (ITVs) consist of inflatable metallic balloons launched two at a time by a
single Scout booster from NASA's Wallops Island Flight Facility. Each ITV contains
a controllable long-wave infrared system for simulating the different thermal signatures
of Soviet satellites, as well as miss distance instrumentation and radio equipment to
relay the data.

Table 4-8. *Soviet Satellites within Reach of the Current and
Potentially Upgraded U.S. ALMV Antisatellite System*

Application	Designation	Number of satellites
Up to 850 kilometers[a]		
Photoreconnaissance	Kosmos	3–4
Signals intelligence	Kosmos	7
Ocean reconnaissance	RORSAT	1–2
	EORSAT	1–3
Communication	Kosmos	3
Manned space station	Salyut, Mir	1
Subtotal		20
850–1,700 kilometers[b]		
Navigation	Kosmos	10
Meteorology	Meteor 2-3	3
Subtotal		13
Total		33

Source: Extrapolated from table 2-1.
a. Excludes early warning and Molniya communication satellites in highly elliptical orbits.
b. Excludes constellation of approximately twenty-four "store-dump" communication satellites for reasons discussed in text.

already tested."[72] Since the highest Soviet test was at 1,710 kilometers (see table 4-2), it is possible to surmise that the maximum ceiling for the current ALMV is probably no higher than 850 kilometers. On the basis of these calculations, table 4-8 lists the Soviet satellites that will be placed at risk if the ALMV becomes operational. They are ordered into two target sets: those satellites operating up to 850 kilometers and those between 850 and 1,700 kilometers, which would become vulnerable if the altitude enhancement program goes ahead.

As table 4-8 indicates, there will be approximately twenty Soviet satellites within range of the presently configured U.S. ASAT. Several of these, notably the new class of signals intelligence satellites and three communication satellites, orbit at the ALMV's extreme range. Excluded from the table are the Soviet Molniya communication and early warning satellites that pass within range at the perigees of their highly elliptical orbits in the Southern Hemisphere. Though F-15 aircraft could probably be relocated to this region, the extreme velocity of the target satellites

72. Department of Defense news briefing by Brig. Gen. Robert Rankine, March 10, 1987.

would almost certainly preclude interception. In fact, the Defense Department has admitted that the present ASAT system "will not have the capability to attack Soviet early warning satellites, even at a low point in their orbit."[73]

Doubling the reach of the ALMV brings a further thirteen or so satellites into range, essentially navigation and weather forecasting systems. Deliberately excluded from this target set is the constellation of approximately twenty-four "store-dump" communication satellites. Because these are quite small—weighing around 40 kilograms—they probably do not present a big enough target for the MV's sensor.[74] In any case, the limited number of U.S. ASAT missiles does not make an attack on such a large constellation a profitable exercise.

In executing an ASAT campaign, the American system has some significant operational advantages over its Soviet counterpart. Compared with the Soviet ASAT, which requires many hours to prepare for a launch, the U.S. F-15s can be activated more rapidly. Moreover, as discussed earlier, the intensity of Soviet ASAT operations is hindered by the limited availability of launch pads and the time needed to refurbish them after use. Furthermore, the time taken to intercept a satellite is much shorter for the U.S. ASAT because it does not have to be launched into orbit like the Soviet interceptor, but must merely pass sufficiently close to its quarry for the Miniature Vehicle to be effective. The fact that it is air launched means that it is also far more versatile in targeting satellites than the fixed-site Soviet ASAT system.[75]

73. *Department of Defense Appropriations for 1985,* Hearings before a Subcommittee of the House Committee on Appropriations, 98 Cong. 2 sess. (GPO, 1984), pt. 1, p. 513.

74. Johnson, *Soviet Year in Space, 1983,* p. 16.

75. In general it is unclear how easy it would be for the ASAT-capable F-15 aircraft either to perform extended missions or to relocate to other air bases. For example, a dedicated ASAT Command Center (ACC) is to be set up at Langley AFB as well as a special cryogen storage and processing plant for the liquid helium and nitrogen necessary to cool the missile's guidance system during the flight. It also appears that the range and duration of each F-15 ASAT flight is constrained less by the amount of aircraft fuel and the endurance of the pilot than by the depletion of the same helium and nitrogen that is carried aloft. See *Military Construction Appropriations for 1985,* Hearings, pt. 3, pp. 559–60; and *Department of Defense Appropriations for 1985,* Hearings, pt. 2, p. 195. It might be possible to space at least two F-15s from Langley far enough apart under the expected path of the target satellite for the second aircraft to receive information on the success of the first engagement directly from ground-based surveillance radars and still have time to launch its own missile if required. To extend the F-15's operational radius to make this feasible would almost certainly require in-flight refueling

Although the direct-ascent American ASAT differs markedly from its co-orbital Soviet counterpart, the methodology used earlier for evaluating a Soviet ASAT campaign is applicable for a U.S. campaign as well. Conceivably the U.S. ALMV could have a single-shot kill probability (*SSPK*) higher than those assigned to the Soviet ASAT, but this advantage cannot be assumed. It is appropriate, therefore, to be conservative and use the same kill probability values. The most significant difference is the number of intercept attempts, or shots, feasible each day. While eighteen aircraft will be converted to the ASAT mission, it is unlikely that all will be available for use at any given moment because of routine maintenance.[76] Fifteen operational aircraft is a more realistic figure. At a minimum each F-15 could attempt one intercept a day (for a daily rate of fifteen shots), and two sorties might be possible (for a daily rate of thirty shots).[77] Twenty-two shots representing an average of 1.5 daily sorties per aircraft supplies a middle-range value.

Four target sets have been chosen for the analysis, individually totaling 30, 20, 15, and 10 satellites. Though 20 seems to be the approximate number of Soviet satellites within reach of the unmodified ALMV, it is prudent to consider a larger target set for several reasons. For one, the Soviets may launch additional satellites as a precaution against U.S. ASAT operations. Operable launch pads permitting, they can also be expected to replace disabled satellites in wartime. Furthermore, if and when the ALMV becomes fully operational, its reach may have been extended to threaten more Soviet satellites. With the same effectiveness requirement (95 percent confidence of success, or .05 overall probability of survival), tables 4-9 and 4-10 record the resultant estimates of U.S. ASAT operations using the above variables.[78]

---

or that the aircraft be "recovered" at another air base. As noted earlier, the depletion of the cryogen liquid for the MV's sensor would be a critical factor; others would be the speed at which the ground-based radars could carry out ASAT damage assessment and relay it to the waiting aircraft, and how fast the pilot could reprogram the missile's guidance system, since the target might be in range for less than eight minutes.

76. It is also unclear whether the U.S. Air Force will procure eighteen of the Carrier Aircraft Equipment (CAE) sets that are used to connect the ALMV to the aircraft.

77. The actual sortie rate could be as many as three a day given the full provision of spares and personnel. See Defense Science Board, *Report of the Defense Science Board 1981 Summer Study Panel on Operational Readiness with High Performance Systems* (DOD; distributed by Defense Technical Information Center, Alexandria, Va., 1982), p. 6-4. See also "F-15s Used for Air Defense Intercepts," *Aviation Week and Space Technology*, vol. 116 (June 7, 1982), p. 69; and Epstein, *Measuring Military Power*, pp. 31–35.

78. Evidence suggests that .95 is indeed the U.S. Air Force's effectiveness require-

Table 4-9. *Estimates of U.S. ASAT Shots Required to Disable a Range of Soviet Satellite Target Sets, by Probability of Kill*[a]

Launch shots per target set

Single-shot probability of kill	Target set				
	1 satellite	10 satellites	15 satellites	20 satellites	30 satellites
High (.75)	2	22	32	43	65
Moderate (.65)	3	29	43	57	86
Low (.45)	5	50	75	100	150

Source: Author's calculations as explained in text.

a. Assumes U.S. ASAT operations are 95 percent effective (Soviet satellites have an overall probability of survival of .05). Total shots are obtained by multiplying the *pre-rounded* number of shots required per target (see equation 3 in text) by the number of satellites in the target set.

Table 4-10. *Estimates of Days Required to Disable a Range of Soviet Satellite Target Sets, by Probability of Kill*[a]

Days per target set

Single-shot probability of kill	Target set			
	10 satellites	15 satellites	20 satellites	30 satellites
At thirty shots a day				
High (.75)	0.7	1.1	1.4	2.2
Moderate (.65)	0.9	1.4	1.9	2.9
Low (.45)	1.7	2.5	3.3	5.0
At twenty-two shots a day				
High (.75)	1.0	1.5	2.0	2.9
Moderate (.65)	1.3	1.9	2.6	3.9
Low (.45)	2.3	3.4	4.6	6.8
At fifteen shots a day				
High (.75)	1.4	2.2	2.9	4.3
Moderate (.65)	1.9	2.8	3.8	5.7
Low (.45)	3.4	5.0	6.7	10.0

Source: Same as table 4-9.

a. Assumes U.S. ASAT operations are 95 percent effective (Soviet satellites have an overall probability of survival of .05).

Several important conclusions can be drawn from these two tables. Table 4-9 indicates that under best-case assumptions of an *SSPK* of .75 the United States would nearly exhaust its planned inventory of ALMVs in attacking fifteen Soviet satellites with 95 percent confidence of success. If the U.S. Air Force plans to attack more targets, it must believe that

---

ment for the ALMV. See U.S. Department of the Air Force, *Supporting Data for Fiscal Year 1985 Budget Estimates, Descriptive Summaries: Research, Development, Test and Evaluation* (Dept. of the Air Force, February 1984), p. 317.

the ALMV's performance will be better than assumed here, or it will have to purchase more missiles.[79] Table 4-10 illustrates the superior qualities of the F-15–ALMV system in performing intensive ASAT operations. Again, under the best-case assumptions (an $SSPK$ of .75 and two sorties a day totaling thirty shots), the United States could disable fifteen Soviet satellites in just over a day. If the sortie rate or number of launch opportunities only permit one sortie per aircraft (for a total of fifteen shots a day), then the same campaign would still only take a day longer.

Tables 4-9 and 4-10 are useful for estimating the force requirements for attacking an expanded target set with the same assumed performance parameters. Thus for the United States to consider a campaign against thirty Soviet satellites would require nearly doubling the planned purchase of missiles even with the highest listed $SSPK$. Under best-case assumptions a campaign of this size would take just over two days to complete and ten days under the worst assumptions.

As in the earlier analysis of a hypothetical Soviet ASAT campaign, these estimates do not take into account potential impediments to U.S. ASAT operations. For example, demands on the same F-15 aircraft for continental air defense tasks could severely curtail ASAT operations, as would competing demands for the ground surveillance radars that provide the essential targeting data. One problem identified by the GAO is that when U.S. strategic forces are put on a Defense Condition (DEFCON) 3 alert, the task of detecting ballistic missiles dominates the priorities of the ground-based surveillance radars, with the result that the ASAT mission suffers from "reduced sensor coverage."[80] What effect this would have is impossible to judge from the open literature.

The Soviets can also be expected to develop countermeasures to defeat or at least complicate U.S. ASAT attacks. The three principal

79. Though the U.S. Air Force has understandably not released its projected effectiveness figures for the ALMV, a 1986 GAO report on the program did caution against unrealistic expectations in this regard. Citing the air force's own Operational Test and Evaluation Center (AFOTEC), it stated that "the original prediction of any weapon system's performance has historically been *extremely* optimistic. As the system matures during development, the performance prediction generally degrades gradually as subsystem shortcomings are countered by engineering redesign wherever possible. However, during operational testing the performance can degrade drastically." See General Accounting Office, *U.S. Antisatellite Program: Information on Operational Effectiveness, Cost, Schedules, and Testing,* Unclassified contents of report B-219105 (June 1986) (emphasis added).

80. Ibid.

methods—maneuvering to evade interception, raising the altitude of a threatened satellite, and deploying decoys—were all addressed in the Reagan administration's 1984 report to Congress on ASAT arms control. As to maneuvering the report states:

> It is not clear that the Soviets have the capability to determine which satellite would be the target of a given attack and thus would have to maneuver several of their satellites each time the U.S. launched or simulated the launch of an ASAT interceptor. Because repeated maneuvers would reduce Soviet satellite lifetimes, maneuver would be a costly countermeasure.[81]

This conclusion is probably true over an extended period, but buying such extra time at a crucial stage in the hostilities may be all that is needed until a replacement satellite is launched. The report went on to add, however, that Soviet satellite maneuvering could be offset by improvements to U.S. space tracking capabilities. The most valuable addition would be the space-based surveillance system currently being considered for deployment. The Defense Department has also acknowledged that deploying this system "would enhance the capability of the [U.S.] ASAT system to engage the next generation of satellites if they used advanced survivability aids."[82] As for the other possible Soviet countermeasures, raising the altitude of a threatened satellite might impair its ability to carry out its mission and be rejected by the Soviets on that ground, while decoys could be countered with changes to the MV's sensor logic.[83]

Deploying a space-based surveillance system might also make it possible for the U.S. ALMV to destroy a Soviet co-orbital ASAT before it has a chance to complete its own mission. At present, with only information from ground-based surveillance radars to rely on, such a feat would be extremely difficult.[84]

81. Ronald Reagan, "Report to the Congress on U.S. Policy on ASAT Arms Control," March 31, 1984, p. 12.

82. *Department of Defense Appropriations for Fiscal Year 1985*, Hearings before a Subcommittee of the Senate Committee on Appropriations, 98 Cong. 2 sess. (GPO, 1984), pt. 3, p. 364. The U.S. Air Force is also seeking to improve the solid propellent rockets on the MV to "hedge against additional maneuvering capability an adversary might build into his satellites." See *Department of Defense Appropriations for 1986*, Hearings, pt. 2, p. 427.

83. Reagan, "Report to Congress on U.S. Policy on ASAT Arms Control," p. 12.

84. For a detailed discussion of the problems involved in such an operation and the possible Soviet countermeasures, see Donald L. Hafner, "Approaches to the Control of Antisatellite Weapons," in Durch, ed., *National Interests and the Military Use of Space*, pp. 251–52.

U.S. Residual ASAT Capabilities

In addition to the planned deployment of the F-15–ALMV, the United States like the USSR possesses some systems with residual antisatellite capabilities.

ABM SYSTEMS. The United States does not now have an operational ABM capability, but the Spartan missiles developed for the Safeguard-Sentinel system are still in storage and presumably could be reactivated and modified for the ASAT role if required.[85] However, these would need a new front end, as the original W-71 nuclear warheads are to be dismantled. If replaced with a similar warhead, they would suffer the same operational drawbacks for ASAT use that face the Moscow ABM system.

As part of its ongoing ABM research program (now subsumed under the Strategic Defense Initiative), the U.S. Army conducted a series of tests with a modified Minuteman ICBM to determine whether ballistic missile reentry vehicles could be intercepted by nonnuclear means outside the atmosphere. Known as the Homing Overlay Experiment (HOE), a successful test was finally carried out on June 10, 1984, after a series of failures.[86] Using an infrared homing sensor like that in the Miniature Vehicle and an unfurlable umbrella-like metal net, the test interceptor destroyed a dummy warhead, launched by an ICBM from Vandenberg AFB, at an altitude of more than 100 kilometers.[87] The U.S. Army is now pursuing more advanced techniques as part of the SDI (see below). The HOE test nevertheless demonstrated a residual capability to intercept satellites in low earth orbit.

LONG-RANGE BALLISTIC MISSILES. Just as the Soviet Union could modify

85. See *Fiscal Year 1984 Arms Control Impact Statement*, Joint Committee Print (GPO, 1983), p. 126. The potential ASAT capability of the Spartan missile was admitted in 1969. See Stares, *Militarization of Space*, p. 120. Interestingly, the launch facilities at Johnston Island in the Pacific, the site of an early U.S. ASAT program, are also maintained in a mothballed state in case atmospheric nuclear testing is resumed. See *Department of Defense Appropriations for 1985*, Hearings, pt. 3, p. 576.

86. Office of Assistant Secretary of Defense, Public Affairs, "Successful Homing Overlay Experiment Intercept Announced," news release 311-84, Washington, D.C., June 11, 1984.

87. Ibid.; Clarence A. Robinson, Jr., "BMD Homing Interceptor Destroys Reentry Vehicle," *Aviation Week and Space Technology*, vol. 120 (June 18, 1984), pp. 19–20; and Charles Mohr, "Army Test Missile Is Said to Destroy a Dummy Warhead," *New York Times*, June 12, 1984.

some of its strategic weapons for the ASAT mission, so the United States has the same option at its disposal. Likewise, the United States would have to confront the same problems: potential collateral effects on friendly satellites and disrupted communications. However, the advent of lightweight, low-yield devices, if they allow relatively discriminating nuclear ASAT attacks, might make this option more attractive.[88]

ELECTRONIC COUNTERMEASURES. Given the widespread deployment of U.S. bases overseas, the United States has, if anything, a much greater opportunity to conduct satellite jamming operations than the Soviet Union has. The U.S. Navy is also believed to have developed operating procedures to jam Soviet ocean reconnaissance satellites (see chapter 5). Understandably, little information is publicly available on overall U.S. ECM capabilities and planning for such operations.

LASER FACILITIES. The most powerful U.S. laser now in existence with a potential ASAT capability is the U.S. Navy's Mid-infrared Advanced Chemical Laser (MIRACL) at the joint-service High-Energy Laser Systems Test Facility, in White Sands, New Mexico. Reportedly, it is a deuterium fluoride continuous wave laser operating at 3.8 microns with a power output of 2.2 megawatts.[89] This wavelength has good atmospheric transmission properties, meaning that beam projection into space is not beyond its capacity. A special beam director taken from the navy's Sealite program at San Juan Capistrano, California, was added to MIRACL at the end of 1985, further improving its ASAT potential.[90]

THE SPACE SHUTTLE. The Soviet Union has long considered the U.S. space shuttle to be a potential ASAT device, because its demonstrated ability to maneuver close to orbiting objects for inspection and retrieval means that the shuttle could tamper with and even capture Soviet satellites.[91] Spacecraft up to about 600 kilometers are probably vulner-

88. The Lawrence Livermore National Laboratory has reportedly designed and tested low-yield nuclear devices that according to their brochure "might serve as the warhead for an anti-satellite weapon." See Jack Cushman, "U.S. A-Bomb Could Wipe Out Satellites," *Defense Week,* vol. 5 (December 24, 1984), p. 1.

89. Defense Marketing Services, Inc., "Sealite/Navy HEL," *DMS Market Intelligence Report* (Greenwich, Conn., 1984); and Michael A. Dornheim, "Missile Destroyed in First SDI Test at High-Energy Laser Facility," *Aviation Week and Space Technology,* vol. 123 (September 23, 1985), pp. 17–19.

90. "Hughes Laser Beam Director Tests Planned at White Sands," *Aviation Week and Space Technology,* vol. 123 (October 7, 1985), p. 18.

91. "Soviets See Shuttle as Killer Satellite," *Aviation Week and Space Technology,* vol. 108 (April 17, 1978), p. 17. The retrieval of a satellite was first demonstrated with the mission to return and repair the Solar Max satellite on April 12, 1984. See Craig

able to an operation of this kind,[92] and under normal conditions, the shuttle's remote manipulator arm would be able to retrieve objects of around 14,500 kilograms.[93] However, since it would be relatively easy for the Soviets to attach antitampering devices, or booby traps, to their satellites, the United States would likely be deterred from carrying out such an operation. Capturing a single Soviet satellite is unlikely to be sufficiently important to tempt the United States into risking a shuttle orbiter. The possible development of Orbital Maneuvering Vehicles (OMVs), controlled from the shuttle orbiter and able to perform many of the same tasks but operating at a considerable distance from it, would reduce this concern, however.[94]

Potential U.S. and Soviet ASAT Systems

Many of the potential U.S. and Soviet ASAT weapons have already been identified in the earlier section dealing with generic threats to space systems. Whether such weapons are deployed will depend on several factors. One is how much support can be generated for pursuing research to a level at which the cost effectiveness of the weapon can be demonstrated. Clearly, perceived advances by an adversary in certain key technologies such as nonnuclear kinetic energy weapons and lasers would fuel such support, as would new military threats posed by the adversary's space systems. Politico-military pressure to develop and deploy new ASAT weapons will also determine whether space arms control is considered desirable to pursue or, if already in place, to preserve. It seems apparent, however, that regardless of the merits of developing more advanced antisatellite weapon systems than those either deployed or currently planned, the key technologies are already being pursued as a result of the growing superpower interest in ballistic

---

Covault, "Orbiter Crew Restores Solar Max," *Aviation Week and Space Technology,* vol. 120 (April 16, 1984), pp. 18–20.

92. As of March 1987 the highest altitude shuttle mission was 51-J, in which the orbiter went as high as 515 kilometers. See "Military Shuttle Flight Sets Altitude Record," *Aviation Week and Space Technology,* vol. 123 (October 21, 1985), p. 26.

93. Rockwell International, *Using the Space Shuttle: A Guide to Shuttle Utilization* (Space Transportation and Systems Group, 1983), p. 11. The maximum weight of 29,500 kilograms may be possible in some cases.

94. See "Robotic Tug for Shuttle," *Defense Electronics,* vol. 16 (October 1984), pp. 57, 59.

Table 4-11. *Potential Near-Term and Far-Term ASAT Weapons*

Near term (to 1995)	*Far term (1995 and beyond)*[a]
Advanced air-launched kinetic energy weapon systems	Ground-based lasers with orbiting or pop-up mirrors
Ground-based direct-ascent nuclear-armed or kinetic energy weapon systems (for low and high altitude use)	Space-based lasers
	Space-based neutral particle beam weapons
Ground-based lasers	Nuclear-pumped space-based X-ray lasers[b]
Space-based kinetic energy weapon systems (directed projectiles, railguns, space mines)	
High-powered radio frequency weapons	

Source: See text.

a. Excludes the possible development of new, ASAT-capable space weapon platforms, such as a manned aerospace plane.

b. Currently prohibited by the Outer Space Treaty (see chapter 6).

missile defense. Long before such defenses—even in their most limited form—become operational, the construction of prototype antimissile systems may provide each side with additional and perhaps highly effective antisatellite weapons. At the very least, antimissile research will create a major stimulus to ASAT research and development. The overlap between the two missions is just too great to avoid such cross-fertilization.

Despite the uncertainties in predicting the pace at which weapons with ASAT capabilities could be deployed in the future, certain technologies are plainly more mature than others. Table 4-11 maps out potential ASAT weaponry for the near term (to 1995) and the far term (1995 and beyond). As noted earlier, these weapons do not have to reach full operational deployment within these dates to provide some capability for ASAT operations.

The development of these weapon systems will inevitably expand the range of threats to satellites. In particular, the opportunity to attack high-altitude satellites promptly and with greater confidence will almost certainly grow. On the basis of today's research programs, it is possible to predict more specifically how the ASAT capabilities of both superpowers could evolve to the year 2000.

Future Soviet Systems

At a minimum, it would not be surprising if the Soviets fielded an improved version of their current co-orbital interceptor. The use of a different booster to extend its altitude reach cannot be discounted either. Indeed, there is already speculation that the Soviets may use the Proton (SL-12) or a new heavy lift launch vehicle that is presently under development.[95] Both would permit attacks against U.S. satellites in the geosynchronous orbit although, as noted earlier, this would be a ponderous capability given the lengthy flight time to such altitudes.

A possible candidate for a new low-altitude ASAT system would be one that emulates the U.S. ALMV. Potential carrier aircraft include the *Backfire* bomber, the Su-27 *Flanker,* MiG-25 *Foxbat,* and MiG-31 *Foxhound* fighter interceptors.[96] An alternative or complementary system would be ground-based conventionally armed direct-ascent missiles. These are most likely already under development for the next generation of ground-based antiballistic missiles.

Yet another option would be a system of orbital space mines. This would not be too hard for the Soviets, since their current ASAT system has many of the principal components of such a weapon. But as noted earlier, maintaining operational space mines does present some significant problems, a fact underlined by the former secretary of the air force, Verne Orr, before Congress: "Some of the principal drawbacks are the amount of propulsion capability and day-to-day ground controller effort required to keep a mine near its potential target; the risk of international repercussions from an inadvertent collision with the nearby target; and international reaction to threatening visibly another nation's satellites over long periods of time."[97]

In the longer term, the most likely area of Soviet ASAT development is in the field of directed-energy weapons. The U.S. Department of Defense has already warned that

> in the late 1980s, [the Soviets] could have prototype space-based laser weapons for use against satellites. In addition, ongoing Soviet programs have progressed to the point where they could include construction of ground-based laser antisatellite (ASAT) facilities at operational sites. These could be available by the end of the 1980s and would greatly increase

---

95. Department of Defense, *Soviet Military Power, 1986*, pp. 49, 52. The limitations of using the Proton booster for ASAT purposes are discussed in Durch, *Anti-Satellite Weapons,* p. 13.

96. Office of Technology Assessment, *Arms Control in Space: Workshop Proceedings,* OTA-BP-ISC-28 (GPO, 1984), p. 27.

97. *Department of Defense Authorization for Appropriations for Fiscal Year 1986,* Hearings before the Senate Committee on Armed Services, 99 Cong. 1 sess. (GPO, 1985), pt. 2, p. 1185.

the Soviets' laser ASAT capability beyond that currently at their test site at Sary Shagan. They may deploy operational systems of space-based lasers for antisatellite purposes in the 1990s if their technology developments prove successful.[98]

Furthermore, "a prototype space-based particle beam weapon intended only to disrupt satellite electronic equipment could be tested in the early 1990s. One designed to destroy satellites could be tested in space in the mid-1990s."[99] The U.S. Department of Defense has also stated that the Soviet space shuttle under development may be used as an ASAT weapon's delivery platform.[100]

Future U.S. Systems

Even though the U.S. ALMV has yet to reach operational deployment there has already been some initial research into possible follow-on systems. In 1984 the then undersecretary of defense for research and engineering, Richard D. DeLauer, informed Congress that "we have directed a comprehensive study to select a follow-on system with additional capabilities to place a wider range of Soviet satellite vehicles at risk."[101] As noted earlier, the near-term options for improving U.S. antisatellite capabilities beyond those currently planned have been narrowed down to either an enhanced air-launched missile or the use of ground-based Pershing II missiles with Miniature Vehicle warheads. If the proposed study demonstrates feasibility, the U.S. Air Force believes that it can begin development in 1988, with deployment possible before the mid-1990s.

For the longer term the air force has also requested roughly $100 million in the fiscal 1988 and 1989 budgets to study the possible uses of ground-based excimer lasers for the ASAT mission.[102] Several demonstrations are expected to determine their feasibility before deployment could begin in the late 1990s. In announcing these long-term plans, the air force openly acknowledged that the laser research was designed to

98. Department of Defense, *Soviet Military Power, 1985*, p. 44.

99. Ibid., p. 45. See also testimony of Robert M. Gates and Lawrence Gershwin, *Soviet Strategic Force Developments*.

100. Department of Defense, *Soviet Military Power, 1985*, p. 55.

101. Quoted in Fred Hiatt, "Anti-Satellite Weapon Research Is Pressed," *Washington Post*, February 28, 1984.

102. Department of Defense news briefing by Brig. Gen. Robert Rankine, March 10, 1987.

complement similar work being conducted under the Strategic Defense Initiative. A two-way relationship, in which SDI research nurtures the key technologies for ASAT weapons, while the ASAT program provides a useful outlet to fund and test antimissile-related systems, is expected to grow in coming years. Many of the prospective antimissile systems being developed under the SDI program will also have inherent antisatellite capabilities.

Under the SDI's kinetic energy weapons program, several projects have this potential.[103] The follow-on system to the Homing Overlay Experiment (HOE) described earlier, known as the Exo-atmospheric Re-entry Vehicle Interception System (ERIS), is an obvious candidate. This will be a single-warhead device, although interceptors with multiple warheads are also under consideration. Besides deploying ground-based antimissile systems, the SDI organization is also planning development work on orbital kinetic energy weapons. One involves the use of a hypervelocity launcher, or "railgun" (known as Saggittar), while another consists of a cluster of infrared-guided miniature homing vehicles similar to the ALMV.

In the directed-energy weapons technology program, extensive research is being conducted on both ground-based and space-based lasers. Aside from the MIRACL chemical laser, the United States is also constructing a free-electron laser at the White Sands test facility. Long-term plans will raise the power output of this facility to perhaps 100 megawatts which, when wedded to the appropriate atmospheric compensation and beam control systems, may be able to threaten satellites out to geosynchronous orbit. With "pop-up" or space-based "fighting mirrors," such lasers will also be able to attack targets over their horizon. A more ambitious project involves the use of nuclear weapons to generate X-ray lasers. Given the problem of propagating X-ray lasers through the atmosphere, such systems would need to be based in space. Work is also under way to examine the feasibility of space-based chemical lasers and neutral particle beam weapons, including prototype demonstrations in space.[104]

Well before the effectiveness of many of these systems for ballistic

103. Details of the various programs being pursued under the SDI are from Department of Defense, *Report to the Congress on the Strategic Defense Initiative* (Washington, D.C.: SDI Office, 1986).

104. David J. Lynch, "Tests Planned for Particle Beam," *Defense Week,* vol. 7 (October 20, 1986), p. 5.

missile defense can be demonstrated, they will have become *de facto* ASAT devices. Indeed, because of the treaty constraints against testing many of these projects "in an ABM mode," it appears as if the Reagan administration intends to test them in ways that resemble ASAT demonstrations to avoid accusations of noncompliance.[105] For example, as part of the SDI program the United States launched two experimental satellites aboard a Delta rocket on September 5, 1986. Part of the exercise was to track the launch of an Aries rocket from White Sands with an infrared sensor. At the end of the test one of the satellites, which incorporated a modified Phoenix missile radar guidance system, deliberately collided with the other. Thus, while the conditions of the demonstration did not replicate the interception of a ballistic missile, they did nevertheless successfully test a rudimentary ASAT device. More such tests are planned in the near future.

The paradoxical drawback to many of these ASAT-capable ballistic missile defense systems is that they will ultimately undermine the survivability, and with it the feasibility, of space-based strategic defenses. Thus, even if many of the technical obstacles to a workable space-based antimissile system are surmounted, its inherent vulnerability to attack could ultimately discourage deployment. In the process, however, a new, more lethal generation of ASAT weapons may have been created.

Conclusion

The current threat to space systems is both varied and considerable. Yet set against the kinds of dedicated ASAT systems that could be developed and deployed in the future, the threat is still relatively immature.

While the current Soviet satellite interceptor poses some threat, it suffers from significant operational constraints that limit its effectiveness. By adding such devices as attack warning sensors, emergency maneuvering aids, and decoys to American satellites within the interceptor's reach, the United States can minimize their vulnerability to attack.

Though still in the development stage, the U.S. Air-Launched Mini-

105. See Peter Didisheim, *The SDI/ASAT Link,* Papers on Strategic Defense (Washington, D.C.: Union of Concerned Scientists, 1985), p. 11.

ature Vehicle system promises to be an inherently superior ASAT weapon. The eventual deployment of the ALMV and its potential upgrading to a higher altitude capability will surely spur the Soviets to develop more advanced and effective ASATs than the one they now possess. According to the U.S. Defense Department, such weapons are already within the Soviets' reach.

The so-called residual ASAT capabilities do pose a threat to space systems, but it should not be exaggerated. Without extensive testing "in an ASAT mode" most residual systems are incapable of rapid, high-confidence ASAT attacks. Some are also realistically limited to certain types of conflict and most, furthermore, can be countered by a variety of survivability measures to reduce their potential effectiveness in wartime.

Unless checked, the ASAT threats of the future will be qualitatively different from, and considerably more potent than, those of today. Besides the development of new, more effective, antisatellite weapons, antimissile systems capable of attacking satellites may also be deployed. Space systems in low earth orbit will become extremely costly and difficult to protect with even the most sophisticated survivability measures. More ominous is the likelihood that satellites at higher altitudes, including those used for early warning and strategic communications, will steadily become more vulnerable.

CHAPTER FIVE

The Utility
of ASAT Weapons

IF THE value of military space systems to each superpower depends largely on contextual factors, so the effect of their loss or threatened loss is likely to vary in the same way. This basic fact is rarely acknowledged, however. Instead, both sides of the antisatellite debate rely on generalities to argue the merits of their cases.[1] The purpose of this chapter is to examine a range of plausible scenarios—from client state conflicts in the third world, to regional superpower conflicts in places like the Persian Gulf, Korea, and Europe, and finally to strategic nuclear war—where the presence or use of antisatellite weapons could conceivably play a role. Within each case, special attention is paid to the incentives to use ASAT weapons, the costs and benefits of such attacks, and the effectiveness of different ways of negating satellites.

There are obvious pitfalls in this kind of analysis. For one, it is unavoidably speculative, since not all the elements of a particular scenario are knowable in advance. Also, details about each side's prospective ASAT capabilities, and moreover the compensatory measures that the other side may take in response, can only be derived from what is known today. In particular, care must be taken to avoid comparing

1. There have been some notable exceptions. See Kurt Gottfried and Richard Ned Lebow, "Anti-Satellite Weapons: Weighing the Risks," *Daedalus,* vol. 114 (Spring 1985), pp. 147–70; William J. Durch, "Anti-Satellite Weapons, Arms Control Options, and the Military Use of Space," prepared for the U.S. Arms Control and Disarmament Agency (Washington, D.C.: ACDA, 1984); and Donald L. Hafner, "Approaches to the Control of Antisatellite Weapons," in William J. Durch, ed., *National Interests and the Military Use of Space* (Cambridge, Mass.: Ballinger, 1984).

future ASAT systems with today's countermeasures, and vice versa.[2] Nevertheless, examining specific contingencies is useful for conveying the complexity of this issue and for reaching more sophisticated conclusions about the utility of antisatellite weapons.

Client State Conflicts

Of the satellites that could be of value and hence potential targets for ASAT attacks in a conflict between client states or proxy forces of the superpowers, those used for intelligence gathering stand out as the most likely candidates. Since the late 1960s and perhaps before, both superpowers have used reconnaissance satellites to monitor crises and conflicts around the world as indicated by such telltale signs as the frequency of launches and the manipulation of orbits to cover specific areas of interest.[3] Though the evidence is fragmentary and sometimes contradictory, it appears that on several occasions the superpowers have provided intelligence derived from satellites to their client states. For example, photos taken by Soviet reconnaissance satellites were reportedly shown to Egyptian officials during the 1973 Arab-Israeli war, though this was later denied by President Anwar al-Sadat.[4] Israel may have benefited from satellite imagery provided by its ally, the United States, in the same conflict, as Sadat charged, though this assertion also is disputed.[5] A less ambiguous case appears to be the 1978 war between Ethiopia and Somalia. Here Soviet-led Ethiopian forces evidently made good use of reconnaissance data transmitted to a ground station at Dire-Dawa.[6] It has been alleged that Argentina received intelligence from Soviet satellites during the Falklands conflict, but British use of U.S. satellite

2. Ashton B. Carter, "Satellites and Anti-Satellites: The Limits of the Possible," *International Security,* vol. 10 (Spring 1986), p. 73.

3. See Paul B. Stares, *The Militarization of Space: U.S. Policy, 1945–84* (Ithaca, N.Y.: Cornell University Press, 1985); and Robert P. Berman and John C. Baker, *Soviet Strategic Forces: Requirements and Responses* (Brookings, 1982), pp. 156–62.

4. Stares, *Militarization of Space,* p. 141. The real source of the photos may have been Soviet MiG-25 reconnaissance planes.

5. Raymond L. Garthoff, *Detente and Confrontation: American-Soviet Relations from Nixon to Reagan* (Brookings, 1985), note 29 on p. 367.

6. Mark Urban, "Soviet Intervention and the Ogaden Counter-offensive of 1978," *RUSI: Journal of the Royal United Services Institute for Defence Studies,* vol. 128 (June 1983), p. 44. Even this report has to be treated with some skepticism, as Soviet satellites at that time were not thought capable of directly transmitting imagery.

imagery seems more probable.[7] More recently, the Soviets reportedly supplied intelligence acquired by satellite to the Libyans, while the United States has done the same for Iraq and Chad.[8]

Useful though this information might have been, it is hard to imagine either superpower attacking the other's satellites to support a client state in need. For one thing, the military incentives are questionable. Unless the United States is prepared to conduct numerous ASAT attacks, the destruction of a single Soviet reconnaissance satellite that is feeding intelligence data—albeit indirectly—to a client state at war with a U.S. ally would probably achieve little, since these satellites can be replaced with relative ease by the Soviet Union. The United States would also have to face the likelihood of a Soviet tit-for-tat strike against an American reconnaissance satellite, which, if destroyed, could not be replaced so quickly because the U.S. space program is not configured for frequent launches of spacecraft. Depending on the location of the conflict, the loss of satellite reconnaissance could also be compensated for by other means. For instance, the Soviets reportedly used MiG reconnaissance aircraft as well as satellites to photograph the 1973 Middle East War and 1978 conflict in the Horn of Africa. The incentives for ASAT use would arguably be even weaker if the roles were reversed, that is, if the Soviets considered attacking a U.S. reconnaissance satellite. Given the higher availability of alternative U.S. reconnaissance systems worldwide, the benefits could be short-lived at best.

Whatever the potential military benefits to attacking satellites in conflicts of this kind, the associated risk of escalating and widening the conflict would discourage the superpowers from using their dedicated ASAT weapons. Even nondestructive interference with satellites such as jamming would have its attendant hazards, as will be discussed shortly.[9] Finally, there are likely to be other, more beneficial and less inflammatory ways for the superpowers to aid warring client states (such

7. See Nicholas L. Johnson, *The Soviet Year in Space, 1982* (Colorado Springs, Colo., Teledyne Brown Engineering), p. 8; and Max Hastings and Simon Jenkins, *The Battle for the Falklands* (W.W. Norton, 1983), p. 182.

8. See Bill Keller, "Soviet Expands Surveillance Off Libya, Weinberger Says," *New York Times,* January 14, 1986; David Hoffman and Bob Woodward, "North Gave Prohibited Data to Iranians, Records Show," *Washington Post,* February 20, 1987; and Bernard E. Trainor, "France and U.S. Aiding Chadians with Information to Rout Libyans," *New York Times,* April 3, 1987.

9. If the capabilities exist, the use of nondestructive methods of interference by the *client* state cannot be discounted either.

as sending proxy forces and military supplies) that do not involve direct attacks against the military assets of the other superpower.[10]

Client State versus Superpower Conflicts

Many of the same arguments apply to conflicts in which the forces of one superpower are directly engaged against a client state of the other. The principal difference is that the engaged superpower's interest in securing a favorable outcome will clearly be greater, perhaps making it more inclined to take action against satellites that directly aid the forces of its adversary. The potential incentives and disincentives to using ASAT weapons in conflicts of this kind can be illustrated by hypothetical cases in the Middle East, Central America, and East Asia.

The first case posits a U.S. reprisal attack against Libya similar to that carried out in April 1986. In planning this operation, the United States might become concerned that intelligence collected by Soviet reconnaissance satellites could be used to pinpoint the whereabouts of a U.S. carrier task force, thus reducing the likelihood of tactical surprise and possibly aiding Libyan forces in a preemptive or counter strike. Attacking Soviet satellites in anticipation that valuable intelligence could be passed from them to the Libyans does not appear to be an attractive course of action, however. Besides compromising U.S. intentions to carry out a reprisal raid, it would directly involve the Soviet Union in the hostilities, which the United States would want to avoid. Furthermore, the possibility of detection would still exist: there are other Soviet reconnaissance assets in the region. And even if the Libyans were informed of its whereabouts, a U.S. task force should be able to repel an attack. Overall, then, the putative benefits of such an ASAT operation do not warrant the risks of widening the conflict. This is not to suggest, however, that the United States could or would do nothing to counter the potential threat from Soviet ocean reconnaissance satellites. As will be discussed shortly, there are a variety of countermeasures short of destroying these Soviet intelligence assets that the U.S. Navy could employ to reduce the probability of detection.

The second case involves U.S. military operations in Central America and the Caribbean Basin. Soviet reconnaissance satellites would again

10. Gottfried and Lebow, "Anti-Satellite Weapons," p. 155.

be the principal concern, although the United States might also want to impede Soviet communications to the region, especially if the conflict involved Cuba. Again, U.S. decisionmakers would have to weigh the potential escalatory effect of attacking Soviet space assets against the possible military benefits. Given the preponderance of U.S. forces in the area, those benefits would surely be marginal. Soviet incentives to aid its client states with attacks against U.S. satellites appear even weaker because of the considerable redundancy that the United States enjoys in nonsatellite alternatives in this region.

The balance of costs and benefits of ASAT attacks in a major war in the Far East, such as in Korea, could be somewhat different. For instance, if most of South Korea once more was overrun and the United States again considered launching an Inchon-type amphibious counter-attack to prevent total defeat, tactical surprise would be far harder to achieve under the watchful eye of Soviet spaceborne surveillance than it was in the 1950s. If the situation were desperate enough, U.S. ASAT attacks to blind these satellites might seem worthwhile to mask the location and likely destination of the amphibious force. Yet even here the benefits might still be short-lived for the same reasons, and the risks just as high.

Would a second Korean conflict offer the Soviets worthwhile incentives for using ASAT weapons? Attacking U.S. reconnaissance satellites might provide some help to North Korean forces wishing to disguise military preparations and other activities, but such extraordinary measures would themselves provide warning to the United States and South Korea. Furthermore, high-flying U.S. reconnaissance aircraft based in South Korea, Japan, and the Philippines would still be able to monitor these areas, though not with impunity. U.S. communication satellites might also become targets for electronic interference and, if developed in the future, more destructive forms of attack. Set against the risk of escalation, the military benefits of such action again appear dubious. While interference with the communication links to and from the region would certainly make the command and control of American forces in the theater more difficult, there is considerable redundancy in the U.S. communication network serving the Korean peninsula, including trans-oceanic cables, commercially leased satellites, and HF radio.[11]

11. For information on the U.S. C³ system in the Pacific, see the special edition of *Signal*, vol. 38 (February 1984); Maj. Gen. Robert G. Lynn, "C³ Modernization in

Superpower versus Superpower Regional Conflicts

In conflicts of the kind discussed so far, the military utility of antisatellite attacks appears to be marginal at best, while the fear of triggering escalation by destroying a rival superpower's satellite seems a greater deterrent to ASAT use than the fear of reciprocal losses. In conflicts in which the military forces of both superpowers are actively engaged, the calculations by both sides are likely to change markedly. Two contingencies will be discussed here: U.S.-Soviet conflict in Southwest Asia and war in Europe. Since the use of ASAT weapons to support U.S. naval operations could be part of either contingency, it is discussed separately.

Southwest Asia

The most frequently discussed scenario involving the use of U.S. troops in this region arises from a Soviet invasion of Iran. Indeed, the formation of the U.S. Central Command (CENTCOM), formerly the Rapid Deployment Joint Task Force, was predicated on this very contingency.[12] Once CENTCOM's forces had been dispatched to the Persian Gulf, the Soviets would be especially interested in gaining accurate reports on its order of battle and logistical support. Given the opposition that the Soviets would probably encounter from U.S. air defenses, *aerial* surveillance of the Gulf region would not be easy, so the Soviets would have to rely heavily on reconnaissance satellites to furnish such information. The denial of satellite overflight, therefore, could prove useful to the deployment and subsequent operations of CENTCOM forces. Furthermore, with U.S. and Soviet lives being lost on earth, neither side would be likely to feel so reticent about attacking unmanned objects in space.

On closer examination, however, the drawbacks from using ASAT weapons in this context would probably outweigh the potential payoff.

USPACOM," *Signal,* vol. 40 (February 1986), pp. 33–39; "Command, Control Capability Upgraded," *Aviation Week and Space Technology,* vol. 118 (February 7, 1983), pp. 71–73; and Herbert H. Schenck, "Cables in the Pacific: The Girdle 'Round the Earth," *Signal,* vol. 39 (May 1985), pp. 127–35.

12. See Joshua M. Epstein, *Strategy and Force Planning: The Case of the Persian Gulf* (Brookings, 1987), p. 2.

Attacking unmanned satellites may seem a minor event in the context of a direct U.S.-Soviet conventional war, but as will be discussed shortly, the net effect could be to escalate the conflict in unforeseen and ultimately undesirable ways.

Besides this, another deterrent to American *first* use of ASAT weapons would be the fear of a Soviet response in kind. Whatever the value of satellite reconnaissance to CENTCOM, the United States would be especially keen to watch for warlike preparations in other parts of the world, particularly Eastern Europe, and moreover maintain surveillance of Soviet strategic forces, neither of which can be readily performed by other means. Furthermore, unless the object of U.S. attacks against Soviet intelligence gathering satellites is to buy a short period of respite from overhead surveillance, the United States would have to bank on a fairly intensive ASAT campaign to prevent Soviet overflight of the Gulf region because of the USSR's replenishment capabilities.[13] U.S. planners might be reluctant to commit such resources in the expectation that the conflict could spread to theaters where ASAT operations would be more fruitful. Even if the attack costs were acceptable, it still might be possible for the Soviets to gain the desired intelligence from a newly launched reconnaissance satellite after several orbits and before the United States had gained sufficient targeting information to intercept it. The Soviets can also be expected to redouble their efforts to gain aerial overflight of the region once denied the use of satellites.[14]

Besides photoreconnaissance satellites, other potential U.S. ASAT targets include signals intelligence (SIGINT) and communication satellites, though the benefits from attacking these seem questionable when set against the effort required. It is unclear what immediate tactical advantages would accrue if the United States successfully disabled Soviet SIGINT satellites, while in the latter case the redundancy in Soviet communications so close to their border is likely to be high even if the United States were able to jam or disable a significant portion of the many constellations of communication satellites.

A Soviet ASAT campaign, on the other hand, could prove more

13. According to the 1984 White House report, the U.S. ASAT program "is structured to provide a number of readily available ASAT systems sufficient to counter expected Soviet surge and replenishment." Ronald Reagan, "Report to the Congress on U.S. Policy on ASAT Arms Control," March 31, 1984, p. 12.

14. See Thomas L. McNaugher, *Arms and Oil: U.S. Military Strategy and the Persian Gulf* (Brookings, 1985), pp. 28–29, for a discussion of Soviet air support to the region.

disruptive to U.S. combat performance, with photoreconnaissance satellites again one of the most lucrative targets. Although the Soviets might consider attacking U.S. satellites preparatory to an invasion of Iran, the tactical advantages of a temporary period of American "blindness" would have to be balanced against the strategic warning such an act would give to the West. It is also likely to guarantee U.S. involvement in the defense of the Gulf, something the Soviets might believe they could avoid or delay by refraining from attacks on American military assets at the outset. Once U.S. forces had been committed to the battle, the Soviets would likewise wish to deny U.S. surveillance and the consequent targeting of its own military forces. The Soviets, however, would have to expect the United States to use SR-71s based in Europe and TR-1s and other reconnaissance aircraft operating from airbases in Cyprus, Turkey, the Gulf region, and possibly Israel.[15] In the future long-range remotely piloted vehicles (RPVs) are likely to provide another source of intelligence, further reducing the impact of Soviet attacks against U.S. reconnaissance satellites.

Of potentially far greater hindrance to U.S. military operations in Southwest Asia would be the loss or disruption of satellite communications. The United States would be heavily dependent on satellites for communications to and from the Persian Gulf and, to a lesser extent, for command and control within the region.[16] Although high-frequency (HF) radio links are available they do not offer, as discussed earlier, the same channel capacity, security, and reliability as satellite communications.[17] At present, the only way, short of using nuclear weapons, for the Soviets

15. See McNaugher, *Arms and Oil*, pp. 57–62, for a discussion of likely U.S. operating bases in the region.

16. See Lt. Gen. Robert C. Kingston, USA, "C³I and the U.S. Central Command," *Signal*, vol. 38 (November 1983), pp. 23–25; and James W. Canan, "Fast Track For C³I," *Airforce Magazine*, vol. 67 (July 1984), pp. 49–51.

17. Col. Thomas B. McDonald III, USA, deputy director of command, control, communications and computer systems for the U.S. Central Command, admitted in 1983 that "we have a formidable obstacle to multichannel HF radio. The maximum single-hop path is usually 12–1400 nautical miles. From a city near the center of AOR [area of responsibility], Riyadh, to the closest HF entry in Incirlik, Turkey is 940 nautical miles. To Clark Air Base in the Philippines, it is 4880 nautical miles." "USCENTCOM C³I," *Signal*, vol. 37 (August 1983), p. 89. Besides Incirlik and Clark AB, the other dedicated HF entry point to the Defense Communications System for operations in Southwest Asia is located at RAF Croughton in the United Kingdom. See *Department of Defense Appropriations for Fiscal Year 1984*, Hearings before a Subcommittee of the Senate Committee on Appropriations, 98 Cong. 1 sess. (GPO, 1984), pt. 2, p. 841.

to attack U.S. communication satellites serving the region is to try to jam them. While the Defense Satellite Communications System (DSCS) III satellites positioned over the Atlantic have some antijamming capability, the Fleet Satellite Communications System (FLTSATCOM) and Leased Satellite System (Leasat) spacecraft are likely to be susceptible to this kind of interference. Future systems using the extremely high frequency (EHF) band, however, will reduce this vulnerability.

Besides U.S. photoreconnaissance and communication satellites, other possible Soviet ASAT targets are the Defense Meteorological Satellite Program (DMSP) spacecraft, which would be providing valuable weather information to local commanders. The effect of their loss would depend on whether the United States could still receive equivalent data from its National Oceanic and Atmospheric Administration (NOAA) satellites, which are also vulnerable to Soviet ASAT attack. The Navstar GPS system is another possible target if the Soviets develop a future ASAT system capable of rapidly attacking multiple satellites in the semisynchronous orbit.

Europe

In the event of an invasion of western Europe by members of the Warsaw Pact, it seems doubtful whether NATO's initial defensive operations would be significantly helped by U.S. attacks against Soviet satellites. The redundancy of Warsaw Pact communication systems in the region, and the apparent reliance on non-space-based reconnaissance assets assigned to front line units, suggest that the loss of Soviet satellites would not greatly degrade the performance of the Pact's ground forces at the front.[18] But since Soviet photoreconnaissance satellites—especially future models capable of real-time surveillance—are employed to monitor the whereabouts of NATO's tactical and theater nuclear forces for subsequent targeting by Soviet conventional forces, the United States might consider it desirable if not essential to use ASAT weapons in the early stages of a war.[19] The military benefits of interrupting the

18. Unless otherwise stated material for this section is from Durch, "Anti-Satellite Weapons," pp. 21–24; Stephen M. Meyer, "Soviet Military Programmes and the 'New High Ground,' " *Survival*, vol. 25 (September–October 1983), pp. 204–15; and Gottfried and Lebow, "Anti-Satellite Weapons," pp. 155–60.

19. See Stephen M. Meyer, *Soviet Theatre Nuclear Forces, Part II: Capabilities and Implications*, Adelphi Papers 188 (London: International Institute for Strategic Studies, Winter 1983–84), p. 19. Communication satellites are also likely to be important for coordinating Soviet attacks on NATO theater nuclear forces.

flow of information to the Soviet Union, however, would have to be balanced against the risk that it might also hinder negotiations for the prompt termination of the war.[20] Furthermore, environmental factors, such as the level of cloud cover and the ease with which NATO theater nuclear forces could stay hidden from overhead surveillance, might remove the need for early ASAT use by NATO.

As the war progressed the incentives for U.S. ASAT attacks would probably increase. NATO would be keen to deny Soviet reconnaissance of its rear areas, particularly concentrations of reinforcements, the movement of materiel, and the location of possible counterattacks— information most readily obtained with the aid of photoreconnaissance satellites. Moreover, as the war took its toll on the alternative reconnaissance systems, the payoff from striking Soviet satellites would also increase, though by how much would depend greatly on the speed at which the Soviets could replace their disabled satellites. Short of destroying the space launch facilities and data-processing sites, the United States could do little to prevent this. Even a short hiatus in Soviet coverage, however, might buy vital time for NATO to redeploy forces and prepare a counterattack unobserved by the Pact.

Still, unless the Soviets had already initiated ASAT operations, the United States would also have to consider the prospects of retaliatory attacks against its own satellites. As discussed in chapter 3, NATO benefits considerably from the services satellites provide, although the availability of alternative means is also high. For communicating to and from the continental United States and among its allies, satellites are particularly useful to NATO. The role of reconnaissance satellites in local engagements is also increasing as more timely intelligence becomes available to battlefield commanders. As NATO begins to place greater emphasis on the doctrine of striking deep into Warsaw Pact territory to counter the Pact's second and third attacking echelons, satellites will almost certainly take on a more direct role in long-range targeting. The accuracy and effectiveness of a wide range of NATO's military systems will also improve significantly with the advent of the Navstar Global Positioning System. Finally, for predicting Europe's capricious weather patterns, meteorological satellites will also be highly valued.

Depending on how confident U.S. planners felt about their satellites' ability to withstand a Soviet retaliatory strike, the fear of losing such

20. Carter, "Satellites and Anti-Satellites," p. 78.

valuable assets could deter U.S. first use of ASAT weapons in a NATO-Pact war. Unlike their Soviet counterparts, U.S. satellites, as noted earlier, could not be easily replaced once lost. The effect on NATO's prosecution of the war could be considerable. As a senior analyst with the U.S. Defence Intelligence Agency argues: "The loss of satellite-derived information would greatly compound the unknowns for US commanders. . . . Information on second-echelon attacks from armies in the western USSR would be denied. Soviet ASAT attacks would deny information about the direction, strength, and timing of the general offensive into Western Europe."[21] The loss of overhead reconnaissance could have even more onerous consequences. In the judgment of Richard Perle, a former assistant secretary of defense:

> If, in wartime, the Soviet Union were to attack critical satellites upon which our knowledge of the unfolding conventional war depended, in the absence of an American antisatellite capability I think it is evident that we would have little choice but to escalate in order to deter continuing attacks on our eyes and ears, *without which we could not hope to prosecute successfully a conventional war.*[22]

Perle uses NATO's critical dependency on satellites as the principal justification for a U.S. ASAT deterrent because the Soviets "having assets in space of their own that they wish to protect might well be deterred from launching an initial attack against our satellite capabilities."[23]

Although this may be true, the likelihood of the United States deterring Soviet attacks in space while simultaneously carrying out an ASAT campaign against Soviet military satellites that pose a threat to NATO operations is particularly questionable. As Perle states, "The Soviets have vital intelligence collection systems in space that in a conventional war could well spell the difference between the ability of this country to carry out its NATO obligations and our inability to do so."[24] However, it is hard to imagine prolonged ASAT forbearance by the Soviet Union while its own satellites are being attacked by the United States. As Donald Hafner has observed:

21. James H. Hansen, "Countering NATO's New Weapons: Soviet Concepts for War in Europe," *International Defense Review,* vol. 17 (November 1984), p. 1624.

22. *Department of Defense Authorization for Appropriations for Fiscal Year 1985,* Hearings before the Senate Armed Services Committee, 98 Cong. 2 sess. (GPO, 1984), pt. 7, p. 3452 (emphasis added).

23. Ibid., p. 3453.

24. Ibid.

The United States would need truly awesome ASAT capabilities and satellite defenses if it hoped to deter Soviet ASAT use, even while the U.S. Air Force destroyed selected Soviet satellites. Every Soviet satellite destroyed would also be one fewer held "hostage" in support of ASAT deterrence. Deterrence would require that such hostage satellites be of great value to the Soviets but pose only tolerable threats to U.S. military forces, and be of greater benefit to the Soviets than what they would gain by attacking U.S. satellites.[25]

Given NATO's expected heavy use of satellites during a conflict in Europe, these requirements would be hard to fulfill.

Conflict at Sea

High or even on top of the list of likely U.S. ASAT targets in wartime are the Soviet ocean reconnaissance satellites. The major concern, as discussed in chapter 3, is that information on the movement of U.S. naval units, particularly carrier battle groups and convoys bringing vital supplies to the combat zone, will be relayed to Soviet cruise-missile-carrying submarines, long-range bombers, and even land-based ballistic missiles. Consequently, according to Richard Perle, "maintaining the sea lines of communication between the United States and its NATO Allies in wartime depends vitally on our ability, if necessary, to neutralize satellites that will disclose the location of our fleet and merchantmen, because if one can localize those naval assets the destruction of them is not difficult."[26] The same concern presumably applies to U.S. naval operations against the Soviet ballistic missile submarine (SSBN) bastions and in support of a Persian Gulf or Korean contingency.

Clearly the objective of "neutralizing" the threat from Soviet ocean reconnaissance satellites is a desirable goal, but the use of destructive means to accomplish it, as opposed to such nondestructive countermeasures as jamming, spoofing, and evasive action, poses some significant dilemmas. If the object is to attack Soviet ocean reconnaissance satellites before they have detected the whereabouts of Western naval task forces, then the United States would face the difficult decision of whether to initiate ASAT operations prior to the outbreak of hostilities at sea (and perhaps even elsewhere), and risk widening or escalating the conflict, or

25. Donald L. Hafner, "Approaches to the Control of Antisatellite Weapons," in Durch, ed., *National Interests*, p. 249.

26. *Department of Defense Authorization for Appropriations for Fiscal Year 1985*, Hearings, pt. 7, p. 3453.

to delay, and risk being discovered and destroyed. If the war had already started, the United States would again face the possibility of a Soviet response in kind that might be more damaging to U.S. interests than the original threat. In both cases the United States could be deterred from using its antisatellite weapon system.[27] Furthermore, for a counterattack on Soviet RORSATs and EORSATs to be truly worthwhile, the United States would have to neutralize the other sources of naval intelligence available to the Soviet Union, such as trawlers, submarines, long-range aircraft, and land-based high-frequency direction-finding (HF/DF) systems.

Although the U.S. Air Force continues to cite the denial of Soviet ocean reconnaissance as the primary mission for its ASAT program, the U.S. Navy has not been noticeably concerned with the threat from these satellites. The fact that the U.S. ASAT is an air force rather than a navy program is some indication of this.[28] In part the navy's attitude reflects a low opinion of the Soviet space-based ocean surveillance system. As Vice Admiral Gordon Nagler protested in congressional testimony, "I do not agree with the statement it is very, very easy to target an aircraft carrier by RORSAT or ELINT."[29] The navy also appears confident of being able to meet the threat by other means. In reference to the fleet's vulnerability to satellites, then Secretary of the Navy John Lehman stated before Congress:

> We have been working this problem a long time. . . .
>   . . .[W]e have built our fleet tactics and our own ECM [electronic counter-measures] and other equipment to deal with that. And it is one of the never-ending challenge and response kinds of problems you have to keep working in the electronic field.
>   But the results of the major fleet exercises we have run in the last two years give us some confidence that we know how to cope with those kinds of collectors.[30]

---

27. See Durch, "Anti-Satellite Weapons," pp. 20–21.

28. Some U.S. Navy officials have privately questioned whether the air force can be relied on to perform this mission given the continental air defense tasks that F-15 aircraft based in the United States will be asked to perform in a major war.

29. *Department of Defense Appropriations for 1984*, Hearings before a Subcommittee of the House Committee on Appropriations, 98 Cong. 1 sess. (GPO, 1983), pt. 8, p. 464. Some of the navy's attitude can also be explained by the institutional bias against admitting—certainly publicly—anything that might suggest the vulnerability of its beloved carrier battle groups.

30. *Department of Defense Appropriations for 1984*, Hearings before the House Committee on Appropriations, 98 Cong. 1 sess. (GPO, 1983), pt. 2, p. 631.

Though the information is understandably sparse, the tactics and countermeasures available to the U.S. Navy are known to include the following:

—*Avoid detection*. A basic prerequisite to avoiding detection is knowing when Soviet reconnaissance satellites will pass overhead. The U.S. Navy's Space Command at Dahlgren, Virginia, in association with NORAD sends out daily reconnaissance vulnerability reports known as SATRANS (satellite reconnaissance advance notices) to fleet units.[31] On the basis of this warning, fleet commanders can choose among several evasive measures. One method is to try to stay out of view of the satellite. Since satellites pass over the earth's surface at predictable times and with predictable separation distances between passes, transit routes can be planned to avoid surveillance by changing the speed of advance at appropriate points en route.[32] This method is especially useful against the USSR's radar ocean reconnaissance satellites (RORSATs).

Detection by Soviet electronic ocean reconnaissance satellites (EOR-SATs), which basically listen for and intercept signals, can be avoided by maintaining communication silence and turning off all long-range radars. Known as emission control (EMCON), the U.S. Navy regularly exercises this condition with its ships and has even developed a special system fitted to its aircraft carriers to implement EMCON rapidly in an emergency.[33] The success of both these methods was demonstrated during the 1985 NATO Ocean Safari exercise in which a U.S. carrier task force apparently evaded Soviet detection throughout its passage across the Atlantic. As its commander, Vice Admiral Henry Mustin, reported afterwards:

> When we came across the Atlantic we disappeared from the face of the earth, as far as the Soviets were concerned, some place off Halifax, and

31. Department of the Navy, *Supporting Data for Fiscal Year 1984 Budget Estimates Descriptive Summaries (u): Research, Development, Test and Evaluation, Navy* (Dept. of the Navy, 1983), bk. 1, p. 393; and Jeffrey T. Richelson, *The U.S. Intelligence Community* (Cambridge, Mass.: Ballinger, 1985), p. 79. The Soviets apparently operate a similar system. See Viktor Suvorov, *Inside the Soviet Army* (Macmillan, 1982), pp. 106–07.

32. For details of how this tactic can be implemented on a transatlantic voyage, see Scott Barclay and L. Scott Randall, *Users Manual for the Satellite Surveillance Avoidance Optimization Aid,* Manual 78-1-89 (McLean, Va.: Decisions and Designs, 1978).

33. See Julian S. Lake, "Silent Ships," *Defense Electronics,* vol. 15 (May 1983), pp. 158–59; and Vice Adm. Robert E. Kirksey, "New Communications Technologies: Their Applications and Implications," *Signal,* vol. 39 (November 1984), p. 28.

only resurfaced where we are today (some 650 km west of Hebrides) because we felt like it and I can tell you they were going bananas trying to find us and some of the comments they made were very interesting.[34]

One problem with operating under emission control conditions is that over a lengthy period it can severely degrade combat effectiveness.[35] Satellites, however, only pass overhead for relatively brief periods, though the presence of other electronic intelligence collectors may dictate prolonged EMCON conditions.

—*Minimize target identification*. Rather than deploy naval task forces in tight concentric formations with the carrier(s) at the center, the U.S. Navy now disperses ships in random patterns over large areas—reportedly up to 56,000 square miles—not only to prevent easy identification by overhead Soviet reconnaissance assets, but also to reduce their vulnerability to nuclear attack.[36] Another tactic is to turn the exposed ships in the direction of the radar emitter to reduce their cross sections and thus make the task of identification more difficult.

—*Deceive the sensors*. A third general category of tactics is to deceive the surveillance sensors with misleading information. In its simplest form this can consist of temporarily sailing ships on false courses as the satellite passes overhead or changing the formation of the task force to thwart logical deductions about its composition.[37] Against RORSATS, specially designed corner reflectors or decoys that can simulate the radar signature of several ships can be placed many hundreds of miles away from the fleet to provide false information to the satellites. The U.S. Navy has evidently issued such countersurveillance decoys to its surface fleet.[38] EORSATs, on the other hand, can be spoofed by fake electromagnetic emissions.

34. Stephen Broadbent, "Protection of Convoy Routes a Key Objective for *OCEAN SAFARI 85*," *Jane's Defence Weekly*, vol. 4 (October 5, 1985), p. 752. See also the testimony of Admiral Watkins in *Department of Defense Authorization for Appropriations for Fiscal Year 1985*, Hearings before the Senate Armed Services Committee, 98 Cong. 2 sess. (GPO, 1985), pt. 8, pp. 3885, 3890; and James Canan, *War in Space* (Harper and Row, 1982), p. 105.

35. See testimony of Adm. Noel Gayler (ret.), *Arms Control in Outer Space*, Hearings before the Subcommittee on International Security and Scientific Affairs of the House Committee on Foreign Affairs, 98 Cong. 2 sess. (GPO, 1984), p. 325.

36. *Department of Defense Appropriations for Fiscal Year 1985*, Hearings before the Senate Committee on Appropriations, 98 Cong. 2 sess. (GPO, 1984), pt. 2, p. 357.

37. "Spoofing Soviet Satellites," *Defense Electronics*, vol. 15 (March 1983), p. 28.

38. See R. L. DuBose, "Radar Decoys for Ship Defense: US Solutions," Special Supplement 2 to *International Defense Review: Electronic Warfare* (December 1985),

—*Jam the satellites.* As a last resort, both RORSATs and EORSATs can be jammed. According to retired Admiral Gayler, "the amount of power available to the ship compared to the satellite, decisively favors the jammer."[39] The very act of jamming, however, can reveal the location of the fleet, so care must be taken to avoid alerting the "listening" EORSATs when transmitting jamming signals to the RORSATs. Stand-off jamming away from the fleet may be one solution to this problem.

In many respects these nondestructive methods of dealing with Soviet ocean reconnaissance satellites are preferable to outright disablement. They are, as noted earlier, less escalatory in certain conflict scenarios. Misleading Soviet forces by deception may also be more productive. Although some of the electronic countermeasures are "perishable commodities" in wartime, in that they might not be effective for very long,[40] the U.S. Navy, by all indications, remains confident that it can deal with this threat without resorting to destructive ASAT methods. Furthermore, even if the satellites do succeed in relaying the location of key fleet units to Soviet weapons platforms, the U.S. Navy, as it readily acknowledges, is hardly defenseless against subsequent attacks.[41]

At present, no other class of Soviet space systems poses the same kind of threat to U.S. naval operations as the ocean reconnaissance satellites. The Soviet navy no doubt takes advantage of its communication, navigation, and weather satellites, but it is questionable whether the United States would gain much by attacking these space assets in a naval conflict. In the future the most worrisome threat would be a Soviet space-based submarine detection system, but as discussed earlier, U.S. Navy officials remain confident that this will not be available for ten to fifteen years at the earliest.

Set against what the United States might gain from possessing an ASAT capability to support fleet operations in wartime, one must consider what it might lose by conceding the same opportunities to the Soviet Union. In 1985 Admiral Watkins, then chief of naval operations, noted the U.S. Navy was "the largest tactical user of space-based

---

pp. 49–50. See also *Department of Defense Authorizations for Appropriations for Fiscal Year 1985,* Hearings, pt. 8, p. 4391.

39. *Arms Control in Outer Space,* Hearings, p. 326.

40. Durch, "Anti-Satellite Weapons," p. 20.

41. See *Department of Defense Appropriations for 1985,* Hearings before a Subcommittee of the House Committee on Appropriations, 98 Cong. 2 sess. (GPO, 1984), pt. 2, p. 195.

systems'' among the American armed services and went on to describe
the data supplied by satellites as the navy's "lifeblood. It ensures our
Navy, one-third the size of our potential enemy, can still carry the day
at sea.''[42] Rhetoric aside, there is no doubt that the U.S. Navy benefits
immensely from satellites for communication, navigation, ocean surveillance, antisubmarine operations, and weather forecasting (see chapter 3). If denied their use in time of war, the operational effectiveness of
the fleet could be severely—perhaps critically—impaired. By being the
biggest beneficiary of satellites, the navy has the most to lose.

ASAT Use as a Catalyst to Nuclear War

Before turning to an assessment of the role of ASAT weapons during
a nuclear war, one must ask how their use or threatened use might
precipitate such a conflict. It is important at the outset to draw a
distinction between two categories of ASAT incidents: those that might
start or accelerate the escalatory spiral leading to nuclear war and those
that might specifically trigger nuclear hostilities.[43] In the first category,
the interference with or destruction of a satellite is perceived by the rival
superpower as an unambiguous sign of hostile intent or, at least, a
willingness to escalate. It does not matter whether that was the intention
or not. What is important is the warlike processes that the action sets in
motion. Thus the ASAT-related incident is not in itself the casus belli
but the initiator of a chain reaction that makes war more likely. In the
second case, superpower relations have already deteriorated sufficiently
for both countries to have placed their nuclear forces on a high state of
alert. In such a volatile situation, an ASAT attack would probably
remove any lingering doubts that war was imminent and perhaps provide
the spark to the powder keg.

With regard to the first category, it is possible to conceive of four
instances in which the actual or perceived use of ASAT weapons could
set the superpowers on the road to nuclear war.

42. Adm. James D. Watkins, chief of naval operations, "Attaining the Weather-
Gauge of Space," remarks delivered at the Naval Space Symposium, Naval Post
Graduate School, Monterey, California, May 21, 1985.

43. Parts of this section are from Paul B. Stares, "Nuclear Operations and Anti-
satellites," in Ashton B. Carter, John D. Steinbruner, and Charles A. Zraket, eds.,
Managing Nuclear Operations (Brookings, 1987), pp. 679–703.

—*Tactical use*. As demonstrated earlier, at the beginning of or during a conventional conflict involving U.S. and Soviet forces, the incentives to use ASAT weapons to gain tactical advantage on the battlefield may become irresistible. But because some satellites support both conventional and nuclear forces, their destruction could prove escalatory. For example, in addition to their tactical applications, photoreconnaissance and electronic reconnaissance satellites would be used to provide status reports on the whereabouts and readiness of each side's strategic nuclear forces. Though these forces are likely to be already on a high state of alert, even the temporary loss of overhead reconnaissance could create dangerous uncertainties about an adversary's ultimate intentions. As William Durch has argued, "If one side views space as a quasi-sanctuary while the other considers it part of the local battlefield, the scale of response to ASAT use could be grossly disproportionate to the attacker's actual intent, whatever the actual operational effect of the attack for either side."[44]

—*Intimidatory use*. Deliberate interference with satellites to exhibit resolve in a crisis provides yet another possible source for superpower conflict. Space, in many respects, offers significant attractions as a medium for brinkmanship. As Air Force General Thomas Stafford has observed: "Conflict in space does not violate national boundaries, does not kill people, and can provide a very visible show of determination at relatively modest cost."[45] But, depending on which satellites are affected, such actions could be perceived as highly inflammatory by an adversary, again causing unintended escalation of a crisis.

—*Retaliatory use*. The use of ASATs in retaliation for other activities may have a similar effect. Horizontal escalation of this sort might be considered either more practicable or desirable than a response in kind. But again, such strategy might prove ill founded and result in unforeseen consequences, not the least being vertical escalation.

—*Misattributed use*. Though unlikely, an accident in space—such as a technical malfunction or collision with a piece of space debris—might be attributed to an ASAT attack and cause a major crisis. The significance of such an incident would clearly depend on the state of superpower relations, the importance of the affected satellite(s), and the details of

44. Durch, "Anti-Satellite Weapons," p. 21.
45. *Department of Defense Authorization for Appropriations for Fiscal Year 1980*, Hearings before the Senate Committee on Armed Services, 96 Cong. 1 sess. (GPO, 1979), pt. 6, p. 3019.

the event. In periods of high tension the inexplicable loss of an important satellite would be the cause of some alarm and suspicion. Such a coincidence is highly improbable, but again it cannot be discounted.[46] A more plausible variation on misattributed ASAT use would involve third parties; that is, other states might want to interfere with U.S. and Soviet satellites, particularly if the superpowers were also involved in the war. But the affected superpower might believe such interference to be the work of the other, again setting off an unwarranted spiral of events.

The second category of ASAT incidents could occur if the situation had deteriorated to a point where on both sides nuclear forces were already primed for launch. Here the incentives to use ASAT weapons— aside from the potential military benefits—would depend on whether war was considered inevitable or still avoidable. If the latter, satellite attacks might be considered too provocative, although they could pale in comparison to the events that had brought the superpowers to the brink of war. If war was considered imminent, then, for the following reasons, the pressure to use ASAT weapons could become irresistible, tipping the superpowers over the brink.

—*Preemptive use.* Given the present redundancy of superpower strategic command and control systems, neither side is likely to feel so dependent on its satellites, at least for basic retaliation, as to make preemptive ASAT use either a compelling fear or a compelling opportunity. Neither side is likely to believe that an ASAT attack, however comprehensive and swift, would preclude nuclear retaliation by the adversary. But either side may believe—especially if prompt high-altitude ASAT systems are developed—that its use of ASATs could limit the extent of the retaliation and improve its likelihood of prevailing in a nuclear conflict. This belief could encourage the use of ASATs to provide an added advantage at the outset of hostilities. For example, while the loss of U.S. early warning satellites would in itself provide a strong indication that a nuclear strike was imminent, it would remove the United States' ability to make prompt judgments about the extent and nature of the Soviet strike until ground-based radars had provided their own assessment. Similarly, while the loss of key communication satellites like Milstar would not prevent the transmission of emergency action messages, it would make the control of subsequent U.S. strategic operations more difficult.

46. See Eliot Marshall, "Space Junk Grows with Weapons Test," *Science,* vol. 230 (October 25, 1985), pp. 424–25.

However, the possible incentives for using ASAT weapons at the outset of a war, in terms of the confusion, disruption, and perhaps even momentary paralysis it could cause to an adversary, have to be set against the equal probability that it could have quite the opposite effect. Instead of reducing the level of retaliation, it might encourage a massive "spasm" response from one's opponent. Although both superpowers can be expected to compensate for the growing vulnerability of their key satellites by ensuring greater redundancy, it might also lead them to adopt measures that could prove destabilizing in a crisis. For example, as one analyst has argued, that fear might encourage raising the level of a nuclear alert much earlier and to a higher level than would otherwise be necessary in anticipation of an ASAT attack.[47]

—*Preventive use*. In addition to the anxieties that an adversary might use an ASAT system preemptively to impede retaliation, there is the concern that its satellites might also be used to aid a first strike. The future deployment of surveillance systems that will permit real-time targeting of mobile land-based systems, command posts, and even submarines is the prime—albeit distant—possibility here. If war is considered likely, the presence of such sensors could provoke ASAT attacks to prevent their use. Though the surveillance systems provide the destabilizing factor in this case, it is still the use of ASAT weapons that would most likely precipitate war.

ASAT Use during Nuclear War

Once an intercontinental nuclear war had begun, the incentive to attack anything that might enhance an opponent's war-fighting capabilities and reduce the level of damage to one's own side would be tempered only by the fear that the conflict might thereby become uncontrollable. Satellites will clearly be high on the list of likely targets. But the ability to carry out ASAT attacks in a carefully orchestrated way for very long in a nuclear war is doubtful. Not only are ASAT deployment sites (launch pads, airfields, and in the future laser facilities) vulnerable, but also the space surveillance systems necessary for targeting satellites will almost

47. See Hafner, "Approaches to the Control of Antisatellite Weapons," in Durch, ed., *National Interests*, pp. 241–42; and Donald Hafner, "Potential Negotiated Measures for ASAT Arms Control," in Joseph S. Nye, Jr., ed., *Seeking Stability in Space* (University Press of America, forthcoming).

certainly be destroyed. Indeed, the anticipated destruction of these facilities might hasten the use of ASAT weapons.

Once the dedicated ASAT systems had been rendered inoperable, either side could turn to the use of nuclear weapons for attacking satellites provided that the targeting facilities had also survived. Although the prospect of collateral damage to friendly satellites might deter either side from early use and perhaps even encourage tacit mutual restraint, the perceived advantages of attacking first (especially if the use of nuclear weapons is considered to be inevitable anyway) might outweigh such concerns. Some have argued, however, that attacks on satellites would soon become irrelevant because of the destruction of the associated ground stations and data-processing facilities. But as the satellite ground segment is made more survivable (principally through proliferation and mobility) and the spacecraft themselves become less dependent on ground stations, the usefulness of ASAT attacks will increase.

The effect of such attacks on the outcome of the war is obviously impossible to gauge. Some have even argued that these attacks "would not significantly affect the course of a nuclear war *once it had begun*."[48] But it seems fair to argue that they would probably make the war less manageable and harder to terminate. As discussed in chapter 3, communication satellites could prove vital for maintaining lines between the national command authorities and any remaining nuclear forces. Similarly, nuclear detection and other space reconnaissance systems would probably be the only source of intelligence for managing these forces in a meaningful way, if indeed their use still had any meaning. The problem, of course, is that the value of those systems as battle management aids marks them as ASAT targets. Once they are lost, the prospect of disseminating cease-fire orders or ensuring compliance with a war termination agreement would inevitably diminish.[49] Thus, while the use of dedicated antisatellite systems will most likely decline rapidly after the first nuclear exchange, the loss of satellite services by other means will contribute to the chaos and make the war less controllable.

Conclusion

The situations in which dedicated ASAT weapons could be of some benefit to the United States appear to be confined to a narrow band on

48. Gottfried and Lebow, "Anti-Satellite Weapons," p. 160 (emphasis in original).
49. Ibid., p. 162.

the conflict spectrum—essentially conventional engagements between the superpowers in places like Southwest Asia and Europe. At lower levels of conflict, the risks of widening the crisis or war outweigh what are already doubtful military benefits, while the worth and relevance of ASAT attacks in a prolonged strategic nuclear exchange are questionable. Even in the conflict scenarios in which ASAT attacks seem to offer some tangible benefits, the presence of alternative, nonsatellite systems and the adversary's ability to reconstitute space assets rapidly could significantly reduce the desired effect.

In judging the potential benefits of using ASAT weapons, both sides would also have to consider the prospect of retaliatory attacks against their own satellites. Though on balance the United States has more to lose in an ASAT exchange, especially if high-altitude weapons are deployed in the future, the Soviets also clearly value the support that satellites provide. In this sense, both sides are likely to think twice before initiating an ASAT attack unless the benefits heavily outweigh the possible retribution. The belief that the United States can deter Soviet attacks on its satellites at the same time it attempts to destroy Soviet satellites is extremely doubtful.

This begs the basic question of whether there is a need for a U.S. ASAT system beyond its role as a deterrent, especially if these weapons can be banned through arms control. For the time being at least, nondestructive methods for neutralizing the most worrisome Soviet space systems, namely those used for ocean surveillance, appear adequate. Although the tactical incentives to develop additional ASAT capabilities could grow in the future, these should be weighed carefully against the broader impact that the possession of such systems could have on strategic stability. Unless Soviet space systems begin to undermine the United States' ability to retaliate effectively, ASATs provide at best marginal benefits for U.S. national security. Moreover, in a severe superpower crisis the potential for their use could prove a serious liability to strategic stability. Overall it is hard to disagree with the assessment that "ASATs possess a considerably greater capacity for transforming a crisis into a war, and for enlarging wars, than they do for assisting in military missions or enhancing deterrence."[50]

50. Ibid., p. 148.

CHAPTER SIX

Arms Control in Space

GIVEN the doubts that exist about the benefits of antisatellite weapons for U.S. national security, it is appropriate to consider whether a negotiated arms control agreement can meaningfully curb their development. The incentives seem obvious. The United States could limit the threat to its more valuable satellite systems and head off a costly, fruitless, and potentially destabilizing arms competition in space. The timing also seems right. The fact that ASAT weapons have yet to be extensively deployed or gain an entrenched constituency suggests that a committed effort to control them would not meet the kind of military and bureaucratic resistence that so often hinders the limitation of more established weapon systems. And since space is a relatively discrete area of activity, one might hope the task could be pursued without becoming hopelessly burdened with the political baggage of other arms control negotiations.

Contrary to this initial assessment, the problems facing space arms control are deceptively large and complex. One of the more challenging is that ASAT weapons cannot be clearly defined or easily delimited. As chapter 4 illustrates, there is a large "grey area" of weapon systems that can be used for ASAT purposes but are either unverifiable (such as electronic countermeasures) or outside the rightful purview of space arms control (such as nuclear-armed ballistic missiles). How to address these residual ASAT systems is a major stumbling block. Even limits on dedicated ASAT weapons will not be easy to negotiate or verify. To monitor compliance and deter cheating in places that may be tens of thousands of kilometers from earth is a formidable task, even with the most sophisticated sensors. The unavoidable similarities between commonplace space activities and possible antisatellite incidents further reduces the level of confidence.

These problems, however, pale beside the latest and potentially largest obstacle to space arms control. Since the Strategic Defense Initiative (SDI) was launched in 1983, resistance to any agreement that might constrain U.S. freedom of action to pursue research on ballistic missile defense has steadily risen. Because of the almost symbiotic relationship between BMD research and ASAT development, placing constraints on ASAT weapons could hamper the antimissile program in major ways. Thus, while antisatellite weapons may not have a large constituency pushing for deployment, the continuing high-level support for the SDI has become an effective surrogate.

The purpose of this chapter is to discuss the obstacles to space arms control in greater detail and assess the feasibility of a range of options for limiting ASAT weapons. The obvious starting point is a review of existing constraints on military activities in space and the most recent space arms control initiatives.

The Current Space Arms Control Regime

Space arms control has a long and checkered history. Beginning in the 1950s, the prospect of space becoming militarized prompted a series of proposals to preserve it as a sanctuary from the arms race. Though the use of military satellites soon dashed hopes for a completely demilitarized zone, a good deal of progress was made in either prohibiting or curtailing weapons-related activities in space. A convenient conjunction of sentiments and interests made this possible.

Space was and continues to be viewed by many in a romantic light, as an area that can be kept free of humanity's baser instincts and desires. A frequent exhortation is that space should be exploited for solely peaceful purposes and for the benefit of all mankind without national claim or jurisdiction. Initially at least, these aspirations dovetailed with hard military logic. Except for the support functions described in chapter 3, there was for a long time little incentive to use space for other military ends, notably weapons deployment. Orbital bombardment systems offered few if any advantages over intercontinental ballistic missiles. ICBMs were also likely to be less accident prone and provocative. Space-based ballistic missile defense systems—though superficially attractive—were deemed technically infeasible or prohibitively expensive. Furthermore, as long as the Soviet military space program remained relatively innocuous, there was little need for a U.S. ASAT system other than a limited capability to hedge against the deployment of orbital nuclear bombs. Moreover, to secure Soviet and international acquiescence in reconnaissance from space, the United States actively encouraged the principle that space be used solely for peaceful, that is, nonaggressive, purposes. Despite early opposition, the Soviets eventually recognized the benefits of military satellites and accepted—if only tacitly—the U.S. conception of peaceful space activities. The superpowers subsequently agreed to a variety of additional measures for regulating the military use of space, although it is fair to point out that this has not always been the principal intent of the relevant agreements.[1]

The earliest space arms control measure of any import was the Limited Test Ban Treaty of 1963. Article 1 of this treaty prohibits "any nuclear weapon test explosion, or any other nuclear explosion," in the atmosphere, under water, and in outer space.[2] Four years later the *deployment* of such weapons in space also was banned, by the Outer Space Treaty of 1967, article 4 of which prohibits the placing "in orbit around the earth any objects carrying nuclear weapons or any other kinds of weapons of mass destruction."[3] The unratified and now expired 1979 SALT II (strategic arms limitation) treaty later extended this prohibition by further banning "fractional orbital missiles" (essentially, ICBMs that do not complete a revolution of the earth).[4] In addition, article 9 of the Outer

1. For further details see Paul B. Stares, *The Militarization of Space: U.S. Policy, 1945–1984* (Ithaca, N.Y.: Cornell University Press, 1985), chaps. 2, 3. The full texts of the agreements discussed in this chapter can be found in *Space Law: Selected Basic Documents*, 2d ed., Committee Print, Senate Committee on Commerce, Science, and Transportation, 95 Cong. 2 sess. (Government Printing Office, 1978); and U.S. Arms Control and Disarmament Agency, *Arms Control and Disarmament Agreements: Texts and Histories of Negotiations* (Washington, D.C.: ACDA, 1982) (hereafter *Arms Control and Disarmament Agreements*).

2. Formally entitled "Treaty Banning Nuclear Weapon Tests in the Atmosphere, in Outer Space and Under Water." Besides its obvious implications, there is one the negotiators of this agreement could not have foreseen: it is a barrier to the testing of nuclear-pumped X-ray lasers in space, which are currently being considered under the SDI program.

3. Formally entitled "Treaty on Principles Governing the Activities of States in the Exploration and Use of Outer Space, Including the Moon and Other Celestial Bodies." This in effect converted UN Resolution 1884 of 1963 into a more permanent agreement.

4. Article 9, 1(C). The Second Common Understanding to article 7 also includes arrangements for the dismantling of the eighteen Soviet fractional orbital missile launchers.

Space Treaty requires international consultations before any planned space activity or experiment if the state conducting it has reason to believe it may cause harmful interference with the activities of other states. The Outer Space Treaty also explicitly states that activities in space be carried out in accordance with international law including the UN Charter, thereby indirectly prohibiting the use of force in space except in self-defense.[5]

A more specific, though admittedly still ambiguous, limitation on harmful interference with satellites is contained in the 1972 SALT I accords. Both the Interim Agreement on the Limitation of Strategic Offensive Forces and the Antiballistic Missile Treaty include articles in which the United States and Soviet Union agree "not to interfere with the national technical means of verification of the other Party."[6] Although a commonly accepted definition of national technical means (NTM) has never been reached, it is generally understood to include reconnaissance satellites.[7]

In light of the SDI's emphasis on research and development of space-based ballistic missile defenses, one of the most important clauses of the ABM treaty is article 5. This states explicitly that "each party undertakes not to develop, test, or deploy ABM systems or components which are sea-based, air-based, space-based, or mobile land-based." Furthermore, Agreed Statement D to the treaty also includes the commitment that if ABM systems "based on other physical principles" are developed in the future, "specific limitations on such systems and their components would be subject to discussion." At the time the agreement was reached the term "other physical principles" was generally understood—certainly by the U.S. delegation—to encompass lasers and particle beam technology.[8] Despite Reagan administration pronouncements to the contrary, the weight of legal opinion is that Agreed Statement D does not provide a loophole for testing such advanced ABM systems in space.[9]

---

5. See *Fiscal Year 1986 Arms Control Impact Statements*, 99 Cong. 1 sess. (GPO, 1985), p. 224.

6. Articles 5(i) and 12 respectively. This provision has been reaffirmed by the 1974 Threshold Test Ban Treaty, the 1976 Peaceful Nuclear Explosion Treaty, and the SALT II treaty, all of which have yet to be ratified by the United States.

7. For a discussion of the possible ambiguities surrounding this clause, see Stares, *Militarization of Space*, pp. 165–66.

8. See ibid., pp. 166–67; and *Arms Control and Disarmament Agreements*, pp. 140, 143.

9. Don Oberdorfer, "White House Revises Interpretation of ABM Treaty," *Washington Post*, October 9, 1985. For a full discussion of this issue, see Alan B. Sherr,

Other, more tangentially related agreements that have often been cited as part of the existing space arms control regime include the 1971 and 1984 Direct Communications Link, or hot-line, improvement agreements. Here both parties agreed "to take all possible measures to assure the continuous and reliable operation" of the network's satellite communication links and terminals. Likewise, the 1973 International Telecommunication Convention obligates each party "not to cause harmful interference to the radio services or communications of other Members." Similarly, the 1971 U.S.-Soviet Accident Measures Agreement calls upon both parties to notify the other in the event of interference with missile early warning and related communication systems, although it does not explicitly prohibit interference with them.[10] Finally, the Environmental Modification Convention signed in 1977 bans the military or hostile use of ENMOD techniques—sometimes referred to as weather warfare—in space and other environments. Table 6-1 encapsulates the current space arms control regime.

Extensive though the space arms control regime may be, there are still significant gaps in its coverage. The development, testing, and deployment of ground-based or space-based *nonnuclear* antisatellite systems, to name the most significant lacunae, are not prohibited by existing agreements. Fixed ground-based ABM systems that can reach targets in space using conventional, nuclear, or directed-energy kill mechanisms are also permissible. Even prohibitions on the harmful interference with satellites are ambiguous at best and incomplete at worst. In short, the scope for further space weapons development within the confines of the current arms control regime is considerable.

Recent Initiatives

Though not widely publicized at the time, a brief but promising set of superpower negotiations took place in 1978–79 that specifically focused

---

"Sound Legal Reasoning or Policy Expedient? The 'New Interpretation' of the ABM Treaty," *International Security*, vol. 11 (Winter 1986–87), pp. 71–93; Abram Chayes and Antonia Handler Chayes, "Testing and Development of 'Exotic' Systems under the ABM Treaty: The Great Reinterpretation Caper," *Harvard Law Review*, vol. 99 (June 1986), pp. 1956–71; and Abraham D. Sofaer, "The ABM Treaty and the Strategic Defense Initiative," ibid., pp. 1979–85.

10. Article 3, Agreement on Measures to Reduce the Risk of Outbreak of Nuclear War Between the United States of America and the Union of Soviet Socialist Republics. For text see *Arms Control and Disarmament Agreements*, pp. 111–12.

Table 6-1. *The Space Arms Control Regime, 1987*

Prohibition	Agreement(s)
Nuclear detonations	Limited Test Ban Treaty of 1963, article 1
Deployment of nuclear weapons and weapons of mass destruction	Outer Space Treaty of 1967, article 4; SALT II Treaty,[a] article 9
Deployment of fractional orbital missiles	SALT II Treaty,[a] articles 7, 9
Testing, development, and deployment of antiballistic missile systems or components	Antiballistic Missile Treaty of 1972, article 5
Use of force in space[b]	Outer Space Treaty of 1967, article 3
Harmful interference with national technical means of verification or specified systems	Antiballistic Missile Treaty of 1972, article 12; Direct Communications Link improvement agreements of 1971 and 1984, article 2; International Telecommunication Convention of 1973, article 35; SALT II Treaty,[a] article 15
Use of environmental modification techniques	Environmental Modification Convention of 1977, articles 1, 2

Sources: *Space Law: Selected Basic Documents*, 2d ed., Committee Print, Senate Committee on Commerce, Science, and Transportation, 95 Cong. 2 sess. (Government Printing Office, 1978); and U.S. Arms Control and Disarmament Agency, *Arms Control and Disarmament Agreements: Texts and Histories of Negotiations*, 1980 ed. (Washington, D.C.: ACDA, 1980).
a. Never ratified by the United States, now expired.
b. Except in self-defense, under article 51 of the UN Charter.

on limiting antisatellite weapons.[11] The three rounds of talks held between the United States and Soviet Union in Helsinki, Bern, and Vienna were instructive in showing that an ASAT arms agreement would not be as easy to conclude as many had first believed. Significant differences emerged between the two sides on such issues as the role of the U.S. space shuttle and the presence of the operational Soviet antisatellite system. Although it became apparent in later rounds that the best that could be hoped for in the near term was an agreement that banned the use but not the testing of antisatellite weapons, even this modest goal caused numerous arguments. Debates over whether the space systems of allied nations would be covered by a bilateral agreement and whether there were mitigating circumstances in which ASAT attacks could be deemed justifiable and legitimate proved significant obstacles.

11. Unless otherwise indicated the sources of information on the 1978–79 negotiations are Stares, *Militarization of Space*, pp. 192–99; and Walter Slocombe, "Approaches to an ASAT Treaty," in Bhupendra Jasani, ed., *Space Weapons—The Arms Control Dilemma* (London: Taylor and Francis, 1984), pp. 149–50.

Nevertheless, by the end of the third round, the framework for a draft banning the use as distinct from the possession of antisatellite weapons had been tentatively agreed to. There was an expectation that further discussions would lead to a successful conclusion. But, as the Carter administration became more preoccupied with the struggle for SALT II ratification and as relations with the Soviet Union deteriorated steadily over Cuba, Iran, and finally Afghanistan, the prospects for further ASAT negotiations receded. While never officially terminated these specific talks have been in abeyance since 1979.

Throughout President Reagan's first term, initiatives for space arms control came almost solely from the Soviet Union. Despite frequent leadership changes, the Soviets put forward a string of proposals, including two draft treaties before the United Nations, and announced a unilateral ASAT test moratorium conditional on U.S. reciprocity. All were accompanied by exhortations on the need to prevent the "militarization of outer space."

The first of the draft treaty proposals, which came in August 1981, appeared to build on the earlier U.S.-Soviet discussions in proposing both a prohibition on the use of force in space and a ban on the stationing of "weapons of any kind" in orbit.[12] Though it was treated by the United States as if it were a propaganda exercise rather than a serious proposal, the draft treaty represented a significant departure from the earlier Soviet position. In addition to dropping their opposition to the U.S. space shuttle (except to its use as a weapon system), the Soviets also signaled that both superpowers could maintain their existing and planned ground-based ASAT systems under the agreement, since only space-based ASAT systems would be banned. Although less than comprehensive, the proposed arrangement nevertheless offered some constraint without curbing each side's existing ASAT programs. But the United States summarily dismissed the Soviet proposal as being defective without making, it appears, any serious attempt to probe the Soviet position or respond with a counteroffer.

Soviet calls to halt the spread of the arms race to outer space continued unabated throughout 1982 and reached a new intensity in the summer of 1983. Whether this new vigor was the result of the announcement in

12. Formally entitled "Soviet Draft Treaty Submitted to the U.N. General Assembly: Prohibition of the Stationing of Weapons of Any Kind in Outer Space," August 11, 1981. See especially articles 1 and 3, in U.S. Arms Control and Disarmament Agency, *Documents on Disarmament, 1981* (GPO, 1985), pp. 333–34.

March 1983 of the U.S. Strategic Defense Initiative or Soviet anticipation of the start of the U.S. ASAT testing program can only be surmised. Whatever the reason, Soviet objectives had unmistakably changed, reflecting, in the view of some, a significant hardening of attitudes.[13] The new Soviet offensive began on August 19 with the declaration by Soviet General Secretary Yuri V. Andropov to a group of visiting U.S. Senators that

> the U.S.S.R. assumes the commitment not to be the first to put into outer space any type of antisatellite weapon, that is, imposes a unilateral moratorium on such launchings for the entire period during which other countries, including the U.S.A., will refrain from stationing in outer space antisatellite weapons of any type.[14]

The next day, Soviet Foreign Minister Andrei A. Gromyko presented a second draft space treaty to the UN secretary general.[15] It was far more comprehensive than the 1981 proposal in prohibiting among other things the testing and deployment of "any space-based weapons intended to hit targets on the Earth, in the atmosphere, or in space," the testing and creation of "new anti-satellite systems," and the testing and use of "manned spacecraft for military, including anti-satellite purposes." Perhaps the most novel aspect of this draft treaty (besides the renewed opposition to the shuttle) was that it also called on parties to "destroy any anti-satellite systems that they may already have" (article 2.4). The Soviets were, in effect, offering to dismantle their existing co-orbital ASAT.[16] In a single stroke, they had become the standard bearers for comprehensive ASAT limits, thus completely reversing the positions held by the two sides at the earlier, bilateral talks.

The official U.S. response was again negative: no counterproposal or even diplomatic probing of the Soviet position was attempted. Instead the draft treaty was criticized for its insufficient verification procedures,

13. See testimony of John D. Steinbruner, *Arms Control in Outer Space*, Hearings before the House Committee on Foreign Affairs, 98 Cong. (GPO, 1984), p. 28.

14. John F. Burns, "Andropov Issues a Promise on Antisatellite Weapons," *New York Times*, August 19, 1983.

15. Conclusion of a Treaty on the Prohibition of the Use of Force in Outer Space and from Space against the Earth, UN General Assembly Document A/38/194 (August 23, 1983).

16. For an interesting exposition of the draft treaties by a Soviet official, see Boris Mayorsky, "The USSR Initiative in the Struggle for Peace in Outer Space," in Nandasiri Jasentuliyana, ed., *Maintaining Outer Space for Peaceful Uses* (Tokyo: United Nations University Press, 1984), pp. 290–97.

its failure to encompass Soviet residual ASAT capabilities, and its prohibition of the space shuttle.[17] The impasse continued for the rest of 1983 and well into 1984, with official Soviet condemnations shifting increasingly away from the U.S. ASAT program to focus on the SDI. The deaths of Andropov and later Konstantin U. Chernenko did little to interrupt the momentum of the Soviet campaign.

Responding to still more calls by the Soviets for an ASAT test ban and in particular to growing congressional dissatisfaction with the official U.S. position, the White House began to moderate its opposition to talks on space weaponry. A flurry of promising diplomatic activity in the fall of 1984, however, ended in nothing more than mutual recriminations.[18] After the reelection of President Reagan, the negotiating thread was once again taken up, resulting in "talks about talks" between Gromyko and Secretary of State George P. Shultz at Geneva in January 1985. Here both sides agreed to resume discussions on strategic and intermediate-range nuclear weapons and committed themselves "to work out effective agreements aimed at preventing an arms race in space."[19] Although three baskets of negotiations along these lines did eventually begin in Geneva, little progress had been made by mid-1987 on the issue of space weapons. Not surprisingly, the chief bone of contention has been the Strategic Defense Initiative.

By the end of 1985, the Soviet diplomatic offensive had become focused almost solely on the SDI, with markedly less attention paid to ASAT weapons.[20] One important exception came just before the first test of the U.S. ASAT against a target in space in September 1985. *Tass* announced that it had been authorized to state that if the test went ahead, the Soviet Union "would consider itself free of its unilateral commitment not to place anti-satellite systems in space."[21]

17. See *Fiscal Year 1986 Arms Control Impact Statements*, pp. 228–29. For other views, see William J. Durch, "Anti-Satellite Weapons, Arms Control Options, and the Military Use of Space," prepared for the U.S. Arms Control and Disarmament Agency (Washington, D.C.: ACDA, 1984), pp. 51–52; and John Pike, "Limits on Space Weapons: The Soviet Initiatives and the American Response," F.A.S. Staff Study (Federation of American Scientists, September 1983).

18. See Stares, *Militarization of Space*, pp. 233–35; and *Fiscal Year 1986 Arms Control Impact Statements*, pp. 233–38.

19. Text of joint communiqué, cited in Dusko Doder, "U.S., Soviets to Resume Arms Talks," *Washington Post*, January 9, 1985.

20. See Walter Pincus, "Soviets Turn Silent on Antisatellite Arms," *Washington Post*, February 7, 1985.

21. "Tass Statement on 'Unilateral Commitment' to ASAT," in Foreign Broadcast Information Service, *Daily Report: Soviet Union*, September 5, 1985, p. AA1.

Paradoxically, the subsequent test appeared to antagonize the U.S. Congress more than the Soviet Union. The reason for this stems from earlier congressionally mandated constraints on U.S. ASAT testing. Beginning with the Department of Defense appropriations bill for fiscal 1984, Congress agreed to release ASAT procurement funds on the condition that it receive, no later than March 31, 1984, a report from the White House on U.S. ASAT arms control policy.[22] Although the report was duly transmitted, it did little to quell growing congressional skepticism of the administration's declared commitment to seeking ASAT arms control. Consequently, the language of the following year's Defense appropriations bill was even more constrictive in allowing only three ASAT tests against objects in space. Furthermore, Congress insisted that before testing could take place, the president had to certify that the United States was "endeavoring in good faith, to negotiate with the Soviet Union a mutual and verifiable agreement with the strictest possible limitations on antisatellite weapons consistent with the national security interests of the United States."[23] Although the certification was again delivered on time, many legislators were angered that it was submitted while Congress was still in recess, thereby effectively preempting potential opposition, and that it contained nothing more than a restatement of the March 31, 1984, report. Many questioned whether the administration was indeed endeavoring in good faith to negotiate an ASAT agreement, especially since the White House text also stated—somewhat contradicting itself—that no such agreement had yet been found to be in the national security interests of the United States.[24] The fact that the September 1985 U.S. ASAT test was carried out against a still-functioning scientific satellite, which the air force claimed to be defunct, rather than against an Instrumented Test Vehicle, did nothing to allay congressional suspicions that the administration was not fulfilling its part of the bargain. As a result, Congress imposed a complete ban on further U.S. ASAT testing against objects in space, subject to Soviet reciprocity, in the fiscal 1986 Defense appropriations bill.[25] The ban was

22. For a concise account of the various congressional actions, see U.S. Congress, Office of Technology Assessment, *Anti-Satellite Weapons, Countermeasures, and Arms Control* (GPO, 1985), pp. 99–101.

23. *Making Continuing Appropriations for the Fiscal Year 1985, and for Other Purposes*, Conference Report 98-1159, 98 Cong. 2 sess. (GPO, 1984), p. 109.

24. See "White House Message on Anti-Satellite Arms," *New York Times*, August 21, 1985.

25. *House Joint Resolution 465, Further Continuing Appropriations for Fiscal Year 1986*, Conference Report 99–450, 99 Cong. 1 sess. (GPO, 1985), sec. 8097, p. 37.

later extended for fiscal 1987. Though the air force can still test against points in space (such as the radiant emissions from stars), the ban is a severe setback to its plans. It does, however, provide some breathing space for the United States to reconsider its opposition to ASAT limits.

The Obstacles to ASAT Arms Control

Even with the necessary political commitment, ASAT arms control confronts serious problems. Five obstacles stand out: the pressure to maintain a dedicated ASAT capability; the presence of an already tested Soviet ASAT system; the unavoidable existence of residual ASAT capabilities; the problem of verifying ASAT limitations; and finally the close relationship between ASAT and BMD development. To a great extent these problems overlap. For instance, doubts about verification largely spring from the presence of residual antisatellite capabilities, which in turn is related to the state of BMD development. As will become evident shortly in the survey of arms control options, the significance of these obstacles varies according to the kind of limitations one is trying to reach.

—*The pressure to maintain an ASAT capability*. Perhaps the most fundamental obstacle to ASAT arms control is the concern that it would leave the United States defenseless against the threat from Soviet space systems. Even though an ASAT agreement need not limit dedicated antisatellite systems entirely (leaving aside residual capabilities as well), some opponents consider even the most modest limitations unacceptable and dangerously shortsighted. Whatever the nature of the Soviet space threat today, they argue, it may be entirely different tomorrow. In fact, as noted before, constraining ASAT weaponry may have the paradoxical side effect of stimulating the development of the very space systems (such as new surveillance satellites) that would make an ASAT capability desirable if not essential. But just as a projection of threats from future Soviet *satellite* systems should be part of any U.S. net assessment of ASAT arms control, so the assessment must also include a projection of threats from future Soviet *antisatellite* systems that might evolve in the absence of constraints. Furthermore, arms control agreements need not be of unlimited duration. If the Soviet satellite threat became sufficiently worrisome, then continued U.S. adherence could be reviewed.

—*The current Soviet ASAT system*. The presence of an operational

Soviet system for intercepting satellites has convinced many that the United States should seek at least a comparable capability before it considers any limitations on its own ASAT system. An active U.S. program, it is further argued, would also increase Soviet incentives to negotiate and provide additional bargaining leverage once discussions began. But the process of "catching up" with the Soviets may actually prejudice the outcome or even resumption of the talks. Reaching an agreement will undoubtedly be harder if there are two—in this case markedly different—systems to take into consideration.

Even in the absence of an operational U.S. system negotiators would face the tricky problem—if a comprehensive ban is the ultimate goal—of dismantling the current Soviet ASAT boosters and interceptor vehicles. Since it is unclear how many of these were manufactured, doubts would remain about covertly deployed stocks. As is often pointed out, the small numbers of high-value U.S. satellites mean that even a handful of covertly deployed Soviet ASATs could inflict considerable damage, although this fear could be mitigated somewhat by increasing the redundancy of exposed U.S. satellites. The monitoring problems would also be mitigated if deployment of the current Soviet ASAT system were allowed under the terms of an agreement, but even then the United States would run some risk of clandestine Soviet conversions and improvements. Ultimately, however, the threat from small numbers of covertly deployed systems has to be balanced against the threat of large numbers of *overtly* deployed ASATs.

—*Residual ASAT systems*. Defining at the outset what constitutes an ASAT weapon and hence what could be subject to control presents another formidable task. According to the Reagan administration's definition an "'ASAT capability' relates to all systems capable of damaging, destroying or otherwise interrupting the functioning of satellites," a formulation which, they are quick to point out, includes a wide range of weapons specifically designed for other purposes but which nevertheless have an inherent potential for use against satellites. These include, as described in greater detail in chapter 4, ballistic missiles, space boosters, electronic countermeasures, experimental antimissile systems such as directed-energy weapons, spacecraft capable of maneuvering into the path of, or detonating in proximity to, other spacecraft, and weapons that could be carried by manned space systems such as the shuttle or Salyut space station. As the administration's ASAT arms control report also noted: "There is little reason to believe that the USSR would use any of these non-optimum capabilities in lieu of the systems with known ASAT capabilities. However, a ban on the one readily identifiable ASAT system could increase the likelihood that other systems would be covertly developed to have ASAT capability."[26]

Clearly the threat from residual antisatellite systems can never be completely eliminated even under the most stringent of arms control regimes. The significance of this threat will therefore depend on how useful such weapons are considered to be, particularly in conflicts below full-scale nuclear war; the effectiveness of the measures that can be adopted to reduce the vulnerability of satellites to these threats; and ultimately the importance attached to constraining the development of new generations of much more effective ASAT weapons.

—*Verification*. The previous two problems are often couched in terms of the difficulties of verifying compliance with an ASAT arms control agreement. Besides the standard problems of monitoring activities at such places as launch sites and experimental research centers, the sheer volume of space that would have to be policed for signs of cheating is enormous—from just above the atmosphere out to geosynchronous orbit and increasingly beyond. As the White House report points out:

> Determining with confidence whether an object hundreds of kilometers above the earth has been damaged could, in practice, be extremely difficult, and from what source it had been damaged could be extremely difficult or impossible. It may be difficult to determine whether a satellite has been damaged by electronic countermeasures. It is also difficult, or in some cases could be impossible, to determine whether an orbiting satellite contains a weapon.[27]

The presence of dual-capable systems obviously makes the verification task doubly difficult. Given the relatively closed nature of Soviet society, monitoring compliance with an ASAT accord—as with any arms control agreement—would be considerably harder for the United States than for the USSR. Also, as skeptics of arms control point out, the smaller number of U.S. satellites would mean that the United States would take a disproportionately higher risk for any shortcomings in monitoring.

Although the problems facing ASAT verification cannot be dismissed lightly, final judgment on whether the potential benefits are worth the

26. Ronald Reagan, "Report to the Congress on U.S. Policy on ASAT Arms Control," March 31, 1984, pp. 5, 6.
27. Ibid., p. 4

risks should rest on an assessment of the probability that *militarily significant* violations could go undetected over a lengthy period. Also, certain precautionary measures can be taken to hedge against Soviet cheating and even "breakout."[28] Unfortunately, too often in verification debates the irreducible margin of uncertainty becomes more important than the overall level of confidence, obscuring the central issue of whether the activities that *could* be verified *should* be constrained.

—*The ASAT-BMD overlap.* Before the SDI was launched the inherent antisatellite capabilities of exo-atmospheric ballistic missile defense systems were not considered a major problem for ASAT arms control, largely because neither superpower seemed much interested in developing advanced antimissile systems after the 1972 ABM treaty.[29] While the ASAT potential of the Galosh missile interceptors around Moscow was discussed during the internal deliberations of the Carter administration before the 1978–79 bilateral negotiations, their possible use short of full-scale nuclear war was not considered credible. The SDI has now changed this situation and in the process immensely complicated the prospects for ASAT arms control.

Although the testing and deployment of space-based antimissile systems are, as noted earlier, expressly prohibited by the ABM treaty, the United States is clearly reluctant to consider another agreement that may place still more barriers in the way of the SDI. Also, as George Keyworth III, the former science advisor to President Reagan, has argued, the current freedom to develop antisatellite weapons provides a useful way for testing ABM-related technologies and components.[30] Thus whatever the merits of ASAT constraints per se, they now have to be judged alongside their potential impact on the SDI. It is almost certainly this by-product of ASAT constraints that explains the Soviet Union's continuing interest in space arms control. Yet as the United States presses on with the SDI, the need to hedge against its possible deployment will probably make the Soviet Union more reluctant to

28. For an excellent summary of the ASAT verification issue, see William J. Durch, "Verification of Limitations on Antisatellite Weapons," in William C. Potter, ed., *Verification and Arms Control* (Lexington, Mass.: Lexington Books, 1985), pp. 81–106.

29. For useful discussions of the overlap, see Ashton B. Carter, "The Relationship of ASAT and BMD Systems," *Daedalus,* vol. 114 (Spring 1985), pp. 171–89; and U.S. Congress, Office of Technology Assessment, *Arms Control in Space* (GPO, 1984), pp. 35–37.

30. See Michael R. Gordon, "Proposed U.S. Anti-Satellite System Threatens Arms Control in Space," *National Journal,* vol. 15 (December 31, 1983), p. 2664.

consider ASAT limits. Antisatellite weapons, after all, represent the most potent countermeasure to a space-based BMD system.

The Benefits of ASAT Arms Control

While these obstacles undoubtably make the task more difficult, one must not lose sight of the possible payoffs from ASAT arms control. These include benefits for satellite survivability and strategic stability; potential cost savings; and contributions to other arms control activities and international space cooperation in general.

—*Satellite survivability*. As discussed in chapter 4, the task of making space systems survivable is made easier when the threat is bounded and, better still, limited to the extent feasible by negotiated measures. Arms control could reduce uncertainty for space system designers and improve the chances that one or more threats would not overwhelm a satellite's defensive systems during its expected lifetime. An unconstrained ASAT arms competition might also discourage the development or deployment of improved space-based systems for early warning, reconnaissance, and other useful military support missions. Though arms control measures would convey the same benefits to the Soviet Union, the lead that the United States enjoys in space technology and its overall higher dependency on satellite services indicate that it would be the chief beneficiary.

—*Strategic stability*. Reducing the likelihood of either side executing a disabling strike against the other's vital early warning and strategic communication satellites naturally lends stability to superpower relations, especially during severe crises. The latitude for misperceptions arising out of incidents in space is similarly reduced. ASAT arms control is not the exclusive method for hedging against such occurrences but, as noted earlier, it makes the task somewhat easier.

—*Cost savings*. Over the long term, the cost savings from constraining ASAT weapons development could be substantial, although this would depend very much on what limitations were enacted. The money authorized for ASAT development could be redirected into enhancing satellite survivability, which would doubtless cost even more in the absence of limitations. Though funds would need to be expended to hedge against ASAT "breakout" and to monitor compliance should an agreement be reached, it is reasonable to expect that the total would fall short of the cost of successive generations of ASAT weapons.

—*Other arms control measures.* Again, depending on the type of limitations imposed, ASAT arms control could buttress the ABM treaty by blocking off an important avenue for circumvention. If made part of a more general prohibition on weapons in space, an ASAT agreement would also forestall the deployment of space-based strategic delivery systems, or "space strike weapons" as the Soviets call them. Space arms control could also improve the climate for space cooperation between the superpowers, and possibly even collaboration in planetary exploration.

With these arguments in mind, what then are the available options for controlling the development of antisatellite weapons?

ASAT Arms Control Options

Like most other weaponry, antisatellite systems can be controlled through limits on testing, deployment, or use. The most comprehensive agreement would constrain all three activities, the least would simply ban the use of ASAT weapons. Although each approach is discussed below as if a bilateral U.S.-Soviet agreement were the goal, unilateral actions, whether they be declarations of intent such as test moratoriums or more discreet types of signaling, should not be discounted.[31] They can be useful as confidence-building measures in advance of formal negotiations or as temporary expedients if talks are slow to resume. And though both superpowers would probably reject a multilateral forum as an arena for meaningful discussions on a topic as sensitive as ASAT weaponry, some agreements could be opened later for multilateral endorsement.[32]

31. For a general discussion of the utility of tacit-informal bargaining, see Barry M. Blechman, "Do Negotiated Arms Limitations Have a Future?" *Foreign Affairs,* vol. 59 (Fall 1980), pp. 102–25; and Kenneth L. Adelman, "Arms Control with and without Agreements," *Foreign Affairs,* vol. 63 (Winter 1984–85), pp. 240–63.

32. Unless otherwise indicated the information for this section is from Donald L. Hafner, "Approaches to the Control of Antisatellite Weapons," in William J. Durch, ed., *National Interests and the Military Use of Space* (Cambridge, Mass.: Ballinger, 1984), pp. 239–70; and "Outer Space Arms Control: Unverified Practices, Unnatural Acts?" *Survival,* vol. 25 (November–December 1983), pp. 242–48; Durch, "Verification of Limitations on Antisatellite Weapons"; and Office of Technology Assessment, *Anti-Satellite Weapons.*

Restrictions on ASAT Deployment

A comprehensive deployment ban would aim to eliminate all ASAT weapons, whether based on earth or in space.[33] Negotiating such a ban, however, would immediately run into the definitional problem outlined earlier. Too fuzzy and broad a definition of ASAT weapons (that is, including most residual systems) would make an agreement unnegotiable, while too narrow a definition could make the final product meaningless. At the outset it would have to be recognized that the threat from residual ASAT systems could not be eliminated entirely, but that restrictions could nevertheless be applied. This would require at the very least a prohibition on testing such systems "in an ASAT mode" so as to reduce the concern that the nondedicated systems could be quickly converted into antisatellite weapons during a crisis or war. Banned tests could include simulations of satellite intercepts by ballistic missiles, the projection into space of directed-energy beams beyond a specified power output, and high-speed rendezvous by orbiting objects.[34] With further improvements to U.S. space-monitoring capabilities, especially with a space-based surveillance system, compliance could be verified with a high degree of confidence. (See the discussion of test restrictions below for more details of U.S. monitoring requirements and assets.)

A complete deployment ban would of course raise the problem of how to verify the dismantlement of existing *dedicated* ASAT systems. Although the United States could readily monitor with its reconnaissance satellites the dismantlement of the two Soviet ASAT launch pads, alternative facilities might be covertly configured for ASAT use. Another complicating factor here is that the SL-11 booster facilities used to launch the Soviet ASAT interceptor are also used for launching ocean recon-

---

33. The most comprehensive agreement would actually be the complete demilitarization of space, which is not discussed here. The reasons demilitarization would not be practical or desirable are straightforward. It would require reversing a long-standing and established practice of using space for military purposes, many of which are arguably beneficial to superpower stability. It would also require distinguishing between and monitoring space activities used for military and nonmilitary ends, an all but impossible task today. Finally, the United States is likely to suffer most under such an agreement, given its higher overall use of military satellites. For the best critique of a proposal for the demilitarization of space, see Hafner, "Approaches to the Control of Antisatellite Weapons," pp. 242–48.

34. Donald L. Hafner, "Potential Negotiated Measures for ASAT Arms Control," in Joseph S. Nye, Jr., ed., *Seeking Stability in Space* (University Press of America, forthcoming).

naissance satellites. Even if the Soviets were prepared to dismantle, in addition to the known launch sites, all their SL-11 boosters and ASAT interceptors, there would still be doubts about covertly deployed stocks and, furthermore, the use of different launch vehicles. Providing on-site inspection of the launch areas might reduce suspicions of this kind, but it could not hope to eliminate them entirely.[35]

Whatever the limits to monitoring Soviet ASAT deployments, the United States would still have high confidence in detecting covert testing of their current satellite interceptor. Stated differently, the Soviets cannot be confident that they could successfully evade U.S. detection, certainly over a prolonged period. Improvements to U.S. space surveillance capabilities would provide a further deterrent to Soviet cheating. Test experience to date suggests that the Soviets are unlikely to have great confidence in the current operational effectiveness of their ASAT; without additional testing their confidence would surely diminish still further. The United States would also be able to monitor the construction of new Soviet launch sites.

For the Soviets, once the U.S. F-15–Air-Launched Miniature Vehicle (ALMV) system becomes operational, the multitude of potential F-15 ASAT operating sites and the small size of the homing device would pose severe if not overwhelming monitoring problems. On-site inspection combined with a weapons "tagging" scheme could help alleviate these problems, but it is unclear whether either side would accept such intrusive measures.

In the absence of an operational U.S. ASAT system, the most serious challenge to the integrity of a deployment ban would come from the development of antimissile systems that could target objects in space. Currently, land-based fixed-site BMD systems are not prohibited under the ABM treaty. Whatever their shortcomings for ballistic missile defense, they could pose a significant threat to satellites. Thus for a deployment ban to be truly effective, additional constraints would have to be placed on the development and testing of ground-based BMD systems such as Homing Overlay Experiment–type interceptors and laser weapons. These measures, however, would effectively mean

---

35. The Soviets have become far more receptive to the principle and practice of on-site verification in recent years. Though not specifically referring to OSI in the context of an ASAT accord, the 1983 Soviet draft treaty did call for additional consultation and cooperation in matters arising from, among other things, "observance of its provisions" (article 5).

confining the SDI to laboratory research and any field testing to within the atmosphere.

A less ambitious step would be to ban new types of ASAT systems—that is, to prohibit antisatellite weapons beyond those already developed by each superpower. Such an agreement has many attractions. First, it would avoid the thorny issue of negotiating and later monitoring the fate of existing ASAT systems. Second, it would allow each side the means for countering threatening satellites that may evolve in the future. Third, as the altitude reach of both the current Soviet and planned U.S. ASAT systems is essentially limited to low earth orbit (less than 5,000 kilometers), it would indirectly enhance the security of the more benign satellites positioned in higher orbits. Of course, precautions would have to be taken to ensure that the existing systems could not be "grandfathered," for example, by extending their altitude reach with new boosters.

Behind these apparent attractions, however, lie some significant problems. Since the F-15–ALMV system is clearly superior to the present Soviet co-orbital ASAT, the Soviets might consider this proposal inequitable and designed to preserve a U.S. advantage. A compromise arrangement permitting a certain degree of modernization of the Soviet ASAT system might solve the problem, but it would be harder to sell politically in the United States and would raise additional verification problems.

Of larger proportions is the problem of ASAT-capable antimissile systems. Advanced research and development in this area could effectively circumvent a no-new-types agreement. Unless both sides accepted this arrangement on the grounds that it would allow research on ballistic missile defense to continue while affording some protection to high-altitude satellites, agreement would have to be reached on permissible types of BMD development and deployment.

One suggested alternative to the no-new-types approach is a one-generic-type agreement. This would establish quantitative performance parameters for permitted ASAT systems. On the plus side, such an arrangement would obviate the need to argue over existing systems and provide some freedom for each side to pursue the development of ASAT technology. On the minus side, it would create a new set of verification problems. Negotiators would have to find acceptable guidelines on permissible development work that gave each side enough confidence that significant improvements in ASAT capabilities could not be achieved covertly. Furthermore, establishing procedures for the replacement of the current systems would in effect raise many of the same concerns that bedevil the total dismantlement of ASAT weapons. Thus such an agreement, however desirable, is likely to be exceedingly difficult to negotiate.

Restrictions on ASAT Testing

A less problematic approach to restraining the development of ASAT weapons is through restrictions of testing. These could range from a total ban to more permissive regimes that place limitations on the type, frequency, or location of ASAT tests. By making testing the focus of ASAT arms control, one can avoid the problems of dealing with embedded systems. Test moratoriums can also be of fixed or unlimited duration, depending on the long-term concerns of the two parties.

The basic premise behind negotiating test restrictions is that confidence in how well a weapon system will perform cannot be achieved and then maintained without regular testing. Doubts will arise about the reliability of equipment, the skill of operating crews, and the adequacy of operating procedures.[36] This uncertainty will be highest for unfielded systems, while confidence in the performance of those already deployed will presumably erode over time.[37]

A ban on all testing of antisatellite weapons has many of the attractions and drawbacks of a comprehensive deployment ban. In addition to prohibiting the testing of dedicated ASAT weapons, such an accord would likewise restrict the testing "in an ASAT mode" of dual-capable systems. As for existing ASAT weapons, the United States would have to accept that in the near term the Soviet co-orbital ASAT would continue to pose a threat to U.S. spacecraft. This concern, however, can be addressed in large part by making the threatened satellites more survivable. The expectation that the operational potency of the Soviet ASAT would wither away over the longer term would also provide some comfort. Any remaining doubts should be set against the putative benefits of constraining more effective Soviet ASAT systems. As the supporters of ASAT test limits point out, the principal goal is to prevent the development of ASAT systems "capable of numerous rapid, high

---

36. Durch, "Verification of Antisatellite Weapons," p. 93.

37. Proponents of test moratoriums point to the drop in performance of the Soviet ASAT system after the four-and-a-half year hiatus in testing between 1971 and 1976. See Hafner, "Approaches to the Control of Antisatellite Weapons," p. 256.

confidence kills of satellites.''[38] The current Soviet ASAT clearly does not fit into this category, but without test constraints, future ones might.

Monitoring a comprehensive ASAT test ban would not be easy, but with additional improvements to U.S. space surveillance systems, the margin of uncertainty can be reduced to tolerable levels. The United States already has an extensive network of space surveillance sensors made up of high-powered radars and electro-optical telescopes that can detect and track orbiting objects up to geosynchronous altitudes (36,000 kilometers) and even beyond (see appendix B). Two examples indicate the high quality of American imaging sensors. In April 1981, concern that the space shuttle *Columbia* may have shed some of its protective thermal tiles during its maiden flight reportedly prompted NASA to request U.S. Air Force assistance in photographing the underbelly of the shuttle for signs of damage. According to one report, attempts to use the Teal Amber facility in Malabar, Florida, failed because of cloud cover, but other air force facilities appear to have been used.[39] Either way it indicated a high degree of confidence that these sensors could produce photos of the detail required. In addition, in 1983 a high-resolution U.S. Air Force camera in New Mexico successfully photographed a disabled Tracking and Data Relay Satellite System (TDRSS) spacecraft in geosynchronous orbit.[40]

Other observers have reported that during *Columbia*'s first mission, a KH-11 satellite was specially maneuvered to photograph the shuttle, though later orbital analysis has cast some doubt on this.[41] Though it may not have occurred in this instance, the use of reconnaissance satellites for special monitoring tasks in space is certainly an option. Other intelligence assets, specifically those used for gathering signals intelligence (SIGINT), would also be useful for verifying an ASAT test ban. For example, they might intercept telemetry from a test vehicle and also determine on the basis of uplink and downlink communications which space vehicles were active.

At high altitudes the monitoring task becomes more difficult. Even viewed with the latest U.S. Ground-based Electro-Optical Deep Space

38. Hafner, "Potential Negotiated Measures for ASAT Arms Control."
39. Joel W. Powell, "Photography of Orbiting Satellites," *Spaceflight*, vol. 25 (February 1983), p. 82.
40. Thomas O'Toole, "Oil Leak Blamed for Flawed Satellite," *Washington Post*, July 13, 1983.
41. Anthony Kenden, "Was 'Columbia' Photographed by a KH-11?" *Journal of the British Interplanetary Society*, vol. 36 (1983), pp. 73–77.

Surveillance (GEODSS) sensors, objects in the geosynchronous orbit appear little more than small dots of light on the screens of the operators.[42] Although the GEODSS system cannot provide high-resolution pictures of space objects at these altitudes, it can nevertheless determine such basic characteristics as whether the object is stable, turning, or tumbling and its rate of movement. Moreover, it can perform these tasks quite rapidly. Each GEODSS sensor can differentiate satellites from stars and space junk in a single field of view within five to twenty seconds. This information can in turn be relayed immediately to the North American Aerospace Defense Command (NORAD) for comparison with their log of space objects.[43] A major limitation, however, is that this can only be accomplished at night and in clear weather.

The possible deployment of space-based long-wave infrared (LWIR) surveillance sensors may offer even better coverage of high-altitude orbits, although the images may not be as detailed as those currently attainable of satellites in low earth orbit.[44] Nevertheless, such a system would provide a considerable improvement to current U.S. satellite detection and tracking capabilities. Since ground-based radars are essentially limited to line-of-sight observations, there are significant periods when space objects cannot be tracked. A space-based surveillance system would fill most of the gaps in coverage (see appendix B for further details). A network of LWIR sensors in space would also be useful for detecting tests of directed-energy weapons such as lasers and neutral particle beams. Additional sensors, such as gamma-ray spectrometers, multispectral imagers, and ionization detectors, would likewise help in monitoring Soviet directed-energy weapon (DEW) testing in space.[45] Given the likely external characteristics of such weapons—a large power source, pointing and tracking equipment, mirrors, and so forth—they

42. See Dale Foust, "GEODSS Update," *Quest*, vol. 6 (Summer 1983), pp. 27–31; Anne Randolph, "USAF Upgrades Deep Space Coverage," *Aviation Week and Space Technology*, vol. 118 (February 28, 1983), pp. 57–58; and "GEODSS Photographs Orbiting Satellite," *Aviation Week and Space Technology*, vol. 119 (November 28, 1983), pp. 146–47.

43. Anne Randolph, "USAF Upgrades Deep Space Coverage," *Aviation Week and Space Technology*, vol. 118 (February 28, 1983), p. 58. Each sensor also has an auxiliary telescope for tracking objects in low earth orbit.

44. For a discussion of space-based LWIR sensor technology, see Office of Technology Assessment, *Anti-Satellite Weapons*, pp. 78–79.

45. Ibid., p. 110. There is some evidence to indicate that the United States has or will soon deploy special sensors for detecting Soviet DEW testing. Wayne Biddle, "U.S. Planning Satellite to Spy on Laser Weapons in Soviet," *New York Times*, July 11, 1984.

Table 6-2. *Current and Potential National Technical Means of Verification (NTM) for Monitoring a Comprehensive ASAT Test Ban*

ASAT type	Current NTMs				Potential NTMs		
	Reconnaissance satellites	Signals intelligence systems	Ground-based radar	Ground-based electro-optical systems	Space-based LWIR sensors	Space-based multispectral imagers	Gamma-ray spectrometers
Ground-based kinetic energy weapon	Launch-site activity	Telemetry; command and control	Maneuvers; impact debris	Maneuvers; impact debris	Maneuvers; impact debris	...	...
Ground-based high-energy laser	Test-site activity	...	Debris	Debris	Thermal radiation[a]	Thermal radiation[a]	...
Conventional space mine	...	Telemetry; command and control	Maneuvers; impact debris	Maneuvers; impact debris	Maneuvers; impact debris	...	...
Nuclear space mine[b]	...	Telemetry; command and control	Maneuvers	Maneuvers	Maneuvers	Gamma radiation[c]	Gamma radiation[c]
Space-based high-energy laser	F.R.C.[d]	Telemetry; command and control	F.R.C.	F.R.C.	Thermal radiation[a]	Thermal radiation[a]	...
Space-based neutral particle beam	F.R.C.	Telemetry; command and control	F.R.C.	F.R.C.	...	...	Gamma radiation from target[e]

Sources: Table adapted from U.S. Congress, Office of Technology Assessment, *Anti-Satellite Weapons, Countermeasures, and Arms Control* (Washington, D.C.: GPO, 1985), p. 110; and William J. Durch, "Verification of Limitations on Antisatellite Weapons," in William C. Potter, ed., *Verification and Arms Control* (Lexington, Mass.: Lexington Books, 1985), pp. 81–106.
a. Thermal radiation from the source and from the target.
b. Assumes nontesting, as testing of a nuclear device would soon be detected.
c. Activated either by cosmic radiation or by particle beam generator.
d. Functionally related characteristics.
e. Ionization would also be detectable.

would be readily observable either from the ground or space.[46] Table 6-2 shows the current and potential national technical means of verification at the disposal of the superpowers for monitoring compliance with a comprehensive ASAT test ban. Confidence in verification should not be judged on the performance of any one monitoring system; the sensors complement one another and if anything work synergistically.

Overall then, despite the enormous volume of space, the United States would have a high degree of confidence in detecting covert testing of dedicated ASAT systems, especially with additional improvements to the current space surveillance network. Though the Soviet Union could conceivably deploy a space mine that might be difficult to distinguish from other satellites (especially at geosynchronous altitudes), its movements and moreover tests of its kill mechanism would be readily observable. Except for nuclear devices, the Soviets would have very low confidence in the operational effectiveness and therefore wartime utility of *untested* systems. The most serious loophole for potential abuse, however, would again be the testing of fixed-site exo-atmospheric BMD systems. These too can be monitored, but testing is permitted under the ABM treaty. Thus, if a comprehensive ASAT test ban is to be rigorously pursued, additional antimissile test limitations are essential. The most obvious would be to prohibit testing of all antimissile systems in space. As a result, the United States and the Soviet Union would not only have to forgo further ASAT development but also accept significant constraints on BMD research.

If the superpowers determine a truly comprehensive ASAT test ban is too restrictive, then there are other, more permissive test regimes that could be acceptable. One would permit testing of just the two existing ASAT systems, although this would run into the same problems as the no-new-types deployment ban discussed earlier. Another would prohibit testing of only *space-based* ASAT systems. The attraction of a test regime of this kind would depend on the meaning of "space based." If it included tests of objects that complete at least one orbit around the earth, then it would in effect prohibit testing of the Soviet co-orbital ASAT without constraining the U.S. direct-ascent system. The ABM treaty nowithstanding, it might also be considered an additional impediment to space-based SDI research.[47]

---

46. Durch, "Verification of Antisatellite Weapons," p. 95.
47. As a general point, agreements specifying impermissible activities in space could

One proposal that has gained a certain amount of support is a ban on testing high-altitude ASATs.[48] Its appeal derives largely from the fact that it goes a long way toward reconciling the competing interests in the ASAT debate. For one thing, it would allow the further development of low-altitude ASAT systems to counter perceived satellite threats in this region. For another, it would allow antimissile research that is essentially confined to low earth orbit to continue. At the same time it would put a ceiling on further ASAT development and enhance the security of the satellites at high altitudes. As for its feasibility, the immense distance between satellites in low earth orbit and those in the geosynchronous orbit is a formidable *cordon sanitaire,* which could not be easily traversed by either conventional or exotic ASAT systems. As noted earlier, traditional rocket boosters would take between three and six hours to reach high-altitude satellites, not a particularly efficient method of attack. Furthermore, for the foreseeable future, ground-based directed-energy weapons (or even those placed in low earth orbit) will not be able to project beams of sufficient power to disable satellites at high altitudes— at least against those that have received moderate hardening. Thus a high-altitude test ban seems to have all the makings of a natural compromise between the protagonists of the ASAT debate.

Attractive as it is, there are serious doubts about whether such an agreement would be acceptable to both sides and, if so, whether it could last very long. Some Soviet commentators have already stated that a ban on testing high-altitude ASATs would be inequitable, given the greater number of Soviet satellites in low earth orbit that would remain at risk.[49] This concern might diminish if the Soviets plan to transfer more satellites to higher orbits in the future. The Soviet's willingness to support such a ban would also depend on whether they believe it would lend tacit approval to BMD testing and deployment in space, thereby undermining the ABM treaty and leaving the way open for the SDI. On

---

run into demarcation disputes about where the atmosphere ends and outer space begins, a problem that may become more acute with the development of true aerospace vehicles that further blur the already ambiguous dividing line between the two media. See ibid., p. 94.

48. Aspen Strategy Group, *Anti-Satellite Weapons and U.S. Military Space Policy* (Lanham, Md.: University Press of America and the Aspen Institute for Humanistic Studies, 1986), pp. 36–37; and Ashton B. Carter, "Satellites and Anti-Satellites: The Limits of the Possible," *International Security*, vol. 10 (Spring 1986), pp. 94–98.

49. See A. G. Arbatov, "Prevention of the Militarization of Space," in *Proceedings of the Thirty-fourth Pugwash Conference on Science and World Affairs*, Bjorkliden, Sweden, July 9–14, 1984, p. 157.

the other hand, a high-altitude ban would permit the Soviets to develop sophisticated low-altitude ASATs as a hedge against U.S. space-based SDI systems as well as U.S. military satellites.

As for its long-term prospects, a ban on high-altitude testing would in effect surrender the area of space close to earth to uninhibited development of ASAT weaponry, which in turn might progressively threaten the high-altitude sanctuary. The vast distances separating the two areas are indeed an effective barrier, but for how long? Either side could gain operational confidence in ASAT weapons at lower altitudes that with relatively little modification could be converted for use in the prohibited zone. Space mines are a notable example. The potential for this conversion would almost certainly raise serious questions over whether an agreement of this kind could be adequately verified and whether it was really desirable. To be effective and therefore worthwhile, a high-altitude test ban would almost certainly need to be accompanied by constraints on ASAT and antimissile activities in low earth orbit.

A somewhat different approach would be to establish common quantifiable limits for ASAT and BMD research and development.[50] The possibility of prohibiting both ASAT and antimissile testing outside of the atmosphere, say no higher than 100 kilometers, has already been mentioned. For kinetic kill weapons, limits could be placed on how fast and how close such systems could approach other objects in space. These would be designed to allow docking between cooperative space vehicles but prohibit fast flybys of the velocity associated with satellite and ballistic missile intercepts. Velocities below several hundred meters per second might be permitted, for example. For laser weaponry, limits could be placed on a laser's power, on the diameter of its primary mirror, or on its overall brightness, which is a function of its power, wavelength, and diameter of the primary beam director mirror. A brightness limit of 10^{16} watts/steradian might be an appropriate threshold. Finally, particle beam weapons could be regulated by limiting the energy levels of their generators. Determining the threshold levels for these ASAT and BMD technologies would depend largely on how much leeway each side wants to leave for meaningful antimissile research and how much of the threat from antimissile systems is acceptable.

50. The following information is from John Pike, "Limitations on Space Weapons: A Preliminary Assessment," prepared for the Federation of American Scientists (February 1987); and Herbert Lin, "New Weapon Technologies and the ABM Treaty" (Massachusetts Institute of Technology, December 1986).

Restrictions on ASAT Use

To many, an ASAT agreement that prohibited only their use would seem next to worthless as an act of arms control. It would be tantamount to allowing unrestricted ASAT development and ultimately do nothing to protect satellites in time of war. The potential value of a no-use or noninterference accord should not be overlooked, however, especially if made part of a more general package of "rules of the road" for operations in space (discussed below). Although the use of force in space and more specifically interference with satellites that amount to national technical means of verification are already prohibited, an agreement clarifying this and extending these provisions to all satellites might help prevent brinkmanship and other acts of harassment in space.[51] It might also help deter ASAT attacks in the "twilight zone" between peace and war by providing an unambiguous legal threshold that states must visibly transgress.

Despite its modest goals, even this apparently straightforward proposal poses some problems. At the outset, a common definition of what constitutes an "ASAT act" would have to be accepted—a difficult task in itself. Should it refer only to those acts that damage and destroy spacecraft or should it include those that can impede their operation, such as electronic jamming?[52] Should allowances also be made for "legitimate" ASAT acts such as those the Soviets pressed for in the 1978–79 bilateral ASAT talks? And should just U.S. and Soviet satellites be covered by a no-use agreement? These questions would all need to be resolved.

Collateral Measures

In addition to agreements that place specific restrictions on the deployment, testing, and use of ASAT weapons, a group of proposals have surfaced that regulate space activities in general. Their principal purpose is to reduce the likelihood of misunderstandings and ultimately conflicts arising out of incidents in space. They can also be designed to improve verification and enhance the effectiveness of unilateral satellite survivability measures.

51. Hafner, "Potential Negotiated Measures for ASAT Arms Control."
52. See Office of Technology Assessment, *Anti-Satellite Weapons,* pp. 115–16.

RULES OF THE ROAD. This option would specify certain behavioral rules for operations in space. The most obvious precedent is the 1972 U.S.-Soviet agreement on the Prevention of Incidents on and over the High Seas, which curbed the growing number of volatile and dangerous incidents between the warships of the two superpowers. Although the characteristics of outer space pose different requirements for an analogous Incidents in Space agreement, some of the same strictures appropriately modified could be adopted; for example, provisions on avoiding collisions in space; outlawing dangerous maneuvers and simulated attacks (for example, high-velocity flybys); banning the illumination or the launching of objects in the direction of passing satellites; and requiring notification of maneuvers near other states' satellites. Furthermore, as set out in the Incidents at Sea agreement, a committee could be established to meet regularly to discuss compliance issues.

KEEP-OUT ZONES. More specific rules governing minimum separation distances between satellites, or "keep-out zones," is another idea that has received some attention. One suggestion is to divide the geosynchronous orbit into specified "self-defense zones," each representing 10° of arc amounting to 7,400 kilometers across.[53] Twelve of these zones could be apportioned each to the Warsaw Pact, NATO, and neutral countries. As the name implies, the purpose would be to provide satellites an extra margin of time and space to react to ASAT attacks with evasive or defensive actions. "Rogue" satellites found transgressing the boundaries of prohibited zones would be subject to attack, although additional regulations permitting certain exceptions (with the appropriate safeguards), and the transit of satellites, could be agreed upon. Suggestions for low earth orbit include prohibiting launches within 100 kilometers and 2° to 3° of the orbital inclination and right ascension of any other satellite.[54] Different rules could be created for other orbits.[55]

Though potentially useful as an added defensive precaution and general confidence builder, keep-out zones in space may not be as practical or even as desirable as many believe. Unless ASAT technology is constrained in some way, even the largest defense zones may not

53. Albert Wohlstetter and Brian Chow, "Arms Control That Could Work," *Wall Street Journal,* July 17, 1985. For a more extensive exposition of this proposal, see Albert Wohlstetter and Brian A. Chow, *Self-Defense Zones in Space,* Report MDA 903-84-C-0325 (Marina del Rey, Calif.: Pan Heuristics, 1986).

54. Hafner, "Approaches to the Control of Antisatellite Weapons," p. 264.

55. See also Office of Technology Assessment, *Anti-Satellite Weapons,* pp. 136–37.

afford much protection to satellites. According to one study, "Maneuverable ASATs armed with either x-rasers [X-ray lasers] or simple nuclear warheads are theoretically capable of killing shielded targets from initial separation on the order of thousands of kilometers within thirty minutes." Moreover,

> a satellite with a spherical shield optimized for protection against x-rasers could be killed in thirty minutes by a hit-to-kill ASAT from an initial separation on the order of thousands of kilometers. The potential vulnerability of critical satellites does not depend on the development of sophisticated beam weapons of any type.[56]

Thus it appears that satellite defense zones would work best in conjunction with other ASAT arms control measures. Yet given the congestion of satellites that already exists in the geosynchronous orbit, it is questionable whether even relatively modest separation distances could be agreed upon. Higher, less-populated areas of space (for example, in supersynchronous orbit) may be a better place to implement this idea.[57]

Keep-out zones would also undoubtedly raise the question of sovereignty in space, with perhaps undesirable consequences. For example, an agreement of this kind might set a precedent for divisions in space relating to commercial activities.[58] It might reopen the whole debate about where the atmosphere ends and with it national jurisdiction, reviving the issue of the legitimacy of satellite overflight. Similarly, the United States would have to be careful that keep-out zones at the geosynchronous orbit would not compromise current intelligence gathering activities or ballistic missile early warning.

CRISIS MANAGEMENT PROCEDURES. Another measure designed to prevent superpower crises arising out of incidents in space is to establish bilateral emergency consultative procedures, either as part of a general rules-of-the-road package or in a separate accord. Like the 1972 U.S.-Soviet Accident Measures Agreement, it could require each superpower immediately to notify the other of accidents, unauthorized activities, or any other unexplained incidents in space that could risk an outbreak of hostilities. Special communication links could be set up, perhaps be-

---

56. Leonard Anthony Wojcik, "Separation Requirements for Protection of High-Altitude Satellites from Co-orbital Antisatellite Weapons" (Ph.D. dissertation, Carnegie-Mellon University, 1985), p. 121.

57. Ibid., p. 123. See also Office of Technology Assessment, *Anti-Satellite Weapons*, pp. 136–37.

58. Office of Technology Assessment, *Unispace '82: A Context for International Cooperation and Competition* (GPO, 1983), pp. 43–44.

tween U.S. and Soviet space tracking centers, or alternatively established channels like the hot line could be used.

The potential benefits of an agreement of this type have to be weighed against the distinct danger that it might backfire. The likelihood of misperceptions over incidents in space may actually be heightened if one state has the right to request information from another. If a state does not supply information on an incident, either because it genuinely does not know or because it fears compromising sensitive information, the room for suspicions may expand rather than shrink.[59]

COOPERATIVE MONITORING PROCEDURES. By making the monitoring of space activities easier, an agreement between the superpowers to notify one another of all space launches in advance could go some way toward reducing suspicions of hostile intentions. At present, under the terms of the 1976 UN Convention on the Registration of Objects Launched into Outer Space, satellite-launching states are obliged, after a launch has occurred, to provide the UN Registry with its date, territory, and location, the basic orbital parameters of the space object, an appropriate designator, and information on the general function of the space object. This agreement could be modified (as permitted under article 9) to include advance notification. Alternatively, a bilateral arrangement could be reached.

Though a prelaunch notification agreement would not allow the relevant monitoring agencies to relax their vigilance, it would make their task somewhat easier and perhaps even cheaper. And like a no-use ASAT agreement, it would erect another unambiguous legal barrier that states with hostile intentions would have visibly to transgress. On the negative side, the common postponements associated with launch activities could be a constant source of irritation and suspicion unless precautions were adopted to prevent this.

Another method to help reduce suspicions of orbiting objects is to allow some form of in-space inspection. While physical inspection of space objects will almost certainly be rejected by both the United States and the USSR, inspection from a predetermined distance and with advance notification might be acceptable. For example, monitoring could be improved by close proximity inspections and by certain "active" surveillance techniques that might otherwise be considered provocative. Nevertheless, inspection could, like the crisis control

59. For a general discussion of this problem, see Thomas C. Schelling, "Confidence in Crisis," *International Security,* vol. 8 (Spring 1984), pp. 55–66.

measures discussed earlier, create more problems than it solves. Safe-guards would have to be reached to prevent co-orbital ASAT attacks under the pretext of inspection. Determining the amount of advance notification is also a tricky question; too much could provide enough time to conceal prohibited activities, while too little could further excite suspicion during a crisis. Even discussing what inspection techniques should be permitted could risk compromising sensitive information on each side's satellites. On balance, the net benefit to present U.S. monitoring capabilities may only be marginal compared with the draw-backs of allowing equivalent rights of external inspection to the Soviet Union. Furthermore, monitoring techniques may become available to the United States in the near future that will obviate the need for close-in inspection.

OTHER POSSIBILITIES. While not arms control measures per se, other possible agreements could include limits on the use and disposal of nuclear reactors in orbit. Although some see a complete ban on space reactors as an indirect way of removing the Soviet RORSAT threat in addition to heading off the use of nuclear power sources for space weapons, these benefits would have to be balanced against the commercial space applications for space reactors and even their use for enhancing satellite survivability. This conflict of interest might be avoided, how-ever, by limiting the power output of space reactors. A registry of satellites using reactors might also be helpful. Agreement on the prolif-eration and disposal of space junk is another potentially useful measure.

Conclusion

Reviewing the various options to curb antisatellite weapons reveals three general points about what space arms control can and cannot do. First, ASAT arms control cannot eliminate the threat to space systems, only bound it. Second, the different approaches to the control of ASAT weapons can work synergistically: the shortcomings of one agreement can to a large extent be remedied by the provisions of another. For example, restrictions on testing ASAT systems in high earth orbit can be buttressed by prohibiting the deployment of specific systems, such as directed-energy weapons, at lower altitudes. Similarly, a rules-of-the-road agreement can help diminish the uncertainties associated with the monitoring of superpower compliance with other accords.

Third, verification of an ASAT agreement can never be absolute. Its acceptance, therefore, should rest on an assessment of the probability that militarily significant violations would remain undetected, the effectiveness of unilateral measures that the United States can take to hedge against this risk, and the overall benefits of the agreement.

Turning to the larger question, Can ASAT arms control address the most important U.S. security concerns, namely, the threat posed by the operational Soviet ASAT system and the indirect threat that Soviet satellites, particularly the ocean reconnaissance variety, pose to U.S. military operations? As discussed in earlier chapters, the United States could go a long way toward reducing the vulnerability of those of its satellites exposed to Soviet dedicated and residual ASAT capabilities. The principal benefit of an arms control agreement would be to prevent transforming what is still a relatively immature threat to one that is altogether more formidable and more difficult to counter unilaterally. Given the problem of monitoring the dismantlement of existing systems, test restrictions provide the most useful approach to constraining the evolution of more sophisticated ASAT weapons. Although such restrictions might entail accepting constraints on the U.S. Air-Launched Miniature Vehicle before it had reached the same level of operational readiness as its Soviet counterpart, the United States could employ, as discussed in chapter 5, nondestructive methods for dealing with the most worrisome Soviet satellites, methods that would not be subject to formal limitation. Adherence to a testing moratorium could be reviewed periodically to assess Soviet compliance and the continuing usefulness of the agreement.

Such test restrictions, however, will be next to worthless unless testing of ASAT-capable antimissile systems is similarly prohibited. A moratorium on high-altitude ASAT tests would allow the United States (and the Soviet Union) to pursue ballistic missile defense research and development in space without forgoing ASAT constraints entirely, yet, as noted earlier, there are significant doubts about such a regime. Certainly, it would be better than nothing, but it might not last very long. Thus in the end the feasibility of meaningful ASAT restrictions rests on the superpowers' willingness to consider further limits on ballistic missile defense research.

CHAPTER SEVEN

Summary and Recommendations

THE United States is confronted with major policy choices that promise to have profound implications for the future military use of space. While space has been irreversibly militarized for a long time, in the sense that both superpowers use satellites for a wide range of military purposes, the development of antisatellite and space-based antimissile systems is a major departure from the predominant trend. Yet the nation seems to be drifting down this new avenue of the arms race without fully considering whether there are practical and prudent alternatives. The Reagan administration continues to maintain that an antisatellite capability is essential to U.S. national security and also that "no arrangements or agreements beyond those already governing military activities in outer space have been found to date that are judged to be in the overall interest of the United States and its Allies."[1] In light of the findings of this study, I believe there are valid and important reasons to question the wisdom of current U.S. military space policy and these assertions in particular.

Does the United States Really Need an ASAT System?

Supporters of the U.S. ASAT program offer three rationales for its deployment. They argue that it is needed to redress the current imbalance

1. Letter from Ronald Reagan to the Speaker of the House of Representatives, accompanying the "Report to the Congress on U.S. Policy on ASAT Arms Control," March 31, 1984.

in U.S. and Soviet ASAT capabilities, to deter Soviet attacks on U.S. satellites, and to counter the threat posed by Soviet space systems. As for the current imbalance, it is certainly true that the Soviets do possess the world's only deployed ASAT system. But as discussed in chapter 4, the Soviet interceptor suffers from significant operational constraints that would limit its effectiveness in wartime. Although important U.S. satellites are within its reach, their vulnerability can to a large extent be reduced by such protective measures as attack warning sensors, emergency maneuvering systems, and decoys. Moreover, if the Soviets maintain their unilateral moratorium on ASAT testing, confidence in the interceptor's operational effectiveness will surely diminish over time.

The next issue is whether the United States could deter Soviet attacks on U.S. satellites by threatening a response in kind. A necessary precondition for successful deterrence is that the Soviets value the services of their satellites more than denying the same benefits to the United States. Otherwise, the threatened loss of Soviet space systems from U.S. ASAT retaliation could not be a compelling sanction. Judged by the level of effort and investment they make to maintain their military space program, the Soviets clearly value the support that satellites provide. Even though, as discussed in chapter 5, the Soviet Union does not have as much to lose in the event of antisatellite exchanges, and would also be better prepared to absorb destructive attacks on its space systems, it would rather not jeopardize key space assets by inciting U.S. ASAT retaliation.[2] Thus, unless the value of satellites became highly asymmetrical in the United States' favor, the presence of a U.S. ASAT system would most likely deter Soviet ASAT attacks.

Although this argument supports the feasibility of deterrence in space, it is only valid if there is something meaningful to deter. If the Soviets continue to observe their testing moratorium, and the United States takes measures to neutralize the threat from the current Soviet ASAT system, then the need for an equivalent U.S. capability—on the grounds of deterrence—progressively diminishes. Should the Soviet Union dismantle its ASAT interceptors, as it has offered to do in exchange for a similar U.S. concession, then the requirement for a U.S. ASAT deterrent would decrease still further. While there would always be the threat from Soviet residual ASAT systems, such as nuclear-tipped ballistic

---

2. I am indebted to John D. Steinbruner and Joshua M. Epstein for discussions on Soviet disincentives to engage in ASAT warfare.

missiles, the presence of their U.S. counterparts would provide a
deterrent if the likely consequences of their use did not.

That leaves the final argument: is a U.S. ASAT capability needed to
counter the threat from Soviet satellites? The analysis of conflict scenarios in chapter 5 showed that the United States could find an ASAT
capability of some use, although those instances appear confined to
conflicts in which both superpowers are engaged. ASAT attacks to help
warring client states would probably provide marginal if any military
benefits, and only at the considerable risk of widening and escalating the
war. Even in situations in which U.S. ASAT attacks might offer some
benefits, the effect could be at best short-lived and at worst counterproductive. Short of destroying the USSR's launch facilities, the United
States would still have to contend with Soviet replacement satellites.
Furthermore, unless the Soviets had already initiated an ASAT campaign, the United States would risk provoking retaliatory attacks against
its more valuable space assets.

The prospect of the United States deterring retaliation while it
simultaneously prosecutes a campaign against Soviet satellites is extremely remote, if not logically preposterous. This raises the additional
question of whether the United States could successfully *defend* against
Soviet ASAT retaliation following a U.S. attack. Were the Soviet ASAT
threat to remain as it is today, a successful defense might be achieved.
But no threat is static, as most prudent military planners will attest. It
can be virtually guaranteed that the Soviets will respond to the deployment of the F-15–Air-Launched Miniature Vehicle (ALMV) with a more
capable system of their own. Notwithstanding additional satellite survivability measures, the probability of a cost-free U.S. ASAT campaign
is very low. Given that the most likely setting for a superpower confrontation is on the Eurasian landmass, where Soviet reliance on satellites
would be *comparatively* low, the United States stands to lose a great
deal more from ASAT exchanges than does the Soviet Union. The
inability of the United States to replace lost or damaged satellites quickly
would compound this loss. Hence the threat of retaliation for initiating
ASAT attacks is more likely to deter the United States than the Soviet
Union.

It is also worth restating, however, that even without a weapon system
dedicated to disabling satellites, the United States is not defenseless
against the threat posed by Soviet spacecraft. On the most worrisome
category of Soviet space systems—namely, those used for ocean recon-

naissance—the U.S. Navy appears confident that it can neutralize the threat with such nondestructive methods as jamming, spoofing, and evasive maneuvers. In many respects these methods are preferable to outright disablement. In a full-scale nuclear war, the United States would also have the option of using nuclear weapons against Soviet satellites and space installations.

In the future the Soviets may develop more threatening surveillance satellites that can continuously track mobile U.S. strategic forces both under water and on land. In that event the United States would almost certainly need to have a dedicated ASAT system at its disposal. Yet all indications are that the technology for such omniscient surveillance will not be available in the foreseeable future.

Finally, regardless of the arguments for and against a U.S. ASAT capability, there are serious questions about whether the F-15–ALMV is the best system. Spending more than $4 billion on what will probably be no more than thirty-five missiles hardly seems cost effective.[3]

What Are the Likely Consequences of ASAT Development?

At a minimum, the Soviets can be expected to deploy an additional, more capable antisatellite system if the United States goes ahead with its ASAT program. Contingency planning if not advanced development work for such a system is almost certainly under way. On the basis of a reasonable technical extrapolation, an ASAT system comparable to the American F-15–ALMV is probably within the Soviets' grasp. So too are more advanced weapons that will be able to threaten critical U.S. communication and navigation satellites positioned at higher altitudes. Indeed, a senior U.S. Air Force official has already declared that "there is no doubt that the Soviets have the technology for high orbit ASAT[s]."[4] For several years the annual U.S. Defense Department publication *Soviet Military Power* has also painted an alarming picture of potential Soviet ASAT weapon systems using lasers and particle beams.

Faced with such a formidable array of threats, the task of protecting U.S. satellites will become progressively more difficult. Yet after spend-

3. Walter Pincus, "Reagan Criticizes Legislators Trying to Kill ASAT Program," *Washington Post,* March 29, 1986.
4. Maj. Gen. J. H. Storrie quoted in James W. Canan, "Bold New Missions in Space," *Air Force Magazine,* vol. 67 (June 1984), p. 92.

ing large sums of money on satellite survivability measures, the best position that the United States can hope to reach is the one that it more or less occupies today, namely, where most of its satellites—certainly those in high-altitude orbits—are relatively safe from all but nuclear attack. Just as likely, however, is that the satellite survivability effort will become either too expensive or just too difficult. As a consequence, in time of war the United States would not be able to rely on the current benefits that satellites provide to its forces. Moreover, because of the growing vulnerability of space systems generally, the United States might also have to forgo the development of new military space systems, regardless of their promise. Worse still, the United States might develop false expectations about the survivability of its space assets, prompting even greater reliance on satellites for wartime missions. That course could be catastrophic for the United States if it ever came to a war with the Soviet Union.

In addition to these military concerns, unconstrained ASAT development also has serious implications for conflict management and crisis stability. The deployment of highly capable ASAT weapons will add new, destabilizing uncertainties to crisis situations, especially if satellites used for the command and control of strategic nuclear forces become vulnerable. Although both sides can be expected to take the necessary precautions to reduce their dependency on spaceborne systems, the presence of ASAT systems could still create, as discussed in chapter 5, an undesirable and potentially unstable situation in a severe crisis. With so much at stake, therefore, the United States should seriously reconsider its need for an ASAT system and its current opposition to space arms control.

Are ASAT Constraints Feasible?

The essence of the Reagan administration's argument against ASAT arms control is that no agreement could hope to address all the possible threats to U.S. satellites, and even the constraints it could impose would not be verifiable. These two objections warrant further review.

The administration asserts that because the United States relies on a comparatively small number of satellites, America would take a disproportionately higher risk in agreeing to an ASAT arms accord. But this is not a valid case against arms control. Rather, it is an argument against placing too much reliance on a small number of satellites, since they will become even more vulnerable in the absence of arms control. With the appropriate precautions to increase the survivability and redundancy of the exposed satellites, the risk from Soviet residual threats can be reduced to acceptable proportions.

The administration's low estimate of its ability to defend U.S. satellites from Soviet attack sharply contrasts with its confidence about defending the space-based system envisioned under the Strategic Defense Initiative. For example, critics of ASAT arms control often assert that the ability of the Soviet Union to jam U.S. satellites and to develop and deploy space mines covertly, under the guise of ordinary space operations, would make any antisatellite weapon ban meaningless. Yet at the same time officials from the SDI program office believe that they can ensure the survival of space-based antimissile systems, presumably against the same Soviet space mines and jamming techniques. Moreover, SDI supporters are confident that they can achieve this against an adversary who is *unconstrained* in its options to attack orbital systems. Testifying on the deployment of space mines against high-altitude targets, Lieutenant General James A. Abrahamson, the director of the Strategic Defense Initiative Organization, told Congress that if the United States hardens its satellites to withstand nuclear effects, a space mine would have to maneuver within two or three kilometers of its prey to be a threat. And it would have to be able to respond instantly to its target's movements. He went on to elaborate:

> If the maneuvering is ground-commanded, I would like to recall for you the practicalities of what our present ECM [electronic countermeasure] capabilities are and ECM is something that we usually deploy on the battlefield and we measure and test. They would be trying to command this thing [a space mine] from the ground, probably at an order of thousands of miles away, maybe up to 22,000 miles away, and the threat would be within a few kilometers of what we are trying to do. . . . [B]ut it is easier to countermand using ECM techniques something a few kilometers away than it is to maintain a communication system that will go across thousands of miles.[5]

If the SDI program office can have confidence in its ability to defend against preemptive attacks in space, even against presumably dedicated

5. *Department of Defense Appropriations for 1986,* Hearings before a Subcommittee of the House Committee on Appropriations, 99 Cong. 1 sess. (GPO, 1985), pt. 7, p. 669.

ASATs, then surely their expectations should be even higher if the Soviet Union's ability to test and deploy such systems is severely constrained. If the official SDI view is ill founded and overly optimistic, as many believe, then one must ask whether the United States would rather live with the lesser threat posed by Soviet residual ASAT systems, knowing that it could do many things to compensate for this vulnerability and still benefit from the services that satellites provide, or alternatively allow the Soviets complete freedom to develop and perfect sophisticated antisatellite systems with the very real prospect that vital U.S. satellites would not survive very long in wartime. Given the choice prudent U.S. military commanders would surely opt for the former.

That certainly seems to be the preference of former U.S. Air Force Chief of Staff General Charles A. Gabriel, who stated in congressional testimony:

> I would rather both sides not have a capability to go to geosynchronous [orbit] with an ASAT. *In fact I would like to be able to agree with the Soviets that we not have any ASATs if we could verify it properly.* Because we are an open society, we need our space capabilities more than they do.[6]

Gabriel's caveat about verification is obviously an important one. As stated earlier the United States cannot hope to monitor compliance with an ASAT agreement or for that matter any arms control agreement with *absolute* certainty. Yet it can monitor with a high degree of confidence the most important part of an ASAT agreement, namely, the deployment and testing of systems that have been specifically designed for the ASAT mission. As one of Gabriel's deputies, Major General Thomas C. Brandt, acknowledged when asked whether the United States could monitor ASAT tests: "We have an excellent capability to monitor the employment of the Soviet ASAT."[7] With added improvements to American space surveillance capabilities, some of which are, ironically, being developed under the SDI or as aids to ASAT targeting, U.S. confidence in monitoring an ASAT test ban should grow still further.[8]

6. *Department of Defense Appropriations for 1985,* Hearings before a Subcommittee of the House Committee on Appropriations, 98 Cong. 2 sess. (GPO, 1984), pt. 2, p. 191 (emphasis added).

7. *Department of Defense Authorization for Appropriations for Fiscal Year 1986,* Hearings before the Senate Committee on Armed Services, 99 Cong. 1 sess. (GPO, 1985), pt. 7, p. 4314.

8. Given the Strategic Defense Initiative Organization's confidence in meeting the surveillance, acquisition, tracking, and kill assessment (SATKA) demands of a multitiered

The verification issue, like the debate over the residual ASAT threat, ultimately comes down to a basic choice. Is it better for the United States to take advantage of an agreement that constrains the most serious threats to U.S. satellites, or forgo such an agreement because it could not monitor every possible violation, but only those that are militarily significant? Again the answer seems clear.

What About the SDI?

The current U.S. commitment to the Strategic Defense Initiative represents both an obstacle and a threat to ASAT limitations. It is an obstacle in that the United States is clearly reluctant to agree to ASAT limits that might constrain its freedom of action to pursue antimissile research. Testing such systems in the "ASAT mode" appears to be the administration's strategy for avoiding some of the more restrictive portions of the Antiballistic Missile Treaty.[9] Also, as ASAT weapons provide one of the principal methods for countering space-based missile defenses, the Soviet Union's willingness to consider ASAT constraints is likely to recede the longer the United States continues to pursue antimissile research and development.

The SDI is a threat to meaningful ASAT limitations because the techniques for intercepting satellites and ballistic missiles are so similar. Since missile defense is operationally more demanding, many of the experimental antimissile systems will become de facto ASAT devices long before they can prove their feasibility for deployment as strategic defense weapons. In effect, the SDI promises to become a breeding ground for new generations of ASAT weapons if nothing else. Finally, deployment of antimissile systems beyond current levels would render an ASAT ban virtually meaningless. The only conceivable exception is the deployment of antimissile systems designed to intercept warheads for the point defense of ICBM silos and critical command and control sites.

Ironically, strategic defense may not be feasible unless constraints

---

BMD system, the relatively modest requirements of ASAT arms control monitoring should be easy to fulfill. See John Tirman, ed., *The Fallacy of Star Wars* (Vintage Books, 1984), p. 256.

9. See Peter Didisheim, *The ASAT/SDI Link*, Papers on Strategic Defense (Washington, D.C.: Union of Concerned Scientists, 1985), p. 11.

are placed on antisatellite weapons. Although SDIO officials believe that they can protect the space-based components of a strategic defense system, their confidence is not widely shared within the defense community. Either way, restricting the threat to space systems would certainly make life a lot easier for SDI planners. A prohibition on ASAT tests and deployments in high earth orbits, for instance, would go a long way toward helping to protect vital early warning and battle management sensors that are likely to be deployed there as part of an SDI system. Even such modest arms control proposals as a rules-of-the-road agreement for space operations could be helpful; in fact Lieutenant General Abrahamson has already expressed an interest in "keep-out zones."[10]

All this suggests that space arms control and antimissile research (and even deployments) are not so incompatible as an initial assessment would indicate. At the same time it is important to underline that strategic defenses—certainly those offering any meaningful protection of populations—are very much a long-term possibility, while the opportunities for constraining antisatellite weapons exist today. The United States can take advantage of these opportunities without forgoing SDI research completely and without abandoning the long-term hope that nuclear weapons may indeed be rendered "impotent and obsolete," to use President Reagan's words. The only prudent way to do this is to pursue in balanced measure a combination of unilateral and cooperative initiatives.

What Should the United States Do?

The most important conclusion of this study is that the benefits of limiting the threat to U.S. space systems through mutual superpower constraints on ASAT development more than outweigh the costs of forgoing a weapon system dedicated to destroying satellites. In short, there is currently no urgent need for a U.S. ASAT system. But constraining the threat through an all-inclusive treaty that prohibits the testing, deployment, and use of antisatellite systems does not seem a realistic goal in the present climate of U.S.-Soviet relations. There are just too many negotiating hurdles to overcome. Moreover, the balance of costs and benefits of ASAT development may change in the future. Thus the

10. *Department of Defense Appropriations for 1986,* Hearings before a Subcommittee of the House Committee on Appropriations, 99 Cong. 1 sess. (GPO, 1985), pt. 7, p. 655.

United States should retain the option to deploy an antisatellite system at a later date.

American policymakers should endeavor to steer a middle course between outright prohibition and no constraint whatsoever. It should be recognized at the outset, however, that even the most stringent bilateral restrictions on antisatellite weapons cannot be a substitute for maintaining—or better still increasing—support for space system survivability measures such as radiation hardening, emergency maneuvering, and antijamming techniques. These are essential if the United States is to minimize the risks associated with ASAT constraints. At the same time it must be recognized that these unilateral measures will be effective only if combined with such limitations. With this in mind U.S. policymakers should pursue the following:

—*Join the Soviets in their ASAT test moratorium conditional on their continued compliance.* The United States should suspend *all* tests in space of the U.S. F-15–ALMV system and not, as currently mandated under the congressionally imposed moratorium, just tests against objects in space. Soviet compliance with the moratorium should be reviewed by U.S. officials each year.

—*Desist from testing all ABM-related weapons in space.* This would include tests beyond the atmosphere of fixed land-based ABM systems, which are currently permitted under the ABM treaty. At the same time the United States should reaffirm its commitment to observe the strictest possible interpretation of the treaty's other clauses, again conditional on Soviet reciprocity.

—*Maintain a minimum ASAT research and development base.* Procurement funding for the F-15–ALMV system should be deleted and the program essentially "mothballed" so that in the event of Soviet noncompliance with the moratorium, it could be readied for further testing and deployment if need be. Limited funds for exploratory research into other ASAT techniques should also be continued.

—*Continue to improve the survivability of U.S. space systems.* Soviet observance of an ASAT test moratorium, or for that matter any other kind of space arms control agreement, should be no cause for laxity with satellite survivability measures. Opportunities for the Soviets to conduct "cheap shot" attacks against U.S. satellites, especially using residual ASAT systems, should be reduced to a minimum by protecting both the satellite portions of space systems and the vital communication links and facilities that support their operations.

—*Increase the redundancy of U.S. space systems.* In addition to making American satellites exposed to Soviet residual ASAT threats more survivable, the United States should also have the capability to replace them quickly if they are destroyed, or switch to alternative, non-space-based systems if need be. Currently, the United States places more emphasis on in-orbit spares and hosting sensors and transponders on a variety of space platforms. While this practice of proliferating sensors should continue, an emergency launch-on-demand capability should also be investigated for such crucial categories of satellites as photoreconnaissance and emergency communication systems. These would be relatively cheap and simple satellites capable of performing the minimum necessary in wartime.[11] At the very least the United States should begin exercises to practice rapid reconstitution of satellites disabled by enemy action.

Similarly the United States should also simulate in its military exercises and war games the loss of key satellites so that it can learn to function without their support—at least for short periods.[12] Obviously, for this to be accomplished with the minimum of disruption and without loss of military effectiveness, functionally equivalent alternatives must be available for use. Therefore the United States should continue to develop alternative systems to perform the most important missions carried out by satellites. Among the alternative methods worth investigating further are over-the-horizon (OTH) radar for detecting ballistic missile launches and OTH electromagnetic pulse sensors for detecting nuclear explosions, novel communication techniques such as ultrahigh-frequency (UHF) meteor burst and adaptive high-frequency (HF) systems, and long-range high-altitude remotely piloted vehicles for post-attack reconnaissance.[13] Despite the additional expense, the United States should avoid at all costs becoming too dependent on satellites, particularly for the execution of nuclear command and control functions. Finally, policymakers should be wary of developing overelaborate war

11. See Edward Bedrosian, *PACSAT: A Passive Communications Satellite for Survivable Command and Control*, prepared for the Defense Advanced Research Projects Agency, N-1780-ARPA (Santa Monica, Calif.: Rand Corporation, 1981).

12. Apparently, the Joint Chiefs of Staff (JCS) have conducted a number of exercises in which the Soviet Union is postulated to use its ASAT system. It was reported that the loss of key U.S. satellites caused considerable disruption. See Jack Cushman, "JCS Exercise Offers Chance to Practice ASAT Scenario," *Defense Week*, vol. 5 (April 9, 1984), p. 1.

13. See U.S. Congress, Office of Technology Assessment, *Anti-Satellite Weapons, Countermeasures, and Arms Control*, OTA-ISC-281 (GPO, 1985), p. 75.

plans based on unrealistic expectations of the endurance of satellites in a nuclear war.

—*Continue to improve U.S. capabilities for surveillance of activities in space.* Upgrading U.S. satellite detection and tracking facilities is essential, not only to maintain confidence in Soviet compliance with an ASAT test moratorium, but also to reduce the likelihood that ambiguous incidents or accidents in space could set in motion an unnecessary and dangerous chain of events. An orbiting network of space surveillance sensors would be particularly desirable.

—*Continue to take measures to reduce the threat from Soviet satellites.* Even though the United States should refrain from deploying its F-15–ALMV system, it need not remain defenseless against the threat from Soviet satellites. As discussed more fully in chapter 5, there are a variety of techniques—fleet tactics and electronic countermeasures among them—that the United States could use to counter the role of Soviet satellites in wartime.

Beyond these unilateral actions the United States should also consider several negotiated agreements.

—*A U.S.-Soviet ASAT test moratorium.* This bilateral accord could take the form of a five-year renewable commitment not to test antisatellite systems or any other weapons in space.

—*A U.S.-Soviet space weapons ban.* This would prohibit the stationing of weapons of any kind in outer space. The agreement could be made available for multilateral endorsement at a later stage.

—*An Incidents in Space agreement.* This should not only clarify and extend the existing prohibitions against interfering with satellites, but also include other rules of the road governing operations in space. In addition, consultative channels and crisis management procedures for the prevention of hostilities arising from incidents in space should be set up. Other collateral measures to address the growing problem of space debris and the safe use of nuclear power sources in space are also desirable.

—*New guidelines and clarifications for permissible types of antimissile research and development.* Defining precise quantifiable parameters for testing generic types of weapons technology would be particularly useful. These negotiations could be conducted within the U.S.-Soviet Standing Consultative Commission (SCC) and take the form of additional common understandings or protocols to the ABM treaty.

Over the long term the United States and the Soviet Union will also need to discuss the militarization of space on a more fundamental level. Placing constraints on the development of weapons for use in or from space does not address the root of the problem. As both superpowers increasingly use space systems for the support of military operations on earth, limits on antisatellite weapons cannot be expected to last very long. The incentives to develop these weapons will become just too great. Thus the United States and the Soviet Union must begin to think about wider guidelines for the military use of space. For example, today's tacit modus vivendi allowing reconnaissance from space will come under increasing pressure, perhaps sooner than many appreciate. To preserve the beneficial and stabilizing aspects of this arrangement, the superpowers may have to arrive at restrictions on destabilizing types of surveillance from space. Similarly, the United States and the Soviet Union will have to adapt as other countries and even private news-gathering organizations develop earth observation satellites with militarily useful capabilities.[14] Flexibility and cooperation on these issues in the short term should be far more productive than allowing the situation to deteriorate with a net loss to international security in the long term.

In sum, if the United States plunges ahead with the development of antisatellite weapons, it can be certain that the Soviet Union will reactivate its ASAT program. Once an ASAT competition begins, the United States will find the task of ensuring the protection of its satellites increasingly difficult, despite ever more elaborate and costly countermeasures. Besides the added uncertainties that the possession of highly capable ASAT systems by both sides will create in crisis situations, America may eventually have to forgo the development of future space systems because of their unequivocal vulnerability. Alternatively, the United States can take a different path, one that combines practical constraints on ASAT weapons with prudent unilateral actions to minimize the attendant risks. On balance the benefits that this course of action offers to U.S. national security more than outweigh the possible costs. At the very least, it is worth exploring before it is too late.

14. William J. Broad, "Civilians Use Satellite Photos for Spying on Soviet Military," *New York Times,* April 7, 1986.

APPENDIX A

U.S. and Soviet Space System Survivability Measures

IT WAS really not until the 1980s that the United States began to look seriously at ways to make its space systems more survivable.[1] Before then, planners saw U.S. satellites as essentially peacetime-only assets and made little or no attempt to integrate their services into wartime scenarios. Moreover, for a long time the threat to U.S. satellites from potential adversaries was not considered very great. Even when the threat began to grow in the 1970s, the cost-conscious mood of the period made even space system planners reluctant to incorporate survivability features into their designs for fear that the added weight and financial penalties would jeopardize their projects.[2] The net result was that the security of U.S. space operations was for a long time a dangerously neglected area.

The satellite ground control facilities, in particular, have long been considered the most vulnerable part of U.S. space operations. Until the new Consolidated Space Operations Center (CSOC) near Colorado Springs, Colorado, becomes fully operational in 1987, the majority of U.S. Defense Department satellites will continue to be controlled from the Satellite Control Facility (SCF) at Sunnyvale, California.[3] Besides

1. See Paul B. Stares, *The Militarization of Space: U.S. Policy, 1945–1984* (Ithaca, N.Y.: Cornell University Press, 1985), pp. 169–70, 185–86, 209–11.
2. Ibid., p. 174.
3. Bruce A. Smith, "USAF Readies Vandenberg, Colorado Center for Military Shuttle Operations," *Aviation Week and Space Technology*, vol. 122 (March 18, 1985), pp. 125–26.

187

Table A-1. *Dedicated U.S. Satellite Ground Stations*

Category and program	Control or receiver sites
Photoreconnaissance	
Keyhole (KH)-11, KH-12	Ft. Belvoir, Va.
Signals intelligence	
Chalet, Magnum, Jumpseat	Ft. Meade, Md.; Pine Gap, Australia; Menwith Hill, U.K.[a]
Ocean reconnaissance	
Whitecloud	Guam; Diego Garcia; Adak, Alas.; Winter Harbor, Maine; Edzell, Scotland; Blossom Point, Md.
Early warning	
Defense Support Program (DSP)	Buckley Air National Guard Base, Colo.; Nurrungar, Australia; Kapaun, West Germany. Six mobile terminals located at Holloman Air Force Base, N.Mex.
Communication	
Defense Satellite Communications System (DSCS) III	Ft. Detrick, Md.; Northwest, Va.; Sunnyvale, Calif.; Ft. Meade, Md.; Wheeler Air Force Base, Hawaii; Camp Roberts, Calif.; Landstuhl, West Germany; Clark Air Base, Philippines
Fleet Satellite Communications (FLTSATCOM)	Norfolk, Va.; Wahiawa, Hawaii; Finnegayan, Guam; Bagnoli, Italy; Stockton, Calif.; Diego Garcia
Leased Satellite System	El Segundo, Calif.; and FLTSATCOM sites with two mobile ground stations at Guam and Norfolk, Va.
Navigation	
Transit-Nova	Winter Harbor, Maine; Rosemont, Minn.; Wahiawa, Hawaii; Point Mugu, Calif.
Navstar GPS	Diego Garcia; Kwajalein Atoll; Ascension Island; Kaena Point, Hawaii; Andersen Air Base, Guam; Adak, Alas.
Meteorology	
Defense Meteorological Support Program (DMSP)	Offutt Air Force Base, Nebr.; Monterey, Calif.; Loring Air Force Base, Maine; Fairchild Air Force Base, Wis.; Thule, Greenland; Kaena Point, Oahu

Sources: William M Arkin and Richard W. Fieldhouse, *Nuclear Battlefields: Global Links in the Arms Race* (Cambridge, Mass.: Ballinger, 1985), app. A; James Bamford, *The Puzzle Palace: A Report on America's Most Secret Agency* (Boston: Houghton Mifflin, 1982), p. 210; Jeffrey Richelson, *American Espionage and the Soviet Target* (New York: William Morrow, 1987), pp. 227, 234, 237; C. Richard Whelan, *Guide to Military Space Programs* (Arlington, Va.: Pasha Publications, 1984), pp. 37, 52, 86; Hughes Aircraft Company, "Leasat," *Fact Sheet* (El Segundo, Calif.: Space and Communications Group, 1979); Richard W. Blank, "The NAVSTAR Global Positioning System," *Signal*, vol. 41 (November 1986), p. 75; and Walter B. Hendrickson, Jr., "Satellites and the Sea," *National Defense* (October 1982), p. 28.
a. Uncertain.

being close to the San Andreas fault, the SCF is extremely vulnerable to terrorist or special forces attacks from the adjacent freeway. Sunnyvale is the hub of the worldwide Air Force Satellite Control Network (AFSCN), which performs the crucial station-keeping tasks discussed in chapter 4. The network is made up of seven tracking stations at Manchester Air Force Station, New Hampshire; Vandenberg Air Force Base, California; Kaena Point, Hawaii; Guam; Thule Air Base, Greenland; Mahe Island, Seychelles; and Oakhanger, England.[4] While CSOC will eventually take over the functions of the SCF, the AFSCN will remain essentially the same.[5] Although most military satellites have other ground stations that support their specific missions (see table A-1), the number is still quite small. Thus it would be comparatively easy for the Soviets to disable the complete network. But, as will be discussed shortly, plans call for shifting control of some of these satellite constellations to mobile ground and airborne facilities in wartime.

Another vital component of the ground segment is the network of facilities responsible for space surveillance. This provides tracking information for day-to-day satellite operations and in the future will give indispensable support for ASAT targeting, satellite-attack warning, and if necessary space arms control monitoring. Since the complete network consists of fixed land-based systems, it would be highly vulnerable in wartime. Appendix B discusses U.S. space surveillance capabilities more fully.

Finally, the two principal launch sites that the U.S. would rely on to replace satellites disabled in wartime—Vandenberg Air Force Base, California, and the Kennedy Space Center, Florida—are both vulnerable to sabotage and military attack from the nearby oceans. To a lesser extent the facilities that would control space shuttle operations, namely, the NASA Goddard and Johnson Space Flight Centers (at Greenbelt, Maryland, and Houston, Texas, respectively) and the White Sands communications and tracking facility in New Mexico, are also vulnerable.[6]

4. See James B. Schultz, "Inside the Blue Cube," *Defense Electronics*, vol. 15 (April 1983), pp. 52–59.

5. James B. Schultz, "Ford to Automate Satellite C² Net," *Defense Electronics*, vol. 16 (August 1984), pp. 37–38.

6. James B. Schultz, "In the Shadows of Space," *Defense Electronics*, vol. 17 (April 1985), p. 81; and *Military Construction Appropriations for 1985*, Hearings before a Subcommittee of the House Committee on Appropriations, 98 Cong. 2 sess. (Government Printing Office, 1984), pt. 3, p. 163.

U.S. Systems

As noted earlier, enhancing the survivability of satellites is a relatively recent initiative. Satellites designed in the 1970s whose operational lifetimes extend into the late 1980s will remain comparatively vulnerable. Although new satellite designs now have to meet stringent survivability criteria laid down by the Joint Chiefs of Staff (JCS), particularly with respect to electronic countermeasures and nuclear effects hardening,[7] there is some concern that even these measures may not be sufficient to meet the potential Soviet ASAT threat of the 1990s. While specific details of the survivability measures incorporated into each U.S. satellite are classified, a general picture can be derived from the open literature.

Reconnaissance Satellites

The KH-11 photoreconnaissance satellites are among the most vulnerable in the U.S. inventory by virtue of their low-altitude orbits. Though they have some ability to maneuver, it is unclear whether this could be accomplished in response to a co-orbital ASAT attack. It is not unreasonable to assume, however, that the latest models have sensors to detect interference and some antijamming capability. The successor to the KH-11 is also expected to have a range of survivability enhancement aids, such as radar warning sensors, decoys, and emergency maneuvering systems.[8] No information is publicly available on the protective measures used by signals intelligence satellites.

Early Warning Satellites

Although the Defense Support Program (DSP) early warning satellites are beyond the reach of the current Soviet co-orbital ASAT, they are still susceptible to radiation damage, electronic jamming, and laser interference. A variety of measures are being implemented to make the DSP satellites more survivable.[9] Apparently, the major components of

7. According to one report, current specifications call for satellites to be hardened to endure a radiation dose of about 0.5 joules (cm²). See Eric J. Lerner, "Strategic C³: A Goal Unreached," *IEEE Spectrum*, vol. 19 (October 1982), p. 53.

8. John Pike, "Anti-Satellite Weapons," *F.A.S. Public Interest Report*, vol. 36 (November 1983), p. 13.

9. Unless indicated otherwise the following information is from Jack Cushman, "AF Seeks Invulnerable Warning Satellites," *Defense Week*, vol. 5 (January 16, 1984),

the improved DSP satellites scheduled to be deployed in the late 1980s will be nuclear hardened. A "mission data rebroadcast" capability using a powerful transmitter will provide some protection against Soviet downlink jamming and the disruption of communication links from nuclear explosions in the atmosphere. For instance, electronic circuitry will automatically reset after a nuclear explosion. It is also hoped that the addition of a second focal plane array operating at a different infrared wavelength will provide extra insurance against laser interference. Attack warning sensors and an emergency maneuvering capability may be added to later models.

Should the on-orbit DSP satellites become permanently disabled, the U.S. Air Force reportedly keeps three spare satellites ready for launch, though it is unclear how soon they could become operational. The availability of launch pads would also be a factor, something that is questionable after an intercontinental nuclear exchange. The on-orbit DSPs that are no longer used are reportedly kept in a "standby mode" so that their "residual capability" can be utilized in an emergency.[10]

The latest models of DSP satellites have been fitted with several features to reduce their dependence on vulnerable ground stations. The introduction of laser satellite-to-satellite cross-links to bypass overseas ground stations is one such measure. Another has been to make the satellites more autonomous, especially in station-keeping tasks. Besides improving the security and hardening of the fixed ground sites, six mobile ground terminals (MGTs) have been procured to provide direct readout of warning information. These are all to be deployed at Holloman AFB, New Mexico, and will be dispersed in an emergency. According to congressional testimony the mobile terminals are "virtually impossible for the Soviets to target,"[11] though some nongovernment experts find this doubtful.[12]

---

p. 12; Craig Covault, "USAF Initiates Broad Program to Improve Surveillance of Soviets," *Aviation Week and Space Technology*, vol. 122 (January 21, 1985), pp. 14–17; and *Department of Defense Appropriations for 1985*, Hearings before a Subcommittee of the House Committee on Appropriations, 98 Cong. 2 sess. (GPO, 1984), pt. 5, p. 438.

10. *Department of Defense Appropriations for 1985*, Hearings, pt. 5, p. 438.

11. *Department of Defense Authorization for Appropriations for Fiscal Year 1984*, Hearings before the Senate Committee on Armed Services, 98 Cong. 1 sess. (GPO, 1983), pt. 5, p. 2469. Other terminals may also be placed on E-3A and E-4B aircraft. See *Air Force Magazine*, vol. 66 (July 1983), p. 19.

12. See Daniel Ford, *The Button: The Pentagon's Strategic Command and Control System* (Simon and Schuster, 1985), p. 214.

Communication Satellites

DEFENSE SATELLITE COMMUNICATIONS SYSTEM. The DSCS II has very little if any protection against radiation and only a limited ability to counter jamming.[13] Furthermore, according to the Defense Department its communication links are "vulnerable to nuclear scintillation and blackout effects resulting from high altitude nuclear bursts."[14] In contrast, its successor—DSCS III—has been specifically designed with a whole range of survivability measures. These include radiation hardening to Joint Chiefs of Staff specifications, multibeam antennas that can "null out" electronic interference, spread spectrum techniques to prevent jamming, and encrypted telemetery and command links to counter spoofing and electronic intelligence gathering.[15] There will also be a minimum of two spares in orbit to replace those lost to enemy action. As for the ground segment, each of the Satellite Configuration Control Elements shown in table A-1 can provide backup services to the primary Satellite Control Facility at Sunnyvale should this be destroyed.[16] The Satellite Configuration Control Elements are also hardened against electromagnetic pulse and other collateral nuclear effects. In the event that these facilities are disabled, the DSCS III satellites can also operate autonomously for "extended periods."[17]

FLEET SATELLITE COMMUNICATIONS SYSTEM. Each of the Fleet Satellite Communications (FLTSATCOM) System spacecraft has been nuclear hardened to Joint Chiefs of Staff specifications.[18] For example, it was reported in congressional testimony that each can withstand an electro-

13. Bruce G. Blair, *Strategic Command and Control: Redefining the Nuclear Threat* (Brookings, 1985), p. 205; and Ford, *The Button*, p. 188.

14. *Department of Defense Appropriations for 1985,* Hearings, pt. 4, p. 669.

15. See *Department of Defense Appropriations for Fiscal Year 1985,* Hearings before a Subcommittee of the Senate Committee on Appropriations, 98 Cong. 2 sess. (GPO, 1984), pt. 3, p. 353.

16. See also Lt. Gen. Winston D. Powers, USAF, and Andrew M. Hartigan, "The Defense Satellite Communications System," *Signal,* vol. 39 (July 1985), p. 56.

17. *Department of Defense Appropriations for 1985,* Hearings, pt. 5, p. 439; General Electric, "DSCS III," brochure prepared for the U.S. Defense Communications Agency, no date; *Aviation Week and Space Technology,* vol. 118 (January 17, 1983), p. 111.

18. *Navy Leased Satellite (LEASAT) and Fleet Satellite (FLTSAT) Programs,* Hearing before the House Committee on Armed Services, 97 Cong. 1 sess. (GPO, 1981), p. 3.

magnetic pulse of up to 50,000 volts per meter.[19] Perhaps the weakest element of the whole system is the UHF communication links, which according to Vice Admiral Gordon Nagler "can be jammed very easily."[20] As noted earlier, this frequency is also highly susceptible to atmospheric disruption from nuclear explosions. And it is unclear what provisions the U.S. Navy has made to ensure backup facilities to the present network of vulnerable Fleet Broadcast stations.

LEASED SATELLITE SYSTEM. Given the nature of the navy's leasing arrangement with Hughes, it seems unlikely that the Leasat System was built to meet the JCS nuclear hardening standards. As in the case of the FLTSATCOM satellites, its UHF communication links are vulnerable to jamming. It is also questionable whether the Leasat System's operational control center at the Hughes headquarters in El Segundo, California, is hardened in any way. Provision has been made, however, for some redundancy in the ground segment: two mobile ground control stations, at Guam and Norfolk, Virginia, have been procured to back up the main facilities.[21]

AIR FORCE SATELLITE COMMUNICATIONS SYSTEM. The AFSATCOM transponder packages hosted by the DSCS III, Satellite Data System (SDS), FLTSATCOM, and other satellites have all been nuclear hardened, presumably to JCS standards.[22] The single-channel transponder possesses some protection from jamming through a system known as a "regenerative repeater."[23] This simply repeats the transmitted messages, which can also be formatted in a way that reduces interference from jamming. According to one analyst, however, the effectiveness of the AFSATCOM system in a nuclear environment "appears very doubtful. . . . Links to ground and airborne terminals are subject to severe weakening from signal absorption and scintillation. A small

19. *Defense Department Authorization and Oversight and Department of Defense Authorization of Appropriations for Fiscal Year 1984,* Hearings before the House Committee on Armed Services, 98 Cong. 1 sess. (GPO, 1983), pt. 5, p. 494. Vice Admiral Gordon Nagler, who reported this fact, went on to state his dissatisfaction with that standard of hardness.

20. Ibid., p. 555. He went on to say that "if we went to war today, we probably very early in the game would have to revert to other means of communication." See also Blair, *Strategic Command and Control,* p. 204.

21. Hughes Aircraft Company, "LEASAT," *Fact Sheet* (El Segundo, Calif.: Space and Communications Group, 1979).

22. Bruce A. Smith, "New Satellite Systems Designed for Survivability," *Aviation Week and Space Technology,* vol. 116 (March 8, 1982), p. 82.

23. General Electric, "DSCS III."

number of high-altitude nuclear explosions could interrupt communications for long periods."[24]

SATELLITE DATA SYSTEM. Besides the upgraded antijamming capability of the AFSATCOM transponders, very little information is publicly available on the survivability features incorporated in the SDS satellites.[25] Although NASA's Tracking and Data Relay Satellite System (TDRSS) may be able to back up the SDS satellites in an emergency, it is unclear how vulnerable it is to jamming and other threats.

NATO III AND IV. Likewise, little is publicly known about the survivability features on the NATO III satellites, although it has been inferred that they have been designed with some radiation hardening and antijamming facilities.[26] The new NATO IV satellites are expected to be far more survivable.

MILSTAR. Given the importance of Milstar to the Defense Department's plans for future strategic and tactical communication, considerable effort has gone into ensuring its survivability in wartime.[27] This includes hardening the satellite to withstand nuclear effects and laser interference; the use of the extremely high frequency band, which facilitates a range of antijamming techniques; nulling antennas; encrypted data and command links; and on-board processing. Moreover the Milstar satellites will most probably possess some emergency maneuvering capability. To reduce reliance on ground stations, each satellite will be designed to operate autonomously for many weeks and will also be able to cross-link data via other satellites. The ground segment will be dispersed, hardened, and proliferated. Selected terminals, such as airborne command posts and mobile command centers, will also be able to control the space segment.[28]

24. Blair, *Strategic Command and Control*, pp. 203–04. See also *Department of Defense Appropriations for 1985*, Hearings, pt. 4, p. 669.

25. Defense Marketing Services Inc., "SDS," *DMS Market Intelligence Report* (Greenwich, Conn., 1984).

26. Larry K. Wentz and Gope D. Hingorani, "Outlook for NATO Communications," *Signal*, vol. 37 (December 1982), p. 54.

27. The information on Milstar survivability features is from *Department of Defense Appropriations for 1985*, Hearings, pt. 5, pp. 436–37; U.S. Department of the Air Force, *Supporting Data for Fiscal Year 1985, Budget Estimates, Descriptive Summaries: Research, Development, Test and Evaluation* (February 1984), p. 432; James B. Schultz, "Milstar to Close Dangerous C³I Gap," *Defense Electronics*, vol. 15 (March 1983), pp. 46–59; and James Fawcette, "Milstar: Hotline in the Sky," *High Technology*, vol. 3 (November 1983), pp. 62–67.

28. Department of the Air Force, *Supporting Data for Fiscal Year 1985 Budget Estimates, Descriptive Summaries: RDT&E*, p. 431.

COMMERCIAL SATELLITES. Finally, the commercial satellites on which the Department of Defense relies heavily are now being protected in minor ways. A Department of Defense directive issued in 1985 requires all national security related communications to be encrypted.[29] The Space Defense Operations Center (SPADOC) is also widening its satellite warning status reports to include commercial satellite operators that provide services to the Defense Department.[30] Since these initiatives do not involve actual defensive measures, they would have little effect in wartime.[31]

Navigation Satellites

The improved Transit satellites are reportedly hardened to withstand some radiation effects and system-generated electromagnetic pulse (SGEMP) but probably little else.[32] In contrast, the Navstar GPS satellites that will replace Transit have been described as "probably the most survivable nonsynchronous satellite system that we have today."[33] Besides each satellite being hardened to withstand nuclear and laser effects,[34] the primary survivability asset of the Navstar system is the size and configuration of the constellation. With eighteen satellites plus several spares in six separate orbital planes at an altitude of 20,200 kilometers, there is considerable redundancy in the event of an ASAT

29. "Defense Dept. Plans New Strategies for Communications Satellites," *Aviation Week and Space Technology,* vol. 123 (December 9, 1985), p. 49.

30. "Space Defense Operations Center Upgrades Assessment Capabilities," ibid., p. 73.

31. The "Captain Midnight" incident, in which the communication satellite broadcasting the Home Box Office television channel was deliberately jammed, gives some indication of the vulnerability of commercially owned satellites. See Donald Goldberg, "Captain Midnight, HBO, and World War III," *Mother Jones,* vol. 11 (October 1986), pp. 26–29, 48–53.

32. K. D. McDonald, "Navigation Satellite Systems: Their Characteristics, Potential and Military Applications," in Bhupendra Jasani, ed., *Outer Space: A New Dimension of the Arms Race* (London: Taylor and Francis, 1982), p. 163; Brendan M. Greeley, Jr., "Navy Expanding Its Space Command to Bolster Readiness," *Aviation Week and Space Technology,* vol. 124 (February 3, 1986), p. 57.

33. *Military Posture and Department of Defense Authorization for Appropriations for Fiscal Year 1983,* Hearings before the House Committee on Armed Services, 97 Cong. 2 sess. (GPO, 1982), pt. 5, p. 552.

34. See Bruce A. Smith, "Orbital Survivability of Milstar, Navstar Vital to Defense Effort," *Aviation Week and Space Technology,* vol. 118 (March 14, 1983), pp. 94–97; and *Department of Defense Authorization for Appropriations for Fiscal Year 1984,* Hearings before the Senate Committee on Armed Services, pt. 5, p. 2713.

attack using conventional or nuclear means.[35] According to the Defense Department, "Until all spare satellites were destroyed, there would be no impact on worldwide GPS coverage. Subsequently, there would be minor reductions in the number of hours per day of coverage for each satellite destroyed." While the department also claims that "the attack would require weeks before the GPS constellation was degraded sufficiently to preclude operational support," there is no mention of the type of ASAT used in this calculation.[36] A rapidly targetable, multiple-shot laser weapon, for example, would reduce this estimate considerably.

The data links between the Navstar satellites and their users employ spread-spectrum signal techniques and encryption. Jamming is not considered a great threat to the system. As reported in congressional testimony:

> To effectively jam the uplink, jammers would have to continuously radiate every GPS satellite for two weeks. Such a feat can only be accomplished with a system of large ground jammers on territory outside the Soviet Union. This type of jamming threat does not exist.[37]

Downlink jamming can only be effective against individual GPS users. This is a low-probability threat, because military users have backup self-contained navigation systems or easy terrain masking techniques if the GPS signal is temporarily lost.[38]

The Navstar GPS spacecraft will use many of the standard measures to reduce dependence on ground stations. Reportedly, each has been designed to be left unattended for as long as two weeks and with some modification for as much as 180 days.[39] In addition to a dispersed ground control network, the system has been designed to operate with only one ground station. Remote Tracking Stations of the Air Force's Satellite

35. *Department of Defense Appropriations for 1984,* Hearings before a Subcommittee of the House Committee on Appropriations, 98 Cong. 1 sess. (GPO, 1983), pt. 8, p. 503.

36. Ibid. It was reported elsewhere that even a constellation as small as five satellites could still provide a limited operational capability for two to five hours a day. See *Department of Defense Appropriations for 1985,* Hearings, pt. 5, p. 437.

37. *Department of Defense Appropriations for 1985,* Hearings, pt. 5, p. 437. Reportedly a "2kw jammer would have to be positioned within one nautical mile of the receiver to deny the use of GPS signals in position fixing." *Military Posture and Department of Defense Authorization for Appropriations for Fiscal Year 1985,* Hearings before the House Committee on Armed Services (GPO, 1982), pt. 5, pp. 732–33.

38. Smith, "Orbital Survivability of Milstar, Navstar Vital to Defense Effort," p. 95.

39. *Department of Defense Appropriations for 1985,* Hearings, pt. 5, p. 437.

Control Facility Network will also be able to provide an emergency backup to the dedicated GPS ground antennas.[40]

Nuclear Explosion Detection Sensors

Like the AFSATCOM transponders, the survivability of the Nuclear Detection System (NDS) packages ultimately depends on the vulnerability of the host spacecraft. Both systems, however, benefit considerably from being proliferated among many different satellite constellations. Besides this redundancy, the NDS sensors have also been nuclear hardened.[41] Moreover, cross-link ranging has been added to provide six months of autonomous operation without ground support. However, the NDS transmissions are vulnerable to nuclear scintillation.[42]

Meteorological Satellites

The Defense Meteorological Satellite Program (DMSP) spacecraft are currently within reach of the Soviet co-orbital ASAT and, as admitted in congressional testimony, there are "no plans to add [a] maneuvering or self-defense capability."[43] However, the follow-on version of the DMSP satellite, the Block 5D-3, will apparently be nuclear hardened and have a special shutter to protect the imaging sensor from laser damage.[44] Another weakness today is that "the uplinks and downlinks are presently vulnerable to jamming."[45] The air force is planning to rectify this with an EHF command and data link on DMSP II, due to become operational in the mid-1990s. The EHF links will also help reduce disruption caused by scintillation and absorption.[46] The DMSP II satellites will also have an emergency maneuvering system. Perhaps the most vulnerable part of the DMSP system is its ground segment. In 1984 the air force admitted: "The command and control ground stations

40. Ibid.
41. "USAF Pushes Survivability of Satellites," *Aviation Week and Space Technology*, vol. 121 (September 24, 1984), p. 72.
42. Blair, *Strategic Command and Control*, p. 273.
43. *Department of Defense Appropriations, Fiscal Year 1986*, Hearings before the Senate Committee on Appropriations, 99 Cong. 1 sess. (GPO, 1986), pt. 2, p. 332.
44. Department of the Air Force, *Supporting Data for Fiscal Year 1985 Budget Estimates, Descriptive Summaries: RDT&E*, p. 937.
45. *Department of Defense Appropriations for 1985*, Hearings, pt. 5, p. 438.
46. Ibid.

Table A-2. *U.S. Space System Survivability Measures*

	Survivability measure								
Mission or Program	Maneuver-ability	Nuclear hardening	Laser hardening	Satellite redun-dancy	Anti-jamming capability	Link re-sistance to nuclear effects	Satellite autonomy	Ground station re-dundancy	Overall survivability rating
Reconnaissance	L(P)	n.a.	n.a.	L	n.a.	L	n.a.	L	Low
Early warning (DSP)	L	M(P)	L(P)	M	L(P)	L(P)	L(P)	L(P)	Low to Medium (P)
Communication									
DSCS III	L	H	n.a.	L	H	M	M	M	Medium
FLTSATCOM	L	M	N	L	L	L	L	L	Low
Leasat	L	n.a.	N	L	L	L	L	M	Low
AFSATCOM	...	M	...	...	L(P)	L	...	L	Low
SDS	L	n.a.	n.a.	L	L	L	L	L	Low
NATO III	L	L	N	L	L	M	L	L	Low
Milstar	H	H	H	M	H	H	H	H	High
Navigation									
Transit-Nova	L	M	N	M	n.a.	L	L	L	Low
Navstar GPS	n.a.	H	H	H	H	H	H	H	High
Nuclear explosion detection (NDS)	...	H	n.a.	H	n.a.	L	H	H	Medium to High
Meteorology (DMSP)	L	H	L(P)	L	L(P)	L(P)	L(P)	L(P)	Low to Medium

Note: L = limited protection; M = medium protection; H = high protection; N = no protection; (P) = planned improvement; n.a. = not available.
Source: Author's estimates.

have no independent capability of generating commands in the event that the Omaha ground station [Air Force Global Weather Central at Offutt AFB, Nebraska] is unable to perform its function. The Omaha facility is above ground, without backup power or air conditioning and is *extremely vulnerable* to severe weather, national disaster, manmade disaster or attack."[47] This will be redressed somewhat with the plans to harden a new command, control, and data relay facility at Fairchild AFB, Washington State, and also by making the satellites more autonomous.[48] The low-altitude National Oceanic and Atmospheric Administration (NOAA) and GEOS meteorological satellites, as noted earlier, provide some additional insurance if the DMSP system becomes inoperable.

Table A-2 encapsulates the survivability measures incorporated in each of the U.S. space programs and gives a general assessment of their overall survivability.

Soviet Systems

Because of the paucity of information on Soviet satellite survivability measures, one can only infer their general approach to this problem. Some insurance against the loss of satellites is provided by the size of most Soviet constellations. The Soviets' low-altitude "store-dump" communication system, which includes at least twenty-four satellites, is an obvious case in point. Moreover the shorter lifespan of most Soviet satellites has fostered a rapid replenishment capability, so that satellites can be launched very quickly if need be, as demonstrated by the high launch rate of Soviet reconnaissance satellites during major international crises. According to one expert on the Soviet space program, "Soviet responses to crises throughout the world suggest that a photographic reconnaissance satellite can be launched within 24–48 hours and higher than normal launch rates can be sustained for at least several weeks."[49] Also, the launch of two satellites during a major strategic exercise in

47. *Military Construction Appropriations for 1985,* Hearings, pt. 3, pp. 412–13 (emphasis added).
48. *Department of Defense Appropriations for 1985,* Hearings, pt. 5, p. 439. The SCF station at Kaena Point, Hawaii, can also be used to receive DMSP data. See *Department of Defense Appropriations, Fiscal Year 1986,* Hearings, pt. 2, p. 332.
49. Nicholas L. Johnson, "C³ in Space: The Soviet Approach," *Signal,* vol. 40 (December 1985), p. 21.

June 1982, during which an ASAT system was tested, may have been a deliberate attempt to simulate the wartime replacement of satellites lost to enemy action.[50]

This ability to replace satellites in rapid fashion is undoubtedly a major strength, but it is only relevant in certain wartime scenarios. In the event of an intercontinental nuclear exchange, launch pads and ground support facilities are unlikely to remain intact very long. This problem can be avoided, of course, by storing spares in-orbit before escalation to general nuclear war, and there is some evidence to suggest that the Soviets are planning to do this.[51]

Finally, it seems fair to assume that Soviet satellite antijamming capabilities are not as sophisticated as the latest U.S. techniques. No further observations about Soviet survivability measures can be drawn from the open literature.

50. Nicholas L. Johnson, *The Soviet Year in Space, 1982* (Colorado Springs, Colo., Teledyne Brown Engineering), p. 25.

51. Johnson, *Soviet Year in Space, 1984,* p. 13.

U.S. and Soviet Space Surveillance Capabilities

SINCE the late 1950s, the United States has operated several systems for surveillance and tracking of objects in space. Some of these were built specifically for this purpose, while others were designed for other missions, such as ballistic missile early warning and missile test monitoring. The current U.S. network, therefore, can be divided into three categories: dedicated, collateral, and contributory sensors. The first two sensor categories are controlled by the North American Aerospace Defense Command (NORAD), while the latter consists of sensors that are under contract to NORAD to provide assistance when requested.[1] The radar and optical systems that make up all three categories are shown in table B-1 and their locations in figure B-1.

Extensive though the network of U.S. ground-based space surveillance sensors is, it does have significant operational limitations. Besides the problem that not all sensors are directly controlled by NORAD or dedicated to satellite tracking, the ground-based radars are limited to line-of-sight observations. Thus there are periods when space objects cannot be monitored.[2] And if a satellite maneuvers between radars there

1. Capt. Dennis K. Harden, "Current Capabilities and Future Requirements of the Air Force Space Surveillance Network," in U.S. Department of the Air Force, *Proceedings of the Tenth Aerospace Power Symposium: The Impact of Space on Aerospace Doctrine* (Maxwell AFB, Ala.: Air War College, 1986), pp. 54–64.

2. *Department of Defense Authorization for Appropriations for Fiscal Year 1986,* Hearings before the Senate Committee on Armed Services, 99 Cong. 1 sess. (Government Printing Office, 1985), pt. 7, p. 4288.

can be a delay before the sensors reacquire and identify the space object.[3] The ground-based sensors can also only detect and track objects of a certain size. NORAD's log of roughly 6,000 space objects does not generally include anything smaller than 10 centimeters in diameter.[4] The numerous pieces of unlogged "space junk" aloft pose a growing risk of collision.[5]

Detecting and tracking objects in deep space—the geosynchronous orbit and beyond—also presents problems. Currently, in addition to the Baker-Nunn cameras and GEODSS electro-optical telescopes, the FPS-79 radar at Pirinclik (Turkey), and the Millstone and ALTAIR radars are used for this purpose. While the GEODSS system is a significant addition to U.S. deep space surveillance, its observations, as noted in chapter 6, are limited to nighttime and good weather. The ground-based radars, on the other hand, do not provide the same degree of resolution as the electro-optical systems, and there are sometimes delays in obtaining observations.[6]

Information on the Soviet space surveillance network is understandably hard to come by. The Soviets have reportedly deployed a dedicated chain of satellite control and tracking stations at Kaliningrad, Yevpatoria, Tbilisi, Dzhusaly, Kolpashevo, Ulan Ude, Ussuriysk, and Petropavlovsk.[7] (See figure B-2.) The Soviets also use a number of ships dispersed around the world for this purpose.[8]

As in the United States, further support for space tracking is provided by the Soviet ballistic missile early warning radars. These include the Hen House radars located at Sary Shagan, Olenogorsk on the Kola Peninsula, Skrunda (Latvia), Nikolayev in the Caucasus, Angarsk near Irkutsk, and Kamchatka; two Dog House and Cat House phased-array radars to the south of Moscow; the large phased-array ABM radar at Pushkino, northeast of Moscow; and six Pechora-type phased-array

3. This apparently occurred during the maneuvers of Kosmos 1603 in October 1984. See "Soviets Orbit Large New Military Electronic Intelligence Satellite," *Aviation Week and Space Technology,* vol. 122 (January 14, 1985), pp. 19–20.

4. Harden, "Current Capabilities and Future Requirements," p. 58.

5. See Eliot Marshall, "Space Junk Grows with Weapons Tests," *Science,* vol. 230 (October 25, 1985), p. 424–25.

6. Harden, "Current Capabilities and Future Requirements," p. 59.

7. *Soviet Space Programs: 1976–80,* Committee Print, Senate Committee on Commerce, Science, and Transportation (GPO, 1982), pt. 1, p. 137.

8. For details see ibid., pp. 125–33; and Bill Baker and Philip Clark, "Shore Leave: The Soviet Achilles' Heel in Space," *New Scientist,* vol. 104 (November 29, 1984), p. 9.

radars that either have been constructed or are near completion at Pechora, Lyaki near the Caspian Sea, Olenogorsk, Sary Shagan, Mikhalevka near Irkutsk, and Abalakova, north of Krasnoyarsk.[9] In addition to these radars, the Soviets also operate high-resolution optical systems similar to the Baker-Nunn cameras.[10]

Little information is publicly available about Soviet space surveillance capabilities, though they undoubtedly suffer constraints similar to those on their U.S. counterparts.

9. See U.S. Department of Defense, *Soviet Military Power, 1986* (GPO), pp. 44–45; and Desmond Ball "The Soviet Strategic C³I System," in *C³I Handbook,* prepared by the editors of *Defense Electronics* (Palo Alto, Calif.: EW Communications, 1986), pp. 210–11. More recent accounts report that three additional Pechora-type large phased-array radars are under construction at Skrunda, Mukachevo (near the Czech border), and Baranovichi (near the Polish border). See David C. Morrison, "Radar Diplomacy," *National Journal,* January 3, 1987, p. 19.

10. Nicholas L. Johnson, *The Soviet Year in Space, 1985* (Colorado Springs, Colo., Teledyne Brown Engineering), p. 10.

Table B-1. *U.S. Ground-Based Space Surveillance Systems*

Name	Sites	Sensor type and designation[a]	Initial operating capability	Primary mission	Range (km)
Dedicated sensors					
NAVSPASUR (Naval Space Surveillance System)	Lake Kickapoo, Tex.; Gila River, Ariz.; Jordan Lake, Ala.	Transmitters	1959	Satellite tracking	24,000
	Ft. Stewart, Ga.; Silver Lake, Miss.; Red River, Ark.; Elephant Butte, N.Mex.; San Diego, Calif.; Hawkinsville, Ga. (HQ. Dahlgren, Va.)	Receivers	1959		
PACBAR (Pacific Barrier Radar)	San Miguel, Philippines	MSR (GPS-10)	1983	Satellite tracking	38,000
	Saipan	MSR (GPS-10)	1990		
Baker-Nunn	San Vito, Italy St. Margarets, Canada	Optical 40-in. telescope	1956	Satellite tracking	80,000
GEODSS (Ground-based Electro-Optical Deep Space Surveillance)	White Sands, N.Mex.	Electro-optical telescopes (two 40-in.; one 15-in.)	1981	Satellite tracking	36,000+
	Haleakala, Maui, Hawaii		1982		
	Taegu, Rep. of Korea		1982		
	Diego Garcia		1986		
	Portugal		1987		
MOTIF (Teal Blue) (Maui Optical Tracking Identification Facility)	Haleakala, Maui, Hawaii	Electro-optical telescopes	n.a.	Satellite tracking	n.a.
Teal Amber	Malabar, Fla.		n.a.		
Collateral sensors					
AN/FPS-85	Eglin AFB, Fla.	LPAR	1975	SLBM early warning	3,500
BMEWS (Ballistic Missile Early Warning System)	Thule, Greenland	MSR (FPS-49A; FPS-50)	1960	Missile warning	4,800
	Fylingdales, U.K.	MSR (FPS-49; FPS-50)	1960		
	Clear, Alaska (all to be converted to LPARs)	MSR (FPS-50; FPS-92)	1960		

Table B-1 (continued)

Name	Sites	Sensor type and designation[a]	Initial operating capability	Primary mission	Range (km)
Collateral sensors—continued					
Cobra Dane	Shemya Island, Alaska	LPAR (FPS-108)	1977	Missile test monitoring	40,000
PARCS (Perimeter Attack Radar Characterization System)	Cavalier, N.Dak.	LPAR	1974	Missile early warning	5,000
AN/FPS-79	Pirinclik, Turkey	MSR (FPS-79)	n.a.	Missile test monitoring	38,000
PAVE PAWS	Beale AFB, Calif.	LPAR (FPS-115)	1980	Missile early warning	5,000
	Otis AFB, Mass.	LPAR (FPS-115)	1980		
	Robins AFB, Ga.	LPAR (FPS-115)	1987		
	Goodfellow AFB, Tex.	LPAR (FPS-115)	1988		
Contributing sensors					
Eastern Test Range (ETR)	Antigua Island	MSR (FPQ-14)	n.a.	Launch support	n.a.
	Ascension Island	MSR (FPQ-15)	n.a.		
Western Test Range (WTR)	Kwajalein Atoll	ALCOR	1972	Launch support	n.a.
		ALTAIR	1981		38,000
	Kaena Point, Hawaii	FPQ-14	1980		n.a.
	Vandenberg AFB, Calif.	FPS-16	n.a.		n.a.
Millstone, Haystack	Westford, Mass.	MSR	n.a.	Satellite tracking	38,000
AMOS (Maui Optical Station)	Haleakala, Maui, Hawaii	Electro-optical telescope	n.a.	Satellite tracking	n.a.

Sources: Nicholas Johnson, *Spaceflight*, vol. 27 (July–August 1985); Capt. Dennis K. Harden, "Current Capabilities and Future Requirements of the Air Force Space Surveillance Network," in U.S. Department of the Air Force, *Proceedings of the Tenth Aerospace Power Symposium: The Impact of Space on Aerospace Doctrine* (Maxwell AFB, Ala.: Air War College, 1986), app. 2, pp. 54–64; Bruce Gumble, "Air Force Upgrading Defenses at NORAD," *Defense Electronics*, vol. 17 (August 1985), pp. 102–04; Joel W. Powell, "Photography of Orbiting Satellites," *Spaceflight*, vol. 25 (February 1983), p. 82; Anne Randolph, "USAF Upgrades Deep Space Coverage," *Aviation Week and Space Technology*, vol. 118 (February 28, 1983), pp. 57–58.

n.a. Not available.

a. MSR = mechanically steered radar; LPAR = large phased-array radar.

Figure B-1. Sites of U.S. Ground-Based Space Surveillance Sensors

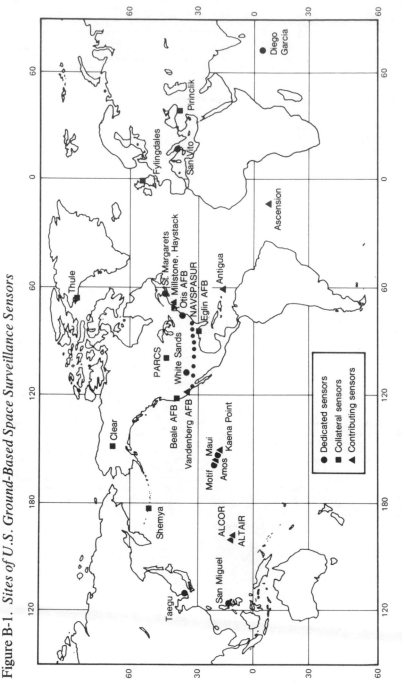

Source: Capt. Dennis K. Harden, "Current Capabilities and Future Requirements of the Air Force Space Surveillance Network," in U.S. Department of the Air Force, *Proceedings of the Tenth Aerospace Power Symposium: The Impact of Space on Aerospace Doctrine* (Maxwell AFB, Ala.: Air War College, 1986), app. 2, p. 60.

Figure B-2. *Sites of Soviet Ground-Based Space Tracking Stations*

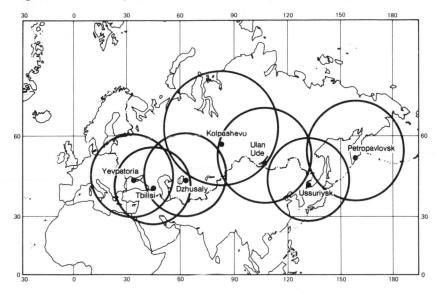

Source: Nicholas L. Johnson, *The Soviet Year in Space, 1985* (Colorado Springs, Colo., Teledyne Brown Engineering), p. 12.

Glossary

Apogee: The farthest point from the earth's surface that a satellite reaches in its orbit.

Constellation: A configuration of satellites of the same type, such as the Navstar Global Positioning System.

Equatorial orbit: A circular orbit above the equator. Satellites placed in this path lie in the equatorial plane and thus have a 0° inclination.

Geosynchronous orbit: A band of space nearly 36,000 kilometers above the equator in which satellites travel at the same rotational speed as the earth around its axis (that is, they have a period of 24 hours). Thus they appear stationary above a specific spot on the equator. Because large areas of the earth are visible from this orbit, it is typically used for communication relay and surveillance.

Ground track: The orbital path of a satellite projected on the surface of the earth.

Inclination: The angle between the orbital plane of a satellite and the equatorial plane of the earth, which for satellites is the 0° reference plane. The inclination determines what portion of the globe the satellite will pass over. For example, a satellite inclined 65° to the equator will travel over the area between 65° north latitude and 65° south latitude.

Molniya orbit: A highly elliptical orbit, typically with an apogee of 40,000 kilometers and a perigee of 500 kilometers. The name derives from the class of Soviet satellites that are placed into orbits of this shape. The most common use of this orbit is to relay messages to the polar regions, which are out of line of sight from the geosynchronous orbit.

Perigee: The closest point to the earth's surface that a satellite reaches in its orbit.

Period: The time a satellite takes to complete one revolution of the earth. Satellites that travel in low-altitude (200–1,000 kilometer) circular orbits have much shorter periods (typically between 90 and 120 minutes) than those in highly elliptical or high-altitude circular orbits (whose periods are typically between 12 and 24 hours).

Polar orbit: An orbit in which a satellite travels over or almost over the earth's two poles. Satellites in polar orbits eventually pass over the entire surface of the earth as it rotates below them. For this reason reconnaissance and meteorological satellites are usually launched into polar orbits.

Semisynchronous orbit: Typically, a circular orbit at roughly 20,000 kilometers altitude inclined between 63° and 65°. The orbital period is about 12 hours. Space-based navigation systems currently use this orbit.

Sun-synchronous orbit: A near polar, circular orbit. Satellites traveling in a sun-synchronous orbit pass over points on the earth's surface at the same local time each day. This is particularly useful for weather forecasting and reconnaissance, since shadows can be compared for any variations.

Supersynchronous orbit: An orbit beyond the geosynchronous orbit (that is, at an altitude of more than 36,000 kilometers). Satellites in supersynchronous orbits have periods longer than 24 hours.

Index

211